The Intellectual Heritage of the Early Middle Ages

The Intellectual Heritage
of the Early Middle Ages

SELECTED ESSAYS BY

M. L. W. LAISTNER

EDITED BY

CHESTER G. STARR

OCTAGON BOOKS

A DIVISION OF FARRAR, STRAUS AND GIROUX

New York   1972

Reprinted 1966
by special arrangement with Cornell University Press

Second Reprinting 1972

OCTAGON BOOKS
A Division of Farrar, Straus & Giroux, Inc.
19 Union Square West
New York, N. Y. 10003

Library of Congress Catalog Card Number: 66-18045

ISBN 0-374-94712-0

Printed in U.S.A. by
NOBLE OFFSET PRINTERS, INC.
New York, N.Y. 10003

Preface

THE following essays by Max Ludwig Wolfram Laistner are issued in his honor. To his revised *Thought and Letters in Western Europe, A.D. 500–900,* this volume may serve as a companion piece, a collection of his shorter but more detailed analyses.

Just as every scholar of mark has a varied influence on the world about him, so he is the product of many diverse forces. Wolf Laistner's ancestors on both sides were German and, in the generations that he knew, were trained in scholarship or music. His paternal uncle, Ludwig, literary adviser to a well-known Munich publishing firm, was a man of letters and a noted student of German folklore. Laistner's father, Max, a pianist and conductor, moved to England in his twenties and there married a daughter of Frederic Weber, organist for half a century at Marlborough House Chapel. Laistner himself was born in London on October 10, 1890, and was reared in a cultured home. His school was Merchant Taylors; his college, Jesus College, Cambridge. He sat for Part I of the Classical Tripos at the end of his second year, took Part II, sec. D (archeology), in his third year, and received his B.A. in 1912.

The two Cambridge teachers to whom Laistner owed most were William Ridgeway and Arthur Bernard Cook. He coached with Cook in the summer of 1910, and again in his last year he attended Cook's mellifluous lectures on sculpture, vases, and the recent excavations at Ephesus. Ridgeway followed a different, Socratic method, which firmly implanted in Laistner the sense that nothing could be taken on trust. Here too a young student could learn that scholars do not bend their intellectual judgments through friendship, for while Cook and Ridgeway were personally close they openly disagreed on some matters, as, for example, Greek religion. Thus stimulated and instructed, Laistner was well grounded in classics and archeology.

Through Ridgeway's favorable intervention, Laistner secured the Craven Studentship, which took him out of England for travel and field work in Greece in 1912–1913; in the following year he was again in Greece, as a student (or fellow) of the British School at Athens. Laistner's first published works, in the *Annual* of the School, were a study of the geometric pottery at Delphi and a joint report with R. M. Dawkins on the excavations of the Kamares cave in Crete. A reading of these first essays makes it apparent that, though Laistner was not to continue on the path of archeology, he early acquired the ability to write in a firm, scholarly tone. In his work at the Kamares cave, one suspects he was as methodical and orderly a digger as he has since been in fields far removed.

The academic career which followed was soon interrupted. After positions as assistant lecturer in classics at Birmingham and then lecturer in history and archeology at Queen's University (Belfast), Laistner spent May 1916–August 1919 in uniform and on government service. During part of this period he was a company quartermaster sergeant, an experience to which his students of later years attributed something of his vigor of expression.

A position as lecturer in classics at Manchester University followed his return to civilian life, and here, quite by accident, he settled upon his main scholarly interest. In 1920 T. F. Tout, the eminent medievalist of Manchester, received a letter from W. M. Lindsay, inquiring for young scholars to form a team to edit early medieval glossaries. Laistner, shaken loose from old moorings by the war, asked Tout to put in his name, received from Lindsay some pages of an early ninth-century manuscript to transcribe, and passed this test to the satisfaction of a very careful judge. So Laistner buckled down to the communal task; on his own he edited the Philoxenus glossary under Lindsay's supervision.

In the same period, the first half of the twenties, Laistner continued to teach, to write, and to review in the field of ancient history, as he was to do thereafter, but the bulk of his energies came to be devoted to the Early Middle Ages. His major points of view on this period and his methods of approach were also established early. His initial path of inquiry, that of detailed study of the actual manuscripts, he has never abandoned; but Laistner has also known how to broaden his conclusions, so based, for the more general reader. In particular, the promptings of a friend soon led him to set down a general survey of the Latin literature of the Early Middle Ages, the masterful *Thought and Letters,* which immediately became a standard guide for students of the era.

Among the external influences on Laistner's career, only one more perhaps needs to be mentioned. In 1921 he had moved to the University of London as reader in ancient history; four years later he accepted the invitation of Cornell University in the United States to take its chair of ancient history. Cornell had been a center of historical studies in America since the days of Andrew Dickson White, George Lincoln Burr, Charles Henry Hull, and others; its atmosphere encouraged individual study. Here men honored each other above all for scholarly attainment. When Laistner first came, each lecturer in history formed a separate department unto himself.

In these surroundings a transplanted English scholar has found for over three decades friendship and stimulus, security and leisure for his unceasing investigations. Quickly acclimated to the American scene, Laistner has held posts both in the American Historical Association and in the Mediaeval Academy of America; but he has also kept part of his heart in England, where he received a Litt.D. from Cambridge in 1944 and more recently became an Honorary Fellow of Jesus College.

It would ill become the present writer to enlarge upon Laistner's contributions to our knowledge of the Early Middle Ages. As a man well trained in the classics and ancient history, Laistner has concentrated upon the problem "of the intellectual heritage transmitted to medieval men from classical and later Roman times." This, surely, is a crucial problem in the history of Western civilization, but all too often it has been summarily solved by a swift generalization. If one hearkens to an angry churchman's contemptuous dismissal of pagan learning—frequently a judgment wrenched out of context—the problem disappears. If one becomes disheartened by the apparently dull mass of commentaries and other ecclesiastical treatises of the Middle Ages, so largely cribbed by one man from the works of his predecessors, a true answer seems impossible.

Yet the essays in this volume show repeatedly the only safe way to proceed and suggest the solid results that can be attained. We need, as Laistner once pointed out, modern "critical editions of the many texts that are still only available in antiquated and faulty publications," and he himself has done valuable work in this field. We need also careful surveys of the extant manuscripts and of the holdings suggested by the medieval library catalogues if we are to have safe guides for determining "the beginning or the revival of intellectual trends." The following essays are in large part a combination of such surveys and an analysis of the valuable, firmly grounded conclusions which result. The unique character of history, after all, is its ultimate basis upon actual fact in historical time, whence comes a realization of the rich diversity of historical development.

To put Laistner's career in its full light, one must note also that his academic duties at London and at Cornell have lain in the field of ancient history proper. For unity the present volume is built about his studies in the Early Middle Ages, but repeatedly he himself has gone back to the ancient world to publish substantial works quite independent of his other field of interest. Alongside his delightful Richard lectures at the University of Virginia (1950) on *Christianity and Pagan Culture*, for instance, one must place his broad survey of *The Greater Roman Historians* as Sather Professor of Classical Literature, University of Californa (1946).

Preface

A scholar's influence on his age may well be transmitted by more than book or learned essay; in Laistner's career, certainly, one must not overlook his serious attention to the task of the reviewer or the responsibility of the educator. As a glance at the bibliography in this volume will show, Laistner has reviewed a remarkably large number of books, including most of the major studies in his special field of research as well as many of the more significant works in ancient history. Three of these reviews are included here, both as independent contributions to knowledge and as examples of Laistner's methods in this field.

When one reads the rest of his critical analyses and notices, one is, I think, deeply impressed by the solidity of his standards and the fairness of his judgment. Anyone who has essayed to pass public judgment on a book must be struck by the conciseness and clarity of Laistner's reviews and must wish for the common sense which Laistner displays toward the aberrant fringe of scholarship. No author need expect Laistner's applause for mere bulk, his endorsement of ill-founded generalizations, or his toleration of partisanship or of religious bias masquerading as scholarship. Laistner's eye is always to the argument and its proof, but his ear listens to the literary style of the work under examination.

When a work is frankly popular, Laistner will accept it on its own terms so long as its author respects the truth. In such reviews one detects what is necessarily muffled in his scholarly papers—that Laistner is a man keenly interested in the modern age, deeply versed in the poetry and music of the European tradition, and more understanding of the foibles of youth and the average man than would be predicted of a confirmed bachelor dwelling in a little white house on a quiet Ithaca street. When a work, on the other hand, is scholarly, it must expect a thorough going-over. Whether it passes the test or not will be made quite clear, and why. Also, parenthetically, the reader will always find out what the book is about!

Upon rereading these reviews recently, I was struck both by the kindness of their author, whether toward beginning scholars or great men past their prime; by the honesty, nonetheless, of the critical verdict; and by the depth of learning against which

Laistner has measured the work under consideration at the moment. Not once in these reviews has Laistner deigned to be clever at the author's expense; certainly he could not repeat Sydney Smith's jest, "I never read a book before reviewing it; it prejudices a man so." Interestingly enough, Laistner's judgment almost always coincides with the standing of a book over the years.

Finally, a few words must be said on Laistner as an educator. His students of past years now holding chairs of history, English, classics, and theology across the United States agree that Laistner has been a great teacher.

Why this has been so, is not easy to determine. At Cornell there are no rigid requirements of course work or reading, and Laistner has never insisted that his students read any particular group of works. Yet somehow when he has casually suggested that one might look at, say, Caesarius of Arles, one goes right over to the library, begins to digest the indignant bishop's fulminations against drunkenness, adultery, and other sins, and so gains a new, somewhat amazing light on the early Frankish period. Nor, again, has Laistner hovered over one's shoulder as the dissertation was written. If a student has had a specific problem, his adviser will give him the best of counsel; but the end product is most certainly the student's.

There, perhaps, is the secret: Laistner has accepted his graduate students as adults. If they have not been ready to take the challenge or have been intellectually weak, they soon discover the fact for themselves and leave; but if they have stayed, they have educated themselves, and at least a part of this process has been the daily observation of Laistner as a model of scholarly honesty, concentration, and incisive judgment. Not to be overlooked, too, has been Laistner's unfailing kindness in opening his home. As he was often at Ridgeway's house in Cambridge and was stimulated thereby, so his students treasure memories of Laistner's vivid talk, ranging swiftly over the foibles of present politics and culture, the peculiarities of historians, and the latest explorations in ancient and early medieval history—all this while his gentle mother sat on a corner of the sofa, sewing, and softening his judgments if they were too blunt for her kind spirit.

Preface

In offering this volume to Wolf Laistner, his friends and students can do no better than quote some lines which he employed in a dedication to his friend and generous adviser, Alexander Souter:

> Te sequor . . . inque tuis nunc
> Ficta pedum pono pressis vestigia signis.

Chester G. Starr

Champaign, Illinois
January 1957

Acknowledgments

THE present editor is much indebted to Eleanor Huzar, Bryce Lyon, and James Seaver for encouragement and aid and to M. L. W. Laistner for his co-operation. Typographical errors in the original publication of these essays have been corrected, and at a few points Laistner has broadened his references; otherwise the argument and text are as they stood originally.

For permission to reprint the following essays and reviews the editor is grateful to Harvard University Press (*Harvard Theological Review*); University of North Carolina Press (*Studies in Philology*); Oxford University Press (*Bede: His Life, Times, and Writings,* copyright 1935); Royal Historical Society (*Transactions*); University of Chicago Press (*Classical Philology*); Mediaeval Academy of America (*Speculum*); Biblioteca Apostolica Vaticana (*Miscellanea Giovanni Mercati*); American Economic Association (*American Economic Review*); and the editors of *Gnomon*.

Contents

Preface   v

Acknowledgments   xiii

Abbreviations   xvii

Christianity and the Past

1. Some Reflections on Latin Historical Writing in the Fifth
   Century   3

2. The Value and Influence of Cassiodorus' Ecclesiastical History   22

3. The Influence during the Middle Ages of the Treatise *De
   vita contemplativa* and Its Surviving Manuscripts   40

4. The Western Church and Astrology during the Early
   Middle Ages   57

5. Ernst Robert Curtius' *Europäische Literatur und Lateinisches Mittelalter*   83

The Venerable Bede

6. Bede as a Classical and a Patristic Scholar   93

7. The Library of the Venerable Bede   117

8. The Latin Versions of Acts Known to the Venerable Bede   150

9. Was Bede the Author of a Penitential?   165

Contents

The Carolingian Age

10. Some Early Medieval Commentaries on the Old Testament   181
11. Fulgentius in the Carolingian Age   202
12. A Ninth-Century Commentator on the Gospel according to Matthew   216

Miscellanea

13. Richard Bentley: 1742–1942   239
14. Michael Rostovtzeff's *The Social and Economic History of the Hellenistic World*   255
15. Henri-Irenée Marrou's *Histoire de l'éducation dans l'antiquité*   267

Bibliography of the Publications of M. L. W. Laistner, 1914–1956   275

Abbreviations

CSEL—Corpus Scriptorum Ecclesiasticorum Latinorum
       (references to volume, page, and line)
GCS—Die Griechisch-Christlichen Schriftsteller
MGH—Monumenta Germaniae Historica
       (references to volume and page)
PG—Migne, *Patrologia Graeca*
PL—Migne, *Patrologia Latina*
       (reference in both to volume, column, and section)

Christianity and the Past

Some Reflections on Latin Historical Writing in the Fifth Century[*][1]

THE historical literature of the Late Roman Imperial Age, even though it is not in itself an inspiring topic, has hardly received as much attention as it deserves. It is true that the works here to be passed under review are not of the first class either as literature or as historical presentations. On the other hand, the day is, or should be, past when the larger periods of human history can be treated in isolation. It is as much the business of the ancient historian to have some knowledge of what really constituted the classical heritage of the Middle Ages as it is the duty of the medievalist to understand something of the achievement of Greece and Rome. It so happens that, when the scholars of the earlier medieval period desired to acquaint themselves with the main features of the old pagan Mediterranean world and of the early Christian Era, it was chiefly to the historical works of the fourth and fifth centuries that they turned. This circumstance alone seems reason enough to justify consideration of a topic to which most students of ancient history pay little heed. The historical compositions with which we are concerned are without exception compilations, but it is

* *Classical Philology*, 35 (1940), 241–258. Reprinted by permission of the University of Chicago Press.

[1] A paper read at the annual meeting of the American Historical Association held at Washington, D.C., on December 28–30, 1939.

well to remember that the writing of large-scale histories had gone out of fashion several centuries earlier. Abridgments of Livy were already replacing the original work in the age of Hadrian, if not before, and after Tacitus Latin historical writings are either epitomes or brief surveys or else they are collections of biographies rather than histories in the stricter sense. It was Suetonius, not Livy or Tacitus, who most profoundly influenced succeeding generations; and this means not merely that lives of famous or infamous persons continued to be composed but that the historical epitomes and short surveys had a strongly biographical cast. The sole exception, in fact, to this broad generalization is Ammianus Marcellinus, and no one would maintain that his book, admirable as it was, exerted any influence in the centuries that followed.

It may be instructive to refer at the outset to Cassiodorus. In the manual that he composed for the monks of Vivarium there is a chapter on historical works, which is headed significantly enough, "De historicis Christianis." [2] These are the authors and books that he enumerates: Josephus' *Antiquities of the Jews* and *Jewish Wars,* both of which Cassiodorus caused to be rendered into Latin; Eusebius-Rufinus' *Ecclesiastical History;* Orosius' *History against the Pagans;* the *Ecclesiastical Histories* of Sozomen, Socrates, and Theodoret, which were translated into Latin in shortened form by Epiphanius at the request of Cassiodorus; the *Chronicles* of Eusebius-Jerome, Marcellinus Comes, and Prosper; and, finally, the literary histories by Jerome and by his continuator, Gennadius. Now this is a very modest historical library, especially when we consider the remarkable size of the book collection at Vivarium. The absence of pagan historians from the list is also noteworthy. Several possible explanations of this scanty historical equipment suggest themselves. It may be that by the middle of the sixth century, when Cassiodorus wrote his treatise, the fourth-century epitomators, not to speak of earlier historians, were hard to come by. On the other hand, as Cassiodorus' primary purpose was to guide his readers in Biblical and theological studies, he may have purposely excluded books, apart from

[2] Cassiodorus *Institutiones* (ed. R. A. B. Mynors) i. 17.

4

Josephus, not written from the Christian point of view. The opening remarks of chapter xvii in the first book of the *Institutiones* rather suggest that this was the case; yet we also know that his attitude to non-Christian writers in general was more liberal than that of most of his contemporaries. Whatever be the truth—and indeed both explanations just put forward may be correct—the books enumerated by Cassiodorus for the most part became the most popular and frequently copied historical works in monastic libraries for centuries after his time.

Before we pass to our main topic, one author of an earlier generation requires brief mention. The *Chronicle* composed by Eusebius of Caesarea was basic and is constantly used either in its original form or more usually in Jerome's Latin version by chroniclers and historians of the fifth and sixth centuries. Only a little less important was his *Ecclesiastical History,* whose greatest value lay in its extensive documentation. Eusebius' achievement in correlating pagan, Jewish, and Christian chronology was more accurate and more complete than anything previously attempted. In the *Ecclesiastical History* his aim was to illustrate as fully as possible the early centuries of church history by inserting as many citations from his sources, including official records, as possible. He was not a great historian, if by that term we mean an author who achieves a well-rounded picture of an epoch, in which the importance of individual persons and episodes are justly appraised as larger or smaller parts of a whole and in which certain broad philosophic concepts serve as a guide through the maze of history and as an aid for the reader toward a true interpretation. But he ranks high among the humbler and then, as in our own time, far more numerous inquirers of whom George Meredith must have been thinking when he declined Thomas Carlyle's invitation to turn from writing fiction to writing history. " 'Carlyle,' said Meredith, 'do you know what historians remind me of?' 'No.' 'They are like a row of men working in a potato field with their eyes and noses turned down in the furrow, and their other end turned towards Heaven.' " [3]

Historical literature in Latin from the last decade of the

[3] D. A. Wilson and D. Wilson MacArthur, *Carlyle in Old Age,* p. 359. I think it

fourth to the middle of the sixth century—or, in other words, from the death of Ammianus Marcellinus to the *Gothic History* of Jordanes—consists of a large number of annalistic compilations and a smaller group of more literary works. Even in the latter some of the characteristic features in earlier historical writings, for example, set speeches placed in the mouth of leading personages, have disappeared almost entirely. The result is a loss of ethos, a quality that we find, though in a varying degree, in all the more notable historical authors of Greece and Rome; for although Livy, for instance, may be open to criticism on various counts, no fair-minded reader of his pages will deny that he has given us a consistent and convincing picture of the national Roman character and of the achievement of Rome as a unifying, and in some ways indeed a civilizing, force in Mediterranean history. The annalistic works composed in the Late Imperial period consist of a few pagan treatises and of a somewhat larger group of Christian chronicles. The pagan epitomists have other characteristics in common besides their brevity. Not only in Eutropius and Aurelius Victor, but also in Rufius Festus, although his *Breviarium* has as its main aim to sketch the steps by which Rome acquired her eastern provinces, the biographical approach to history is very marked. The characterization of the early Roman emperors is the conventional one which can be traced back ultimately to Tacitus and Suetonius. Tiberius in Eutropius is a man "gravi crudelitate, scelesta avaritia, turpi libidine." [4] Aurelius Victor's estimate is of the same type, but a little more circumstantial. Nero is even more obviously drawn as the conventional tyrant. Again there is often a complete ignorance of historical development, to use no stronger term. The same writer, Rufius Festus, who says of Armenia that it was lost by Nero and recovered by Trajan, even more astonishingly alludes to the three Punic wars with the words "ter Africa rebellavit." [5] Victor is not so crassly ignorant as this, but he too confines himself to a brief mention of Roman disasters at Parthian

---

probable that Meredith, consciously or subconsciously, had in mind a passage in Aristophanes (*Clouds* 191–194).

[4] Eutropius vii. 11. 1.   [5] Rufius Festus xx. 1; iv. 3.

hands and says not a word about Corbulo or the settlement of the Armenian question in A.D. 66. He is also fond of moralizing, perhaps a legacy from the rhetorical schools. People, we learn, had high hopes of Caligula, but things turned out very differently when he came to the throne, "as though in accordance with a law of nature which expressly (*ex industria*) changes good men to bad, cultured men to boors, and so on." [6] On Aurelian's death his troops sent to Rome and asked the senate to choose a successor. "Thus both sides vied with one another in modesty and restraint (*pudore ac modestia*), a virtue rare among men especially in questions of this kind, and almost unknown among soldiers." [7] In Eutropius we observe an utter lack of interest in the inner history of the later Republic. The Gracchi and the constitutional issues of the years 60–49 B.C. are completely ignored, and of Sulla we are merely told that he composed the commonwealth. And, when we are informed by a writer who lived under a fourth-century despotism that Julius Caesar "began to act more irresponsibly (*insolentius*) and against established Roman liberty (*contra consuetudinem Romanae libertatis*)" and that he was responsible for actions that were kingly and almost despotic, we seem to see young Eutropius declaiming his first *suasoria* on tyrannicide to an approving teacher! [8] Still, with all his shortcomings, Eutropius is the best of these pagan abbreviators of history. His chronology is fairly accurate, though he lapses into vagueness here and there; he occasionally introduces a brief mention of occurrences outside the history of Rome, as when he states that in the very year in which Rome defeated the Latins Alexandria was founded by Alexander the Great. A little later he also refers to the early treaty between Rome and Egypt.[9] The *De Caesaribus* is the only genuine treatise by Aurelius Victor, but there are three others, all quite short, which have come down to us under his name. The *Origo gentis Romanae* is a worthless little compilation about legendary Rome down to Romulus and Remus. Its author has the same fondness for fantastic etymologies that we find a little later in Fulgentius and Martianus Capella. The

[6] Aurelius Victor *De Caesaribus* iii. 5.   [7] *Ibid.* xxxv. 11.
[8] Eutropius vi. 25. 1.   [9] *Ibid.* ii. 7. 3; ii. 15.

7

De viris illustribus begins with Proca, king of Alba, and ends with Antony and Cleopatra. It is composed in the concentrated and depressing style of a biographical dictionary, and its historical value is slight. Thus, for instance, the writer says of Cicero, "praetor Ciliciam latrociniis liberavit," which suggests confusion of the Lex Gabinia with the Lex Manilia and a telescoping of Cicero's support of Pompey in 66 and his governorship of Cilicia fifteen years later! [10] The *Epitome de Caesaribus,* though it purports to be an abbreviation of Aurelius Victor's book, contains matter not found in the earlier work and in addition continues the lives of the Caesars from Valentinian and Valens down to Theodosius I. The influence of the rhetorical schools and the desire to furnish them with suitable material for their exercises are apparent in the obiter dicta that the author puts into the mouth of emperors or their subjects. The subsequent fate of these compilations, as suggested by their presence or absence in medieval library catalogues and by the number of extant manuscripts, is not without interest. The most widely read was Eutropius. The *Epitome de Caesaribus* comes next; it was used by Servatus Lupus and Christian of Stavelot in the ninth century, and there is ample evidence for its continued popularity.[11] The *De viris illustribus,* too, seems to have enjoyed a fair success, but the use of Rufius Festus was probably rather restricted. Least known of all, it would appear, was the *De Caesaribus* and the *Origo gentis Romanae.* That the *Epitome* was greatly preferred to the genuine Victor was no doubt due to two causes: its author continued the lives down to Theodosius and added a good deal of anecdotal material which enlivens Victor's rather dry presentation, though contributing nothing of historical value.[12]

[10] Ps.-Victor *De viris illustribus* 81. 3.

[11] See Lupus' letter to Charles the Bald. This is No. 37 in Léon Levillain's edition (*Les Classiques de l'histoire de France au moyen âge,* Vol. 10). For Christian of Stavelot cf. my article in *Harvard Theological Review,* XX (1927), 135 [see No. 12 in this volume]. Christian also appears to have known the *De viris illustribus* (cf. *ibid.,* p. 136).

[12] For the evidence of the medieval library catalogues the reader should consult Max Manitius, *Handschriften antiker Autoren in mittelalterlichen Bibliothekskatalogen (Zentralblatt für Bibliothekswesen,* Beiheft 67), where the information is listed under individual authors. It is not suggested that this information is

The majority of Christian chroniclers are content to follow the lead of Eusebius, though with less success and less authority. Indeed their works are for the most part conscious continuations of Jerome's Latin version of Eusebius. They are, in short, lists of kings, rulers, and magistrates chronologically arranged, with occasional sentences or brief paragraphs recording notable events in a given year. The *Chronicle* by Prosper of Aquitaine is a little more ambitious and consequently more valuable than most. It contains a substantial amount of Biblical material, and it is not built up simply round the names of rulers, but often approaches the form of a running commentary on events. Prosper also includes references to literary events, like the birth and death of authors and the madness and death of Lucretius, his source being Jerome, and in the imperial section of his *Chronicle* he inserts paragraphs on various heresies. Here his authority seems to have been Augustine. It is, moreover, significant that the fullest treatment is reserved for Pelagianism and Semipelagianism, still a very burning question in Gaul in Prosper's day. The work of Sulpicius Severus is in a rather different category. In the only surviving manuscript it is called *Chronica*, but it is a continuous narrative divided into two books. The first is devoted to Biblical history down to the Babylonish Captivity; the second covers the long period from the fifth century B.C. to the author's own time, but Sulpicius omits that part of the story contained in the Gospels and Acts of the Apostles as too sacred to abbreviate or tamper with. In

---

final or definitive; but it is sufficiently copious to justify general inferences regarding the relative popularity of these works in the Middle Ages. Eutropius survives in four or five manuscripts, and the catalogues record seventeen of various dates, from the tenth to the fourteenth century, and a dozen from the fifteenth, most of these last being from Italian collections. Our present text of Rufius Festus is based on five manuscripts, but the *Breviarium* is unknown in medieval book lists before the fourteenth and fifteenth centuries. The genuine treatise by Victor is preserved in only two manuscripts; the *De viris illustribus* and especially the *Epitome* survive in a good many more. Our text of the *Origo gentis Romanae* depends on the same two codices that contain the genuine Victor. In the catalogues only a work on the Caesars is found. Of the eleven cases recorded by Manitius, four show by their description—*a Caesare usque ad Theodosianum*—that the *Epitome* is meant. This circumstance, coupled with the evidence from Lupus and Christian, seems to me to make it very probable that most, if not all, the entries in Manitius refer to the *Epitome*.

its literary character, therefore, the book belongs to the same category as Eutropius' *Breviarium;* it is a short history, not a chronicle. Brief though it be, it is the best piece of historical narrative written during the century that we are considering. Sulpicius twice informs his readers that he has used secular or pagan sources; unhappily he does not particularize.[13] He also alludes to an anonymous treatise on Babylonian chronology, and he was familiar with *Acts of Martyrs* of the Diocletianic persecution, but does not cite from them lest his book become too long.[14] He is at great pains to fix the chronology of persons and events as precisely as possible.[15] Where the evidence is conflicting and there is no way of determining where the balance of probability lies, he leaves the matter open.[16] That he is not always right when he thinks that he has solved a problem matters little, in view of his genuine, scientific desire to obtain and probe all the evidence that he can. Thus he devotes a lengthy passage to the regnal years of Samuel and Saul and finally accepts the testimony of Acts 13:21 on this point. This, as a matter of fact, was an old crux. Several centuries after Severus it was taken up again by the Venerable Bede, who first accepted the same solution as Severus, but subsequently revised it.[17] In another case he not unreasonably exonerates the author of III Kings from the charge of making an error and attributes the corruption to the carelessness of successive generations of copyists.[18] His method is seen at its best in the sections devoted to the history and date of Esther and Judith. Esther, we are told, lived in the time of Artaxerxes, but there were two kings of that name. Severus concludes that she flourished under the younger Artaxerxes; for Ezra wrote at the time of Artaxerxes the Elder, and it would be extraordinary if Ezra had failed to mention so illustrious a woman. Judith is reported to have lived after the Captivity, but under which Persian

---

[13] Severus i. 1. 4; ii. 14. 6; the phrase is *mundiales historici.*
[14] *Ibid.* ii. 5. 7; ii. 32. 6.
[15] Cf. *ibid.* i. 3. 5; i. 15. 2; i. 28. 7; i. 29. 7; i. 36. 3; i. 40. 1; i. 46. 5; ii. 27.
[16] *Ibid.* i. 28. 7.
[17] M. L. W. Laistner, *Bedae Venerabilis Expositio Actuum Apostolorum et Retractatio,* pp. xv–xvi, 57, 131.
[18] Severus i. 40. 2.

ruler is doubtful. He is called Nabuchodonosor, but Severus could find no Persian king of this name after the Captivity. Many thought that the king was Cambyses, but Judith's heroic deed occurred in the twelfth year of the ruler's reign, whereas Cambyses ruled only seven years. Severus therefore concludes that the Persian monarch was Ochus and that Bagoas in Judith is ,the same man who is mentioned in secular authorities as Ochus' contemporary.[19] The same rational approach that he used in this and in other cases of disputed chronology we find elsewhere in Severus' book. The first bird sent by Noah out of the Ark when the waters subsided was a raven. It did not return to the Ark, and Severus explains this by suggesting that the bird could not resist the lure of the corpses left behind when the flood receded.[20] Or again, he remarks of Ezra that he did nothing to rebuild Jerusalem, "thinking, I believe, that it was a more important task to reform a people of corrupt manners." [21] One of the most remarkable passages in the *Chronica* occurs where Severus, who had been trained in his younger days in Roman law, reproduces in his own words the penal ordinances of the Jews. Jacob Bernays long since compared Severus' version with the Hieronymic translation of Exodus and pointed out that Severus' summary is written in a precise legal phraseology worthy of the best third-century jurists. Indeed, the passage would have suggested to Severus' educated readers a comparison with the early ordinances of Roman law.[22] In the last section of his book Severus stands out as a strong supporter of orthodoxy. Just as Cicero had alluded to members of his own political party as *nostri*, so Severus uses *nostri* and *noster* of those who were orthodox and opposed to Arius during that long and bitter doctrinal controversy.[23] To the student of ecclesiastical history the best-known passage in our author is probably the concluding portion, in which is preserved the only contemporary account of Priscillian and Priscillianism.

[19] *Ibid.* ii. 13–14.   [20] *Ibid.* i. 3. 3.   [21] *Ibid.* ii. 10. 5.

[22] The brilliant essay of Bernays, which first appeared in the publications of the Prussian Academy and was reprinted in the *Gesammelte Abhandlungen,* ed. Hermann Usener (Berlin, 1885), II, 81–200, is still quite indispensable. For the passage from Exodus see *ibid.,* pp. 132–40.

[23] Severus ii. 39. 1 and 2; ii. 44. 1 (*noster Foegadius*).

While strongly disapproving of the heresiarch and his tenets, Severus is unsparing in his criticism of Priscillian's chief accusers and bitterly opposed to the calling-in of the secular authority: "It was a monstrous and unheard of crime that a secular judge should pass judgment on an ecclesiastical offense." [24] We cannot doubt, even if we admit that some of his indignation was caused by the discourteous treatment meted out to Martin of Tours by Ithacius and others, that Severus staunchly upheld the authority of the church and of her appointed representatives. But this only makes more remarkable the severe strictures that he passes on some of the clergy in his time. The unjust and rapacious behavior of the Levites is held up as a warning example to ministers of the church. He concludes his account of the Diocletianic persecution by remarking that "the martyrs vied with one another in rushing into the glorious contests, and in those days martyrdoms with a glorious death were sought after more greedily than men now seek bishoprics with base ambitions." [25] Surprise has sometimes been expressed that Sulpicius Severus' *Chronica* had so little success. The book survives in a single manuscript of the eleventh century, and it is mentioned only once in a medieval library catalogue; a copy existed at Murbach in the Vosges in the ninth century. [26] The commonest explanation put forward of the book's lack of popularity is that Severus' elegant and compressed style did not appeal to the literary taste of the earlier Middle Ages, when the more rhetorical and embellished periods of Orosius, Fulgentius, or Martianus Capella were greatly admired. But is not this a very weak argument? Why, if it were true, did Eutropius' *Breviarium* enjoy such success? And did Jerome's *Letters* written in a Latin of all but Ciceronian purity owe their appeal only to the authority of the author? Jacob Bernays doubtless went too far in seeing veiled allusions to contemporary abuses in Severus' narrative of Old Testament history.

[24] *Ibid.* ii. 50. 5: "Saevum esse et inauditum nefas, ut causam ecclesiae iudex saeculi iudicaret."

[25] *Ibid.* i. 23. 5–7; ii. 32. 4.

[26] Manitius, *op. cit.*, p. 234.

And yet besides the two passages already mentioned there is the fierce denunciation of Gallican clergy in his day with which he concludes his account of Priscillian and his own chronicle. [27] Thus it may be suggested that the real reason why Severus' *Chronica* was virtually forgotten until the days of the Humanists was his critical spirit, shown in various ways but most clearly, and for his reputation most disastrously, in his censure of church dignitaries.[28]

If posthumous popularity were proof of greatness, then assuredly Orosius would rank among the leading historical writers of all time. The best of his modern editors speaks of the *immensa codicum copia*—there are some two hundred extant manuscripts of the *Historia adversus paganos*—and Manitius lists one hundred and eight copies in medieval library catalogues.[29] Allusions to, or quotations from, Orosius in medieval authors are innumerable. In recent times there has not been wanting, among a certain school of historiographers whose dogmatism is usually in inverse ratio to their actual knowledge, a tendency to belaud Orosius as an author who, whatever his faults, made some attempt to compose a world-history. Yet the opposite judgment of one critic—Krüger, who is better qualified than most to express an opinion—that Orosius' *History against the Pagans* is not history at all but apologetic is a good deal nearer the truth. Orosius is completely under the domination of his thesis. Now, while it is perfectly true that every man is entitled to write the kind of book that he wishes, it is also true that the reader has the right to form his own judgment of the finished product. And, since Orosius, whatever his ultimate purpose, professed to write history, we are justified in appraising the historical worth of his book. He had undertaken its composition at the suggestion of Augustine, whose disciple he was. Its purpose, briefly stated, was to demonstrate that the pagan assertion that the disasters which befell

[27] Severus ii. 51. 8–10.
[28] Severus' reputation as a hagiographer, of course, did not suffer. His *Life of St. Martin of Tours* earned an immediate and lasting success.
[29] *Op. cit.*, pp. 243–247.

the Roman Empire in the opening years of the fifth century were due to the Romans' neglect of their national gods and religion was false by showing in some detail how earlier civilizations had suffered or even been submerged under disasters no less great than those that threatened Rome in Alaric's day. The first book, after a geographical introduction, portrays the earlier history of the Mediterranean area down to the reputed date of Rome's foundation. The second deals with Persian history after Cyrus, Greek history to Cunaxa, and Roman affairs down to the Gallic invasion of 387 B.C. Book iii is devoted to the wars of the Diadochs; Book iv, to the history of Rome down to the destruction of Carthage. The remaining three books are in the nature of things concerned almost wholly with Roman history. Orosius no doubt deserves credit for weaving together in the earlier part of his work the political and military experiences of different Mediterranean states, but there was nothing startlingly new in this. Quite apart from the fundamental work of Eusebius on pagan, Jewish, and Christian chronology, other far earlier authors had taken as their theme a subject wider than the history of a single state or a single epoch. The first five books of Herodotus are a survey, in part at least inspired by the earlier researches of Hecataeus, of divers countries making up the huge Persian Empire. Hellenistic writers, like Timaeus and, to a less extent, Polybius, had composed their histories on a grand scale, and even Diodorus, poor creature though he may have been, had attempted a universal history. Of these, Polybius alone was consciously writing under the influence of a philosophy of history, though he did not always follow its guidance very consistently. Orosius, in common with other men of his age, was influenced by a mystical belief in numbers. There is a special virtue in the number 7, so his history is divided into seven books. It was 1,164 years from the refoundation of Babylon by Semiramis to its destruction by the Medes and 1,164 years from the foundation of Rome to its capture by Alaric. The dreams and number symbolism in the Book of Daniel afford further material for the historian's ingenuity. It is a natural result of Orosius' purpose that he stresses the ghastly events of the past and, as De Labriolle wittily remarks, parades a kind of museum of historical horrors, before which Orosius' contemporaries would blush at their own complaints.[30] In spite of Orosius' avowed aim in writing his book, we might make every allowance for his bias and find his work a notable achievement in historical composition, if he could be shown to be accurate in his presentation and, in the absence of great critical powers, at least to have treated his sources with respect. Only too often the opposite is true. He used Justin's abbreviation of Pompeius Trogus extensively, yet time and again we find him embellishing his authority with sensational additions or imagined psychological explanations. He alludes to the authority of Livy—actually what he used was an abbreviation of Rome's greatest historian—and then proceeds to misquote or misunderstand him. Livy, for instance, had related that, when in 491 B.C. Romans and Volscians were at war, the Romans suffered a famine, the Volscians were visited by a pestilence. Orosius makes the Romans experience both disasters. His mistakes are very numerous, and there is here only room to cite a few typical examples. Hannibal is made to march from the Pyrenees to the summit of the Alps in nine days, whereas Livy had written that the Punic army reached the top of the Alps from the foot on the ninth day. Livy alludes to a certain Q. Terentius Culleo who was present at Scipio's triumph; Orosius transforms this person into Terence, the poet, who was not born until about fifteen years later! Through misunderstanding Eutropius, Orosius makes the Romans suffer two separate defeats on the Trebia. Galerius is said to have committed suicide, although Orosius' source, Eusebius-Rufinus, related this *felo de se* of one of Maximin's officers. Constans is confused with Constantius and made to march to war against Persia. Here again the error is apparently due to a careless reading of Eutropius. Gaugamela, we are told, is situated near Tarsus (*apud Tarsum*); it is not clear whether this is crass ignorance of geography or a confusion with the Battle of Issus, although the historian had briefly described this battle in an earlier chapter. According to Eusebius-Jerome an earthquake in the early years of the emperor Constantius had destroyed many cities in the eastern provinces. Orosius changes the *multas* of his authority into

[30] Pierre de Labriolle, *Histoire de la littérature latine chrétienne* (3d ed.), p. 679.

plurimas, and this kind of alteration is very frequent and characteristic of Orosius' sensational but unhistorical method.[31] Our last example, too, is instructive, because in it we can compare Orosius with his contemporary, Rufinus. The latter, in narrating the death of Valentinian II by hanging, remarks, "causis etiam nunc latentibus," but adds various beliefs currently held about the occurrence. The most popular was that Arbogast was responsible, but others thought that Valentinian was driven by despair to take his own life, and there were certain bishops to testify to Arbogast's innocence. Now this method of suggesting that the truth was in doubt, while giving rumors common at the time of the event, is honest and has its parallel in Herodotus, Thucydides, Livy, and elsewhere. But Orosius makes a circumstantial murder story out of his materials, which recalls the detective fiction sponsored by the Crime Club! "Through the treachery of Arbogast, they say, Valentinian was strangled and then was hung up by a rope so that people might think he had committed suicide." [32]

When Orosius deals with contemporary events, he is often exceedingly vague. He has recourse to phrases like *ut aiunt, ut quidam ferunt, ut alia tradit opinio, ut fertur,* which suggest that he is using oral traditions or oral sources of information. This is, of course, nothing new—the same thing is found in the classical historians—but we need to be sure of two things if we are to have confidence in the author's narrative: his critical faculty and the reliability of his witnesses. That the former is frankly deficient in Orosius has been demonstrated by a number of examples; the latter is much harder to estimate. Still, to judge by the character of the information supplied, the intelligence or even truthfulness of Orosius' informants was not usually of high caliber. There is one striking exception. The account and eulogy of Athaulf is based on oral testimony obtained from a highly placed Gaul. To me it reads far more convincingly than Orosius' other characterizations, and it is not, so far as I am aware, contradicted by evidence from other sources.[33] The phenomenal suc-

[31] Orosius ii. 5. 6; iv. 14. 3; iv. 19. 6; iv. 14. 7; vii. 28. 13; vii. 29. 6; iii. 17. 1; vii. 29. 5.

[32] *Ibid.* vii. 35. 10.

[33] *Ibid.* 43. 2–8. Orosius met his informant in Bethlehem when both men were on a visit to Jerome.

cess of Orosius' *History* is not difficult to explain. It is very readable; its style is sufficiently rhetorical to satisfy the prevailing
taste of his early medieval readers; its scope is wide and its information, though too often inaccurate, is copious; but, above all,
it was undertaken at the behest of Augustine and gave practical
expression to, or rather illustrated, however imperfectly, one
facet of his many-sided philosophic theory. We can only regret
that he could not intrust the task that he wished done to a more
highly trained and profound intelligence.

The popularity of Rufinus' *Ecclesiastical History* rivaled that
of Orosius in the Middle Ages. Books i–ix are a compressed and
not always accurate rendering of Eusebius; Books x and xi are
Rufinus' own contribution and cover the period from 324 to 395.
"The tenth and eleventh books we have compiled partly from
the traditions of our forebears, partly from what our own recol-
lection had embraced, and these two books like two little fishes
we have added to the loaves described above," that is, the *History*
of Eusebius.[34] Rufinus is admittedly a careless translator. Since
we are here concerned only with his place as a historian, we must
confine ourselves to Books x and xi. Even in the case of these,
it is still a moot point whether they were really as original as
Rufinus claims. But even if Rufinus was heavily indebted to
Gelasius of Caesarea, there remains enough of what is indisput-
ably his own work to allow us to form some judgment of his
historical method and value. He gives us an occasional glimpse
of his informants. There are the monks of the desert with some
of whom he had conversed. There is Theodorus, who as a strip-
ling had suffered torture at the time of the Antioch riots under
Julian the Apostate. Rufinus does not indeed introduce long
speeches into his narrative, but he does enliven it with short
passages in *oratio recta*, for example, when he relates the scan-
dalous trial of Athanasius for magic or the conversation between
that remarkable man and Constantius. Or, again, he reproduces
what purports to be the actual prayer of Theodosius at the critical point of a battle.[35] He is staunchly orthodox, as appears especially in the passages devoted to Athanasius and Arius. Unlike
Severus, however, he employs the word *nostri* in a general way to

[34] Rufinus *E.H.* (ed. Th. Mommsen), p. 952 (9–12).
[35] *Ibid.*, pp. 983–984, 986–987, 1038 (11–15).

signify Christians as distinct from pagans. The western half of the Empire he ignores almost entirely, although he does record the election of Ambrose as bishop of Milan. He is very partial to miracles, as when he describes the finding of the True Cross by the Empress Helena or tells the story of the temple columns in Pontus that were placed in position by superhuman agency after the human builders had failed to set them up.[36] We may fully agree with Mommsen that Rufinus is a valuable source for the earlier Christian legends and for events contemporary with his own life and that in respect both of reliability and of lively descriptive power there are few passages in the extant literature of that age as good as the chapters in which Rufinus relates the rooting-out of the Serapis cult in Egypt.[37] He had lived for six years in that country, and his narrative is based on his own observations as an eyewitness. That he is less sensational than Orosius I have had occasion to show already by reference to an incident told in both authors. Rufinus' story of Helena and the True Cross suggests a comparison with Sulpicius Severus, who narrates the whole episode with a remarkable economy of phrase in eighteen lines. Rufinus' account is nearly three times as long; for, apart from the fact that he writes more diffusely than Severus, he inserts picturesque details, such as that the site on which the Cross was found had been previously occupied by a shrine of Venus, or that the inscription in three languages placed on the Cross of Christ had also been discovered. Moreover, the circumstances by which it was determined which of the three crosses was the True Cross are told briefly and impersonally by Severus. Rufinus introduces the bishop Macarius and reproduces his prayer. He tells us further how the wood of the Cross and the nails became relics, and how Helena invited the virgins, in whose care some of these relics were left on the site, to eat with her and with exemplary humility waited on them herself. The whole of this passage and the narrative of Egyptian events to which I have already referred seem to me to illustrate both the strength and the weakness of Rufinus as a historian. Given a congenial topic, he writes descriptive passages with the skill of a good reporter who records his own observations or, failing that, has enough imagi-

[36] *Ibid.*, pp. 969 ff., 975–976.   [37] *Ibid.*, pp. 1025–1035.

nation to bring a scene vividly before the eyes of his readers. On the other hand, he is less critical or more credulous than Severus, although we must not forget that Severus, who in the *Chronica* writes with great restraint, though not with disbelief, when dealing with miraculous occurrences, was also the biographer of St. Martin of Tours. In the *Life* of that saint Severus displays as implicit a faith in the miraculous as any of his contemporaries.

It is not my intention to enter into so dangerously controversial a subject as the miracles recorded in this age. But two points are worth stressing. The attitude of rationalist historians, especially of the nineteenth century, was certainly futile and unscientific. However much they may themselves have disbelieved miracles, they should have remembered that to the men of the early Christian centuries and of the Middle Ages these supernatural occurrences were a reality which affected their lives and conduct. In consequence they deserved serious and indeed sympathetic treatment by the modern inquirer who would seek to understand the minds of men in those ages. Second, belief in miracles—always excepting those connected with Christ Himself and those of the Apostolic Age—only became widespread in the later fourth century and then rapidly found its way into literature of all kinds. This fact has been well brought out by the greatest living authority on the subject, Père Delehaye, who finds the chief reason for this greater credulity in the growth of monasticism and more particularly in the ascetic practices of the monks, accompanied as they often were by visions and by a belief on the part of the masses in the healing powers of persons endowed with especial sanctity.[38]

Very brief mention must suffice for two other histories. About A.D. 489 Victor, bishop of Vita, published an account of the Vandal persecutions in Africa between 428 and 484. Two-thirds of this narrative are an eyewitness's record. The author also introduces official documents, for instance, several of Huneric's edicts and the *libellus fidei* drawn up by Eugenius, bishop of Carthage. Victor's book is not pleasant reading, for it is a blood-curdling tale of atrocities. Yet the passionate indignation of its author, though it may make him a little less than fair to the Arian persecutors

[38] Cf. *Analecta Bollandiana*, XXXVIII (1920), 73 ff.

of orthodoxy, gives this little history a vivid freshness that we miss in much of the other historical writing put out in the later Imperial Age. It is a valuable record of episodes about which our other sources tell us little. In spite of a certain seeking after rhetorical effect and occasional solecisms in the language, the total effect is more moving than the cold-blooded and more studied narrative of Orosius in his more horrifying passages. The *Gothic History* of Jordanes, although it was not published until the middle of the sixth century, deserves notice as an early attempt to compose the national history of one group of the invaders who overran the western Empire. Jordanes betrays some admiration for Rome and for emperors like Theodosius I and Justinian. Unlike the other historical works that we have considered, the *Gothic History* contains speeches of some length, notably an address put in the mouth of Attila. It is, however, a mere abbreviation of a much longer lost work by Cassiodorus, and the fact that it is now our only source for much of our knowledge of the Goths must not blind us to its poorness as a historical compilation. We may even question whether Cassiodorus' larger work was comparable to national histories like Gregory of Tours' *History of the Franks* or Paul the Deacon's *History of the Lombards*.

To sum up: the historical writing of our period, if it lacks both originality and distinction, is not contemptible. It stresses the value of chronology; and, while it contents itself in the main with compilation, at its best it displays reasonable and even critical use of the materials with which it works. The ancients at least never forgot that the writing of history is an art—it is only in our own time that it is too often debased to the status of an inexact science—and consequently much importance was always attached to language and literary form. Apart from the chronicles, which for the most part are too jejune in their treatment, all these historical works show, though in a varying degree, the influence of the rhetorical schools. Nearly all are written in good correct Latin. Only Victor of Vita commits occasional barbarisms which make his book a valuable source for students of vulgar Latin; while Jordanes is frankly uncouth, not so much because he has confused vernacular with literary

Latin as because the Goth has not acquired a complete mastery over the language of the western Empire. Yet our final conclusion must be that historical composition, either for the interest of its subject or as a literary exercise, was not highly regarded in the fifth century as it had been in the Hellenistic Age or in the first century of our era. The intellectual achievement of the century and a half from Ambrose to Caesarius of Arles is to be seen rather in the more direct service of religion and the church, in apologetic, polemic, expository, and hortatory works. If the greatest humanist and scholar of his age had carried out his half-formed plan, then this period might have had one history worthy to rank as a literary and intellectual performance with the best that it has to offer in other fields of literature. Jerome in the opening chapter of his *Life of Malchus* writes:

I have purposed—if the Lord gives me life and if my detractors cease to persecute me who am now a fugitive and shut off from the world—to write a history from the advent of our Savior down to our own time, from the Apostles to the dregs of our age, and to describe how and through whom Christ's Church came to birth, how growing up it waxed by persecutions and was crowned with martyrdoms; and how after reaching the Christian Emperors it became yet greater in power and wealth, but declined in virtues.

Who would not gladly exchange Jerome's latest works, his anti-Pelagian tracts and even his unfinished commentary on Jeremiah, for the history which he had projected some twenty-five years before, soon after he took up his residence permanently in Palestine?

~ 2 ~

The Value and Influence of Cassiodorus' Ecclesiastical History*

MOST students of history or literature have had at some time the experience of encountering statements or generalizations made by a writer of an earlier generation and then finding them repeated without question by his successors working in the same field of inquiry. What is more, if dissentient voices have been raised, they have often been overlooked or disregarded. The prevailing estimate of Cassiodorus' Ecclesiastical History affords an excellent example of the manner in which erroneous opinions have been repeated *ad nauseam* from one generation to the next, although more than thirty years have passed since two scholars of the first rank, Bidez and Parmentier, provided at least some of the evidence needed for a more just evaluation of Cassiodorus' book. There are two essential questions which seem to call for fresh investigation. The first is concerned with the value and accuracy of the compilation, the second with its diffusion during the Middle Ages and its popularity as a work of reference.[1]

* *Harvard Theological Review*, 41 (1948), 51–67. Reprinted by permission of the Harvard University Press.

[1] The following abbreviation has been used throughout, HT = Historia Tripartita.

Some years after political conditions had forced Cassiodorus to withdraw from public life, he founded his monastic community at Vivarium in southern Italy. He built up his famous library in order to make possible the study of secular and religious works by his monks; and, as a general guide to their reading, he composed his treatise, Institutiones, in two short books, the first devoted to sacred, the second to profane letters.[2] He did not, however, consider the study of only Latin writers to be an adequate preparation for the monastic student. Hence one part of his general plan was to make available in Latin dress Greek works which for one reason or another seemed to him of essential utility. He refers to the Greek books which he caused to be translated, and he names several of the helpers to whom the actual task of translation was entrusted. Amongst the historical works for which he thus assumed a general responsibility was a condensed version of the Ecclesiastical Histories composed by Socrates, Sozomen, and Theodoret. Epiphanius, the translator, was responsible also for Latin renderings of several Greek theological works; otherwise nothing is known about him. Cassiodorus refers twice to the undertaking. He explains its origin and purpose briefly in the Preface, which is certainly from his pen even if his share in compiling the actual history was purely advisory or editorial; and he included an even shorter statement in that chapter of the Institutiones (1, 17) where he describes the historical section of his library.

Epiphanius began by turning into Latin the abbreviated version of the three Histories put together a decade or two before by a certain Theodore, Reader at the church of S. Sophia in Constantinople, but Cassiodorus makes no mention of this fact. Theodore's work, although it has never been printed, is still extant in the same manuscript at Venice (Marcianus 344: saec. xiii) which, as far as it goes, contains the best surviving text of Sozomen.[3] From Book 2, chapter 8, however, Epiphanius pro-

---

[2] The best treatment of Cassiodorus' activities at Vivarium is now to be found in the brilliant book, Les Lettres grecques en Occident, by Pierre Courcelle (Bibliothèque des écoles françaises d'Athènes et de Rome, Fasc. 159; Paris, de Boccard, 1943), pp. 313–388. Cf. my review in Classical Philology for October, 1947.

[3] Cf. J. Bidez, La tradition manuscrite de Sozomène et la Tripartite de Théo-

ceeded independently. There are a few more borrowings from Theodore here and there; after that Epiphanius, with or without the guidance of Cassiodorus, makes his own selections from the Greek originals. The name by which this Latin version became known, Historia Tripartita, explains its origin and seems obvious enough; nevertheless it is hard to say when it first came into use. Theodore Lector called his book a *syntaxis* or compilation. Cassiodorus' contemporary, Liberatus of Carthage, obtained material from Epiphanius' version for his account of Nestorianism and Monophysitism; he calls it "the ecclesiastical history lately translated from Greek into Latin." [4] Gregory the Great refers to a passage "in historia Sozomeni"; actually it is in Theodoret, but Gregory's mistake is readily understandable if he was using HT. Isidore of Seville obtained material from HT for his Chronicle and two notices in De viris illustribus, but did not indicate his source. After that evidence is lacking for a long while; but in the ninth century the title, Historia Tripartita, is well established, though by no means in universal use. It is found in the official report of the Synod held at Paris in 825 and it is employed by individual writers, for example, by Amalarius of Metz and Jonas of Orléans. Others, like Ratramnus of Corbie and Hincmar of Rheims, prefer to name the particular Greek author, for instance, "Socrates in his Ecclesiastical History," although they quote the Latin translation. Walahfrid employs both methods.[5] The library catalogues of the ninth century show a similar variation in usage. Some mention only the three Greek authors and call the book, "Ecclesiastical History," while one lists it as "Tripartite History of Socrates, Sozomen, Theodoret." Whereas the cataloguer at Reichenau with his entry, "Tripartitae II," believed in extreme brevity, his confrère at St. Gall went to the opposite extreme with his, "The Ecclesiastical Histories of Cassiodorus Senator derived from three authors, to wit, Sozomen, Theodoret, and Socrates,

dore le lecteur (A. Harnack und C. Schmidt, Texte und Untersuchungen XXXII [1908], Heft 2b), pp. 35 ff.; and generally, O. Bardenhewer, Geschichte der altkirchlichen Literatur 5 (1932), pp. 117–118.

[4] Cf. Bidez, *op. cit.*, p. 46, where the whole of Theodore's Preface is printed; Liberatus in PL 68, col. 969C.

[5] De exordiis, chs. 20 and 26 (ed. Knöpfler, pp. 45 and 76–77).

twelve books in one volume." Gradually the short title, Historia Tripartita (or Tripertita), without mention of either the Greek authors or of Cassiodorus or Epiphanius, became more and more usual, and in the library catalogues of the twelfth century and later it predominates. Yet authors of the twelfth century still introduce quotations from HT with a reference to the Greek historian cited. William of Tyre inserted two considerable passages from Book 6 into his own History, assigning them correctly to Sozomen and Theodoret "in the Tripartite History." John of Salisbury introduced a citation with the comment: "Hence Socrates—not the Socrates of antiquity, but the writer whom Cassiodorus in his Tripartite History praises as a historian—remarks." [6]

We may now turn to the first of the two questions which call for reconsideration, the value and accuracy of HT. Adverse judgments on it go back a long way. They are as old as Beatus Rhenanus whose book, Autores Historiae Ecclesiasticae, published at Basel in 1523, contained Rufinus' translation of Eusebius' Ecclesiastical History together with Rufinus' two additional Books and HT. He added the documents in Theodoret in the Greek text, using a manuscript at Basel which is still extant.[7] In modern times the most detailed criticism of HT was made by Adolf Franz whose book on Cassiodorus appeared in 1872. After pointing out that the translator's knowledge of Greek was imperfect, he listed many examples of mistranslations in HT and also examples of careless arrangement in the material selected. As often happens when a notable book on a special topic has appeared, Franz' judgments were adopted more or less without question by subsequent writers. They appear in the standard literary histories of Schanz, Manitius, Bardenhewer, Moricca, and Labriolle, as well as in occasional articles. Manitius asserts that the translator had before him a text marred by many errors, while M. van de Vyver indulges in a little hyperbole when he suggests that a monograph would be necessary to de-

<hr>

[6] PL 201, 403A (from HT 1058B–C) and 309D–310A (from HT 1051D); Policraticus (ed. C. C. Webb) II, 214, 10 ff.

[7] L. Parmentier, Theodoret: Kirchengeschichte (Die griechischen christlichen Schriftsteller der ersten drei Jahrhunderte, Leipzig, 1911), p. LXVI.

scribe the many mistakes of which Epiphanius was guilty.[8] That the critics of HT were neither accurate nor just was first demonstrated by Bidez in 1908 when he published his study of the surviving manuscripts of Sozomen. Three years later Parmentier's admirable edition of Theodoret appeared. Both of these scholars were fully aware that Epiphanius had from time to time made "boners," which occasionally are even amusing.[9] But they showed that the Greek manuscripts used for HT were superior, and that by the help of Latin manuscripts of HT it is often possible to correct readings where the extant Greek codices differ. What is more, the Latin text can be used to restore the true reading in places where the surviving Greek text is defective or corrupt. In short, a study of the examples listed by Parmentier in his Introduction and a perusal of the apparatus criticus accompanying the text of Theodoret fully demonstrate the injustice of Cassiodorus' modern detractors.

In the Preface to HT Cassiodorus observes that the three Greek writers, in treating the same events, had not all been equally detailed or shown an equal amount of care; hence some parts were better in one author, some in another. Hitherto it has not been noticed that the selection of passages included in HT implies considerable exercise of the critical faculty. This, it can hardly be doubted, was Cassiodorus' own contribution, in other words, his editorial function was real, not nominal. Regarded from the point of view of historical accuracy Socrates' book is unquestionably the most valuable and the most accurate of the three. Sozomen, a far better stylist, is more agreeable to read. Theodoret's History with its strongly partisan outlook belongs, like Orosius' History, in spirit though not in form to apologetic

[8] M. Manitius, Geschichte der lateinischen Literatur des Mittelalters I, p. 51. In the Nachträge published in II, p. 793 he alludes to the work of Bidez and Parmentier, but he does not point out that their researches invalidated his earlier opinion. M. van de Vyver (Speculum 6 [1931], pp. 264–265), refers to Bidez in a footnote, but his estimate of HT and the fact that he repeats a mistake in Bidez' book suggest that he had not read it very carefully. On p. 51 Bidez had stated that Epiphanius used Theodore Lector down to Book 2, chapter 3. This was either a slip or a misprint; and on p. 55 he says correctly that Theodore's Syntaxis was followed down to Book 2, chapter 7.

[9] For example, the confusion between ὠδῖσιν and ᾠδαῖς, so that παρθενικαῖς ὠδῖσιν in HT become *virginum cantibus!* See Parmentier, *op. cit.*, p. LII.

rather than to historical literature. This feature, which a modern student would regard as a defect, would appear as a merit to the men of the Middle Ages. Besides, although all three introduce documentary material into their books, Theodoret in this respect is much more lavish than the other two. Examination of the selections in HT leads to a significant result. The excerpts from Socrates, the soundest historian of the three, greatly exceed in number those from Sozomen or Theodoret. In Books 4, 9, and 10 Sozomen comes in a bad third, nor are the extracts from him in Books 7 and 8 numerous. He is in the lead only in Book 6. Not a few of the passages taken from Theodoret are documentary or else contain material which is omitted by Socrates and Sozomen. Theodoret is, for example, the only one of the three to give in full the report of the Council of Sardica (HT 4, 24) or Athanasius' letter to the African bishops concerning the Synod of Rimini (HT, 5, 30) or the letter from the Synod of Constantinople to George, bishop of Alexandria (HT 5, 42); and there are other instances of the same thing. Books 11 and 12 of HT come entirely from Socrates who carried the story down to 439. Sozomen appears to have done the same, but the surviving version of his History does not extend beyond 421. One may perhaps surmise that the last section was already missing in the codex used by Epiphanius. Theodoret's account ended with events of the year 428.

If the selection made by Cassiodorus thus shows more care and critical acumen than he has generally been credited with, there was also some excuse for Epiphanius' occasional lapses as a translator. As Parmentier has justly observed, it was no easy task to render into adequate Latin certain of the Greek documents. Many dealt with difficult and obscure points of dogma, and it is probable that already by the middle of the sixth century corruptions had crept into the Greek text. Besides, why should Epiphanius or Cassiodorus be singled out for special obloquy? Rufinus, whose facilities were better and for whom there was therefore less excuse, was not always an accurate translator. This fact has been recognized but his versions have not been judged as harshly as HT has. And, while it would be invidious to particularize, one could readily point to translations published in our own day which are disfigured not just by verbal infelicities but by errors falsifying the author's meaning. Parmentier rated HT more highly than Bidez. The reason is not far to seek. He consulted three extant manuscripts of HT, whereas Bidez had been content to work with Garet's text as reprinted in Migne's Patrology. But Garet was certainly one of the less distinguished members of the Congregation of St. Maur. Mynors has called Garet's edition of the Institutiones a "disappointing and misleading work." The same estimate may be applied to his edition of HT. It thus becomes evident that some of the criticism levelled against Cassiodorus or Epiphanius should by right be directed at the Benedictine editor. A final judgment on the merits and defects of HT will only be possible when a trustworthy edition based on a collation of the best codices becomes available. In the meantime the evidence scattered through the apparatus criticus of Parmentier's Theodoret is highly significant.

The popularity of HT during the Middle Ages has often been stressed in a general way, but without an adequate investigation of the facts. Even those who, like Thiele, have not been content with generalizations but have taken the trouble to collect some evidence are still misleading because their inquiries have not gone far enough.[10] In the first place all the available evidence seems to point to the conclusion that for several centuries after its composition HT was not widely used. For a long time it could not compare in popularity with Orosius' History or even with Rufinus' version of Eusebius. On the other hand, Rufinus' continuation went no further than A.D. 395, and Jerome's adaptation of Eusebius' Chronicle ends with the year 378. Orosius carried his story down to 419, but his book was not an *ecclesiastical* History; and, moreover, in his later books he concentrated mainly on events in the western half of the Empire. Continuations of Eusebius-Jerome by western chroniclers were many,

[10] See Hans Thiele, Studien und Mitteilungen zur Geschichte des OSB 50 (1932), pp. 415–417; the information in L. W. Jones, Divine and Human Readings by Cassiodorus (Columbia U.P., 1946), pp. 56–57, is also insufficient, being taken from Thiele with some additions from Manitius' third volume. There are many omissions even in M. Manitius, HSS antiker Autoren in mittelalterlichen Bibliothekskatalogen, pp. 319–322.

but the only one which met with lasting success was Prosper's. The Chronicle of Hydatius survives in a single manuscript; the same thing is true of later compilers, like John of Biclaro and Marius of Avenches. Besides, the emphasis in these continuations was wholly or almost wholly on western affairs. The one chronicler who appears to have enjoyed a somewhat wider diffusion and who at the same time gave information about the Byzantine world was Marcellinus Comes.[11] Since HT was the only work in Latin to offer detailed information about the Church in the eastern half of the Empire for forty odd years after the death of Theodosius I, one might have supposed, arguing *a priori*, that its popularity would be ensured from the beginning. Yet the evidence points to a different conclusion. Extant manuscripts copied before c. 900 are scarce, and in library catalogues of the ninth century the book appears only seven times, in four German and three French collections. Obviously at least one manuscript of very early date must have survived, the archetype of the oldest that we now possess, and there may well have been two or three venerable codices. The mere fact, however, that extant manuscripts of early date— there are none of the eighth century—are few shows that HT only made headway very slowly, compared, for instance, with Cassiodorus' commentary on the Psalms.[12] It does not appear

[11] The Liber pontificalis, apart from its specialized nature, making any references to eastern affairs merely incidental, only becomes a detailed record from the end of the sixth century. Cf. the judicious summary of Bardenhewer, *op. cit.*, 5, p. 302.

[12] M. Courcelle, whose account of Cassiodorus is otherwise so good, is utterly misleading in what he says about extant manuscripts of these two works. He asserts (*op. cit.*, p. 351 with note 7) that "quantité de manuscrits carolingiens" of HT survive and, in support of this statement, he lists seven. One of these (Sangall. 561) contains saints' lives with, as far as can be judged from Scherrer, at most a few excerpts from HT. Casinensis 302, according to Lowe (Beneventan Script, p. 349), is written partly in ordinary minuscule (saec. x/xi), partly in Beneventan (saec. xi ex.). Vattasso dates Vat. lat. 1970 in the tenth century, while Stevenson, whose dates are less reliable, says of Vat. Pal. 823, "saec. ix vel x." Reifferscheid, on whom M. Courcelle relies, dated Vercelli CI "saec. ix–x" and Naples VI D 18 "saec. x." In short, under the term "carolingien" M. Courcelle lumps together manuscripts varying in date by two centuries or more. He follows a similar procedure in note 2 on the same page when he lists codices of the commentary on Psalms. For the information of the interested reader a more accurate enumeration of truly early manuscripts of that work follows. The dates are not mine but have

to have been much consulted by continental authors of the eighth century, and in England it seems to have been unknown at that period. Levison has noted a reminiscence from HT in Boniface's correspondence, Alcuin cites from it once, and his contemporary, Paulinus of Aquileia, was certainly familiar with it.[13] From Alcuin's time on the writers on the Continent betray increasing interest in the book, with the incidental result that it began to receive more attention also in the scriptoria. How is this change of attitude to be explained? The treatises composed in the ninth century, in which quotations from HT occur, suggest a probable answer.

There were two topics which engaged the attention of scholars in that age for which HT supplied useful material—the various doctrinal "errors" of the Greek Church and the duties of rulers coupled with the problem of their relation to the ecclesiastical authority. It is surely no accident that so many citations from HT in the literature of the ninth century are found in works bearing on one or other of these two subjects. The Synod of Paris in 825 addressed itself once more to the task of refuting Iconoclasm. Opposition to it and also to the extreme form of image-worship approved by the Council of Nicaea in 787 had been stated with great fulness a generation before the Synod of Paris in the so-called Libri Carolini. Doctrinally the position of their author or authors was midway between the two extremes sanctioned and enforced successively by imperial authority in the East. The Libri Carolini are full of quotations from Patristic literature, but I could find no trace of HT. The purpose of the Synod held at Paris is expressly stated: ". . . sententias colligere contra eos qui imagines non solum ab aedibus, sed etiam a sacris vasis indiscrete abolere

---

been assigned by expert palaeographers, Lindsay or Lowe or, in one case, Bruckner: Autun 20A (saec. viii–ix); Durham B.II.20 (saec. viii med.); Laon 26 (saec. ix in.); Munich 14077–78 (saec. ix[1], since Lindsay did not include mss of the later ninth century in his *Notae latinae*); Paris 12239–12241 (saec. viii med.); St. Gall 202 (saec. ix med., period of Grimalt); Schaffhausen, Ministerialbibl. 78 (saec. viii–ix); and Troyes 657 (saec. viii ex.).

[13] W. Levison, *England and the Continent in the eighth century*, p. 141, note 1, points out that I was mistaken in deriving a passage in Bede's commentary on Mark from HT. For Boniface, see *ibid.*, p. 283; Alcuin, PL 101, 97 B–C (= PL 69, 909D–910A): Paulinus, MGH: Epist. IV, 526, 35 ff.

praesumunt." There follows in the surviving report of the Synod a collectaneum of passages from the Fathers. Included are quotations from Books 1, 2, 6, 9, and 10 of HT. But the Greeks had some sympathisers in the West, notably Claudius of Turin. Against him Jonas of Orléans composed a tract, De cultu imaginum, which again is largely a cento of citations from earlier writers, and again HT supplied some of the ammunition for the verbal battle.[14] Controversy died down for a while, only to flare up afresh when the Patriarch Photius in 866 issued an encyclical. This brought to the fore once again various doctrinal differences between the two Churches, the chief of which now concerned the dogma of the Procession of the Holy Spirit. Pope Nicholas I, who invited the Carolingian divines to reply formally to the Patriarch's charges, had himself cited a passage from "Theodoret" in a letter addressed in the previous year to the Emperor Michael. In the most penetrating of the works composed in answer to the papal request, Ratramnus of Corbie's Contra Graecorum opposita, passages from HT find a place.[15]

The ideal Christian ruler and the relationship between Temporal and Spiritual Authority were discussed by Smaragdus, Jonas, Hincmar of Rheims, and Sedulius Scottus. Although his use of HT in the tract against Claudius of Turin proves Jonas' familiarity with HT, he does not seem to have consulted it when engaged in writing De institutione regia for the young king Pippin; nor does Smaragdus seem to have known the book. But Hincmar in the short essay, De fide Caroli, quotes episodes from the lives of Ambrose and Theodosius I as narrated in HT.[16] Sedulius made more extensive use of it than any other scholar of the age. He included extracts from it in his Collectaneum, while in his treatise, De rectoribus Christianis, there are, in addition to many brief phrases or reminiscences, eight long quotations from that source. The extended excerpts are what one would have expected in view of the purpose of Sedulius, to write a kind of "Mirror for Princes." They record episodes in the life

[14] MGH: Concilia II, 484, 25–27, with quotations from HT on pp. 487 and 503; PL 106, 345C, 346B, 346C, 349C.
[15] MGH: Epistulae VI, 481, 18, quoting from HT 4, 6; PL 121, 307C, 336A, 344B.
[16] PL 125, 969B and 974B–D from HT 9, 20–23.

31

of Constantine, the virtues of Flaccilla, wife of Theodosius I, and, of course, Theodosius' penance at the behest of Ambrose. A letter of Athanasius bids temporal rulers to learn and to yearn for heavenly things, and Valentinian I replies with suitable modesty when consulted by a bishop on a point of doctrine. Nor are a notable miracle at the siege of Nisibis in 350 and Julian's death in the Persian war forgotten.[17] There are traces of HT in a few other authors of the ninth century. It was one of the historical works used by Freculph of Lisieux for his History. He appears to have been a pupil of Helisachar who from c. 822 was abbot of St. Riquier and who may have taught there at an earlier date. The extant catalogue of St. Riquier, drawn up in 831, lists a copy of HT.[18] We have already seen that Amalarius and Walahfrid quote from it.[19] Later in the century the papal librarian Anastasius evidently consulted the same copy of HT in the Lateran to which Nicholas I had turned for his quotation when writing to the emperor Michael.[20]

It is thus apparent that by the end of the ninth century HT was well established, and it is not difficult to trace its continued use in the centuries that followed. A few examples must suffice to illustrate the trend and the kind of works for which HT provided useful material. Odo of Cluny relates in his own words the story of Theodosius II's humility towards an arrogant monk of whom Odo dryly observes, "ut credo, non bene compos mentis suae erat." A certain Adalger addressed a brief hortatory tract to a nun, Nonsvinda, for which HT provided suitable exempla. Here and there he indicates his source, but his indebtedness went much further than this; for example, the long description of the controversy between Theodosius I and Ambrose, filling two columns in Migne, is repeated verbatim and without ac-

---

[17] See S. Hellmann, Sedulius Scottus (Munich, 1906) whose edition of De rectoribus provides full information about Sedulius' sources. For the Collectaneum see *ibid.*, p. 97.

[18] G. Becker, Catalogi bibliothecarum antiqui 11, 193.

[19] See page 24 above and MGH: Epistulae V, 248, 19 ff., where Amalarius quotes HT on the subject of the Quartodecimans and Lenten fasting.

[20] MGH: Epistulae VII, 419, 25–26 and 421, 3–4; for Nicholas I see above, page 31.

knowledgment towards the end of this Admonitio.[21] Hagiographers also found Cassiodorus' compilation serviceable, as we see in the Miracula Gorgonii, of which more hereafter, and in Gozwin of Mainz' Passio S. Albani.[22] The numerous writers who contributed, taking one side or the other, to the controversial literature which concerned itself with the Investiture Strife and abuses in the Church, such as simony and the incontinence of the clergy, found HT a handy source for quotations. Passages were taken from Books 2, 7, 9, 10, and 12, some recurring more than once. Thus the story of Paphnutius' intervention at Nicaea in the matter of clerical marriage and its prohibition (HT 2, 14) and the story of Ambrose's election to the see of Milan (HT 7, 8) recur three times.[23] Finally, HT became a normal source of information for historian and chronicler, as can be seen in the works of Marianus Scottus, Sigebert of Gembloux, Otto of Freising, and others of later date.[24] But it is needless to labor the point further; rather one must turn to the even clearer evidence furnished by the catalogues of medieval libraries and by the extant manuscripts of HT.

The lists of medieval libraries containing a copy of HT that are given by Thiele and more recently by Mr. L. W. Jones are incomplete even for the period—down to the end of the twelfth century—to which they confine their attention. Nor, as far as I am aware, has any list of surviving manuscripts ever been drawn up. Yet this is essential evidence. It is more conclusive than many of the quotations or reminiscences found in authors; for it is sometimes impossible to be sure that a medieval writer is citing or repeating a story from the primary source. An example will illustrate this. Among the many miraculous episodes related by Theodoret was one that occurred at the siege of Nisibis in 350 and led to the repulse of the Persian forces under Sapor. The holy Ephrem having prayed from the top of a tower

[21] PL 133, 535A; 134, 922C, 932B, and particularly 934D–936D (= PL 69, 1145A–1146D).
[22] See Manitius, *op. cit.*, II, p. 473, with the references there given.
[23] See the excellent index to MGH: Libelli de lite, I–III, where this pamphlet literature has been conveniently collected.
[24] Cf. MGH: Scriptores V, 525, 11 ff.; VI, 307 and 310; XX, 200 and 201.

which commanded a view of the besieging army, swarms of mosquitoes and other insects appeared and attacked the Persian elephants and horses, filling the trunks of the one and the eyes and ears of the other. This tale was included in HT (5, 45). Soon after the middle of the tenth century an unknown writer composed a brief work, Miracula S. Gorgonii. This minor piece of hagiography was written to glorify the patron saint of Gorze, a monastery in Lorraine. Its author after relating one of the saint's miracles recalls by way of comparison the miracle at Nisibis. The modern editor of the Miracula and Manitius have assumed that the hagiographer took his story directly from HT, but this is far from certain.[25] He narrates the tale in an abbreviated form and in his own words. But the story had been used by Sedulius in De rectoribus Christianis; and it is known that the library of Gorze in the eleventh century possessed a copy of Sedulius' treatise. This codex is lost but formed the basis for a printed edition issued in 1619. The date of the lost manuscript is uncertain, but it was closely related to an extant manuscript of the late ninth century, so that it too may have been copied at that date or not much later.[26] Thus it is at least an even chance that the hagiographer took his illustration from Sedulius rather than from Cassiodorus.

The two lists that follow do not pretend to be complete. It is likely that other scholars may be able to make additions, especially to the list of extant manuscripts. Where a manuscript in a medieval catalogue can be identified or at least brought into relationship with one that still survives, the fact has been noted in round brackets.

HT in Medieval Library Catalogues

Saec. IX:
  Lorsch
  Reichenau
  St. Gall
  St. Riquier
  St. Vandrille

---

[25] MGH: Scriptores IV, 245, 10 ff.; Manitius, *op. cit.*, II, p. 196.
[26] See the full discussion in S. Hellmann, *op. cit.*, pp. 12–13.

Unidentified French library (Becker, *op. cit.*, 21, 4)
Würzburg
Saec. X:
 Cremona
 Tegernsee (Gozbert)
Saec. XI:
 Arras
 Chartres (Cf. Chartres 10: saec. ix)
 Fécamp
 Massay
 Pomposa
 Ripoll
 Toul
 Trier
 Wessobrunn (Cf. Clm 22015: saec. xii)
Saec. XII:
 Angers, St. Aubin (now Angers 676: saec. xi)
 Bamberg, Michelsberg
 Bec
 Bury St. Edmunds
 Corbie
 Durham
 Maillezais
 Moissac
 Peterborough
 Prüfening
 St. Amand (now Valenciennes 498: saec. xii)
 St. Bertin (cf. Boulogne 102: saec. xi)
 St. Maur-des-Fossés
Saec. XII–XIII:
 Cluny
 Crépy
 Limoges
 St. Pons de Tomières
Saec. XIII:
 Canterbury, Christ Church
 Marchiennes (Cf. Douai 297: saec. xi)
 S. French or Italian library (L. Delisle, Cabinet des MSS, III, p. 5)
Saec. XIV:
 Admont (now Admont 89: saec. xi)
 Constance

Heiligenkreuz (Cf. Heiligenkreuz 80: saec. xiii?)
Klosterneuburg
Ramsey
St. Martin des Champs (Cf. Paris, Mazarine 1641: saec. xi)
Saec. XV:
Aggsbach
Canterbury, St. Augustine's
Erfurt, Amplonius (an epitome only?)
Erfurt, Salvatorberg
Melk
Vienna, Dominicans
Saec. XVI:
Fulda
Syon

Extant Manuscripts of HT [27]

Admont 89. saec. xi.
Angers 676. saec. xi, St. Aubin.
Avignon 1348, foll. 131–236v. saec. xiv ex., Chartreux de Bonpas.
Berlin, Cod. Elect. 395, foll. 1-111. saec. xi et xii, Marienfeld.
Books 5 to 7 followed by Letters of Innocent III.
Berlin, Cod. Elect. 856. saec. xiv, Magdeburg.
Bern 116. saec. xv.
Boulogne 102. saec. xi, St. Bertin.
Brussels, Bibl. des ducs de Bourgogne 655. A.D. 1447.
Cambrai 685. saec. ix, Cathedral.
Parmentier dates this codex saec. x/xi. Was he misled by fol. 1 which contains a list of books in the Chapter library written in what is probably a tenth-century hand? See Molinier in Catalogue général 17, p. vii.
Cambrai 688. saec. xii, Cathedral.
Cambridge, Peterhouse 167. saec. xiii.
Cambridge, St. Johns College 169. saec. xiii, Hereford (Franciscans).
Cambridge, Sidney Sussex College 30. saec. xiv [2], English.
Charleville 4. saec. xii, Belleval.
Charleville 201. saec. xiii, Signy.
Chartres 10 (21). saec. ix, St. Père.
The work is assigned to Socrates, Sozomen, and Theodoret and

---

[27] I wish to thank my friend, Mr. S. H. Thomson, for consulting several catalogues inaccessible to me, and particularly for drawing my attention to the codex in Cracow. He also informs me that the manuscript collection there is intact.

Cassiodorus is not mentioned. This manuscript was destroyed in the last war.

Copenhagen, Gl. kgl. S 165 fol. saec. xv, Italian.

Copenhagen, Gl. kgl. S 166 fol. saec. xi.

Cracow, Jagiellonian Library 417 (CC. II. 1). saec. xiii.

Dijon 573. saec. xii, Cîteaux.

Douai 296. saec. xii, Anchin.

Douai 297. saec. xi, Marchiennes.

Edinburgh, University Library 178, saec. xii, English.

Eton College 131. saec. xiv/xv.

Florence, Laurentian Library, Fesul. CLIX. saec. xv.

Florence, Laurentian Library, Plut. LXVII, cod. XXII. saec. xv.

Glasgow, Hunt. 204. saec. xv, French.

Glasgow, Hunt. 217. saec. xi et xv.

Heiligenkreuz 80. saec. xiii?

Leningrad F.I.11A. c. A.D. 815, Noirmoutier.

There is no reason to question the accuracy of the entry on fol. 1, to the effect that the manuscript was copied at the instance of Adalhard of Corbie while he was an exile on the island in the Loire. See the description of the codex by Olga Dobiash-Rozhdestvenskaia, Codices Corbeienses Leninopolitani (Leningrad, 1934), 156. The manuscript was written by many hands in the so-called Corbie ab-script, a style of writing which would require long practice. Hence, as she points out, one can assume that the copyists were monks who had accompanied their abbot into exile.

Leyden, Voss lat. fol. 62. saec. xi.

London, B. M. Addit. 19961. saec. ix aut x.

London, B. M. Addit. 19967. saec. xii.

London, B. M. Cotton Vitell. C. XII, foll. 1–112. Date?

The later part of the present manuscript (foll. 114 ff.) comes from St. Augustine's Canterbury and was written saec. xi/xii. Cf. N. R. Ker, Medieval Libraries of Great Britain, p. 27.

London, B. M. Harley 3242. A.D. 1519, Trier.

London, B. M. Royal 13.C.X. saec. xiii.

London, B. M. Royal 13.D.3. saec. xiii in., Rochester.

London, Chester Beatty 45. saec. xii ex., Guisborough.

Cf. The Library of A. Chester Beatty, Plate CV.

Madrid, Archivo historico nacional. No p-m. A.D. 1400.

Metz 189. saec. xi in., St. Arnulf. This manuscript was destroyed in the last war.

Monte Cassino 302. saec. x/xi et xi ex.

Munich 2685. A.D. 1328, Alderspach.

Munich 6376. saec. x, Freising.

Munich 12237. A.D. 1463.

Munich 13070. saec. xii, Regensburg.

This is one of the two MSS listed by Manitius (*op. cit.,* I, p. 51). The other, Clm 11302, according to the catalogue contains the Latin Josephus, not HT.

Munich 14374. saec. xi, St. Emmeram.

Munich 17126. saec. xii, Scheftlarn.

Munich 18466. saec. xi, Tegernsee.

Munich 22015. saec. xii, Wessobrunn.

Munich 23448. saec. xii et xiv.

Extracts from Books 7–9 and 12.

Naples VI.D.18. saec. x.

New Orleans, Howard Memorial Library. Paper. A.D. 1475, Kempen.

Oxford, Bodl. Canon. pat. lat. 109. A.D. 1465.

Oxford, Bodl. Laud. misc. 440. saec. xi ex.

Oxford, Bodl. Laud. misc. 606. saec. xii ex., Bordesley.

Paris, Bibl. Mazarine 1641. saec. xi, St. Martin des Champs.

Paris, B. N. lat. 5082. saec. x/xi.

Paris, B. N. lat. 8960. saec. xi.

Paris, B. N. lat. 9714. saec. xv.

Paris, B. N. lat. 12525. saec. xii, St. Germain.

Paris, B. N. lat. 16046 and 16047. saec. xv, Sorbonne.

Two copies of HT, one on paper.

Paris, B. N. Nouv. acq. 1603. saec. ix ex., Tours.

E. K. Rand, A Survey of the MSS of Tours, No. 162, with plate 169.

Paris, B. N. Nouv. acq. 1746. saec. x.

Paris, B. N. Nouv. acq. 2379, saec. xi.

Prague, University Library 51 (I.A.41). saec. xv.

Reims 1354. saec. xi, St. Thierry.

Cf. F. M. Carey, Studies in honor of E. K. Rand, p. 59. This is one of the two codices used by Garet. The other, once in the Abbaye de Lyre, I have failed to trace. It is not in the municipal library at Évreux, which possesses many MSS from Lyre.

Trier, Seminarbibliothek 23. saec. xii.

Troyes 250. saec. xii, Clairvaux.

Troyes 266. saec. xii.

Turin DLIX. saec. xi.

Utrecht 256. saec. xv?

Valenciennes 498. saec. xii, St. Amand.

Vatican City, Pal. lat. 823. saec. ix aut x.
Vatican City, Pal. lat. 824. saec. x.
Vatican City, Vat. lat. 1970. saec. x.
Vercelli CI (158). saec. ix-x.
Vienna 374. saec. xiii.
Vienna 3141. saec. xv.
Vienna 4496. saec. xv.

The material collected in the foregoing pages does not pretend to be exhaustive. Yet it may be hoped that it is sufficiently copious, so that further evidence, whether drawn from medieval authors or provided by manuscripts that have been overlooked, will not seriously change the general conclusions presented. *Autres temps, autres goûts!* During the later fifteenth century, between 1472 and 1500 or shortly after, HT was printed four times, at Augsburg, Cologne, Paris, and Strasbourg, the Commentary on Psalms only once, at Basel in 1491.[28]

[28] See Gesammtkatalog der Wiegendrucke 6 (1934), Nos. 6163 to 6167.

3

The Influence during the Middle Ages of the Treatise *De vita contemplativa* and Its Surviving Manuscripts[*]

IT IS a familiar phenomenon in the history of the world that literature and learning may flourish even in times of war and of political and economic unrest; and Gaul in the late Roman imperial age furnishes a good illustration of this truth. Assuredly times were troubled and often dangerous; yet the schools of rhetoric and the governing class of Gallo-Romans, of whom Sidonius was a typical example, kept alive the love and study of pagan letters. If their own contributions to literature were not of a very high order, at least their preoccupation with the greater writers of the past helped to some extent to preserve these for posterity. More vital was the contribution made by Gaul to Christian thought and literature. From Hilary of Poitiers (c. 315–367) to Caesarius of Arles (470–542), that is to say, through nearly two centuries, Gaul produced a remarkable series of Christian prelates, teachers, and writers. And, though the country became for a time a centre of doctrinal controversy, it is fair to say that even the champions of Semipela-

[*] *Miscellanea Giovanni Mercati,* II (Città del Vaticano, 1946), 344–358. Reprinted by permission of the Biblioteca Apostolica Vaticana.

gianism made up in intellectual vigour what they may have lacked in strict orthodoxy.

Among the literary productions of this age is a treatise which for many centuries exerted a far wider influence than has generally been recognized. In recent years, moreover, the *De vita contemplativa* has been rather neglected by students of Patristic literature. There is still no edition of the text answering to the requirements of modern scholarship, nor has its popularity in the Middle Ages been adequately realized or indeed been seriously investigated. It is not necessary to dwell on the few facts known about the author's life nor yet to discuss the literary merits of his book, since others have dealt adequately with these topics.[1] Pomerius reveals his thorough rhetorical training not only in his style, but through reminiscences of pagan authors in the third Book. He cites Virgil and borrows a phrase from the younger Pliny. He also quotes from Cicero's *Tusculan Disputations* and, although there appears to be no direct quotation from the *De officiis,* his discussion of the four cardinal virtues as defined by pagan philosophy suggests familiarity with that work.

The only text of the treatise now commonly available is that in Migne's *Patrologia latina* (59, 415–520). It is a reprint from the edition of Prosper's works issued at Paris in 1711 under the editorship of J. P. le Brun des Marettes and D. Mangeant. Degenhart, as an addendum to his brief study of Pomerius' style, published some variant readings from four manuscripts in Munich. But his contention that the text as it appears in Migne nearly always is superior to that in the *codices monacenses* is too sweeping.[2] The only one of these manuscripts that is of early date (Clm 18524 *b*) contains only a few fragments from Book I. On the other hand, the text of the Council of Aix-la-Chapelle in 816, as printed in the *Monumenta Germaniae his-*

---

[1] Cf., for instance, O. Bardenhewer, *Geschichte der altkirchlichen Literatur* IV, pp. 599–601 and G. Fritz in *Dictionnaire de théologie catholique* XII, coll. 537–543. For the style and language of Pomerius see F. Degenhart, *Julianus Pomerius* (Programm, Eichstätt, 1905) and Sister M. A. C. Prendergast, *The latinity of the de vita contemplativa of Julianus Pomerius* (Catholic University of America: Patristic Studies, LV, 1938).

[2] Degenhart, *op. cit.,* p. 29.

torica, is based on several manuscripts of the ninth century and is a safer guide for the text of those chapters from Pomerius that are reproduced *verbatim*.[3] Several of the readings which Degenhart either rejects or prints without comment are probably correct, for example:

Migne 59, 430 A *dedant]* *ditant.* This reading is found also in the text of the *Concilia* (var. lect. *ditent).* From the footnote in Migne it is obvious that the manuscripts collated by Mangeant varied greatly *(laedant, dent, edant, ditent).* *Ditant* makes perfectly intelligible sense. By *deliciae* in this passage Pomerius means not so much the pleasures of sense as luxuries in the form of costly estates or possessions. This is clear from the context; for he goes on to warn against the snare of seeking worldly honours and paying more attention to popularity with others than to one's own conscience. *Ditari divitiis* occurs later in the treatise (456 C).

467 A *deliciarum]* *litium* in the oldest of the Munich manuscripts. Degenhart remarks, "wohl ein Schreibversehen," but again the context suggests that *litium* is what Pomerius wrote; for his next words are, *non ardor animosae contentionis exanimat.* He is thinking of costly law-suits and is harking back to an earlier passage in the book (459 C): The man who lives a simple life and is untroubled by the worry of worldly affairs, whom *nullus litigator infestat, nullus calumniosus exagitat,* is in a position to strive after the good life.

467 A *iniuriosum]* *inrisorem* in the oldest of the Munich manuscripts and certainly what Pomerius wrote. Cf. 484 D – *simplicitatem spiritualium fratrum inridenter exagitant.* This is an admirable example of the way in which a common word *(iniuriosum),* which was originally a marginal gloss on an unusual word in the text *(inrisorem),* in time was transferred to the text and ousted the correct reading. The phenomenon is likely to occur with any author who was master of a large vocabulary including words that were rare, if not obsolescent. I have elsewhere pointed out examples of the same process in manuscripts of Bede's works.[4]

---

[3] *MGH: Concilia aevi carolini* I, pp. 342 ff.
[4] Cf. Laistner, *Bedae Ven. expos. act. apost. et retract.,* p. xxiv and in *Journ.*

468 A *indulgeant*] *indulgeatur.* Degenhart makes no comment, but it is probably the right reading. Pomerius elsewhere (487 C) employs the impersonal passive construction with this verb and with a number of others.[5]

469 B *pro – – teneritudine*] *propter teneritudinem.* Degenhart rejects the variant, citing *pro abstinentia* (470 C) in support of his view; but he overlooks *propter abstinentiam* in 470 B and 471 A.

In addition there are some readings which even Degenhart admits to be preferable, *observatione* for *ostentatione* (438 D), *prodit* for *perdit* (457 A), and *necessariorum* for *necessarium* (467 C). The reading *incertos* in two Munich manuscripts for *incestos,* though wrong, is palaeographically interesting. Confusion of r and s suggests a possible Insular exemplar in the background. Mangeant appears to have collated some eight or ten manuscripts. All save one were in Paris and none was older than the tenth century. His *Cameracensis* is presumably Ms 204 in the municipal library at Cambrai. The portion containing Pomerius' treatise was, according to the *Catalogue général,* copied in the tenth century also. Mangeant's text was, for the time when it was published, superior; but early manuscripts are so numerous, and the possibilities suggested even by Degenhart's few variants are so many, that a new text–critical edition is much to be desired.

When we turn to the history and influence of the treatise in the Middle Ages, the first question to arise is that of authorship. It has been commonly asserted that from the seventh or eighth century onwards the real author of the book was forgotten until the just claims of Pomerius were established beyond cavil by Sirmond. In a very broad sense this assertion is approximately true; yet the fact remains that, although the treatise was usually attributed to Prosper of Aquitaine, the authorship of Pomerius was never at any time during the Middle Ages entirely obliterated. Sirmond and his contemporaries knew of several manuscripts in which the work was assigned correctly to Pomerius. The *codex pervetustus* at Beauvais is now in the

Theol. Stud. 43 (1942), p. 186.
[5] See the instances collected by Sister Prendergast, *op. cit.,* p. 63.

Bibliothèque nationale at Paris (Nouv. acq. 1065). The manuscript formerly in the Abbaye de la Trappe survives as Ms 146 in the municipal library at Alençon, as the correct attribution of the *De vita contemplativa* to Pomerius shows.[6] Sirmond also noted that the oldest collection of canons brought together in France credits Pomerius with the authorship.[7] But there is still further evidence. In the Acts of the Council held at Paris in 829 there are half a dozen short quotations from the *De vita contemplativa*, besides a general reference to it. In three places the author is called Pomerius, in the others, Prosper.[8] Degenhart has pointed out that in Clm 18524 *b*, the ninth century codex which was once at Tegernsee, the author of extracts from Book I is twice called Pomerius (foll. 119 *v* and 120) and twice Prosper (foll. 122 and 123). A tenth century book-list from St Emmeram and the twelfth century catalogue of the library in Bec both give the right attribution.[9] In a fifteenth century manuscript now in Berlin (Cod. elect. 306) the treatise begins on fol. 1*v*. with the words, "incipit prologus Iuliani Pomerii de vita contemplativa." But on fol. 1*r*, which is otherwise blank, some wiseacre has written, "non sunt Iulii Pomerii sed Prosperi Aquitani." [10] It is a reasonable assumption that Pomerius already appeared as the author in the manuscript from which the Berlin codex was copied.

The question of authorship was further complicated by the confusion of Julianus Pomerius with Julian of Toledo. Alcuin, for example, in his treatise against Elipandus, alludes to the *Prognostica* of Julianus Pomerius "culled from the flowers of the

[6] Cf. Mangeant's introduction and the still valuable account in *Histoire littéraire de la France* II (1735), pp. 665–675. For the Paris Ms see *Bibl. de l'école des chartes* 76 (1915), p. 17; for the Ms at Alençon see *Catalogue général* (in octavo) II, p. 528.

[7] For the so-called *Collectio Andegavensis* and surviving Mss of it cf. H. J. Schmitz, *Die Bussbücher und das kanonische Bussverfahren.*

[8] *MGH: Concilia aevi carolini* II, 620, 25; 623, 5; 624, 25.

[9] G. Becker, *Catalogi bibliothecarum antiqui*, No. 42, 356, Iulianus Pomerius de activa et contemplativa; No. 127, 86, in uno volumine. admonitio Basilii ad monachum. instituta Basilii. Pomerii de vita contemplativa lib. III.

[10] V. Rose, *Die HSS der kön. Bibl. zu Berlin. Verzeichniss der lat. HSS* II, 1, 87. In a thirteenth century Ms now at Florence (Plut. XVII. dext. cod. 8) the treatise is assigned to Augustine, but in the margin another hand has written: "Iste liber est Prosperi et non Augustini." Cf. A. M. Bandini, *Catal. codd. lat. bibl. medic laur.* IV, col. 538.

holy Fathers." [11] This error was perpetuated, for we find the *Prognostica* assigned to Pomerius in the catalogues of St Riquier (s. ix), Bobbio (s. x), Lindisfarne (1095), and Reading (s. xii ex.).[12] We shall see, moreover, that there is some doubt about an entry in the Corbie catalogue of c. 1200. Yet a further source of error was this: Pomerius dedicated his book to a certain bishop Julianus—his see is uncertain—and this prelate might be identified with Julianus Pomerius. In Ms 204 at Cambrai (s. x) the treatise which begins on fol. 69 is headed: "Incipit prologus libri Prosperi ad Iulianum Pomerium"!

It is not easy to account for the fact that the genuine author of the *De vita contemplativa* was almost forgotten, but at least one can suggest contributing factors. Prosper, besides being a champion of Augustinian doctrine in Gaul, was a writer of varied interests, a poet and chronicler as well as a theologian. The attribution to him, therefore, of a work which was clearly influenced by the teaching of Augustine and composed by a man little mentioned even by his contemporaries, is quite understandable. Most of what we know about Pomerius comes from Isidore and from pseudo-Gennadius. They mention two other works by him which seem to have been lost quite early. The fact that Isidore criticized one of them, because it lapsed from orthodoxy in one section, may also be significant. But, above all, the works which gave information about Pomerius appear to have been rare in the early Middle Ages. Thus, outside Spain only three manuscripts of the late eighth or ninth century are known to contain the *De viris illustribus* of Isidore, and the oldest Spanish manuscript to survive (Escurial d. I. 2) can be dated to the year 976.[13] This scarcity forms a striking contrast to the abundance of early codices in which the *Etymologies,* and indeed most of the other writings, of Isidore are preserved. Similarly, whereas there is no lack of early manuscripts containing Jerome's *De viris illustribus* and Gennadius' continuation, only very few of them have the additional chapters which

---

[11] *PL* 101, 266 B.

[12] Becker, *op. cit.,* No. 11, 141–142; 32, 568; 72, 26; *English Historical Review* 3 (1888), p. 121.

[13] Cf. C. H. Beeson, *Isidorstudien,* p. 81; G. von Dzialowski, *Isidor und Ildefons als Litterarhistoriker,* p. 68.

were subsequently added to Gennadius' treatise. Of these chapter 99 describing Pomerius is one.[14] Later manuscripts containing the material added by pseudo-Gennadius are numerous; but by the eleventh century the attribution to Prosper of the *De vita contemplativa* had been so widely accepted that the statements of Isidore and pseudo-Gennadius were generally ignored.

The false attribution did not, however, affect the success of Pomerius' book. It is no exaggeration to say that from the middle of the eighth to the later ninth century its authority all but rivalled that of the leading Latin Fathers. As early as 747 Boniface, in a letter addressed to Cuthbeorht, archbishop at Canterbury (740–760), quotes or paraphrases a passage from *De vita contemplativa* I, 16. He introduces the passage with the words, "quidam sapientum dicebat"; but, as he uses precisely the same phrase to usher in a quotation from Jerome, one cannot deduce that this vagueness reflects Boniface's uncertainty about the authorship of the treatise.[15] The truth is that, although he mentions Augustine by name twice and alludes to Bede as the author of homilies and of a commentary on Proverbs, he is chary of referring to authors by name and sparing of direct quotations. A decade or two after Boniface's letter Chrodegang of Metz in his *Regula canonicorum* cites three short passages from the treatise, calling its author Prosper.[16] Near the end of the eighth century Paulinus of Aquileia made extensive use of "Prosper's" book in the *Liber exhortationis,* addressed to Eric, Margrave of Friaul. Although he follows Pomerius' thought closely, he treats the text with some freedom; for example, he changes the verb from the third person singular to the first person plural, and also makes additions of his own. Thus, while his debt to Pomerius is great and obvious, his quotations are so free that they are valueless for determining what kind of text of Pomerius he used.

When we pass to the ninth century, the most remarkable testimony to the esteem felt for the *De vita contemplativa* is pro-

[14] Cf. the long list of Mss in E. C. Richardson's edition of Jerome's *De viris illustribus* (*Texte und Untersuchungen* 14, 1896).
[15] *MGH: Epist.* III, 352, 1; cf. *ibid.,* 343, 20.
[16] *PL* 89, 1060 C–1061 A. The quotations are from II, 9, 10, and 11.

vided by copious citations in the Acts of Church Councils. There is a brief citation in the proceedings of the Council held at Chalon-sur-Saône in 813.[17] Then at the Council of Aix-la-Chapelle in 816 no less than five chapters from Book I and six from Book II are reproduced *in toto*. Pomerius is in the most select company. His authority is invoked side by side with that of Jerome, Augustine, Gregory the Great, and Isidore.[18] The chapters quoted in the main deal with practical matters: the manner in which the priest should order his life and be an example to his flock; the necessity of correcting evil livers; the relations of the priest to the Church of which he is, as it were, an official; and the desirability of the priest's living a life of poverty, property being held by the Church. In addition we find a description of the priest whose carnal life renders him unworthy of his high office, and a definition of true, in distinction from worldly, riches. In the official record of the Council held at Paris in 829 Pomerius' authority is again appealed to, but the quotations are all brief; and he is twice cited in a Capitulary of Louis the Pius.[19] In view of the importance attached by the heads of the Church to the *De vita contemplativa* it is not surprising to find the bishop of Cambrai, Halitgar, excerpting passages from Book I and especially from Book III for insertion in his *Liber de paenitentia*. He does not always reproduce his author word for word, but makes small alterations here and there. The *Regula canonicorum* printed in Migne's *Patrology* among the works of Amalarius of Trèves and approved at Aix in 816 contains most of the same long quotations that were inserted in the Acts of the Council held in that year.[20] In the letter dedicatory to Lothar II which precedes his little tract, *De anima*, Hrabanus Maurus observes that he has used Cassiodorus and made some additions "ex libro Prosperi." It is by no means certain, as Manitius assumed, that he is referring to the *De vita contemplativa*, but the possibility cannot be ruled out. His indebt-

[17] *MGH: Concilia aevi carolini* I, 275, 23–25.
[18] *Ibid.* I, 342; 347; 351; 353; 356; 381; 382–385.
[19] *Ibid.* II, 611; 613; 620; 623; 673; 709; *MGH: Capit. Reg. Franc.* II, 31, 10 and 36, 5.
[20] As Dom Germain Morin has pointed out (*Dict. de Théol. Cath.* I, col. 934), there is no adequate reason for attributing this compilation to Amalarius.

edness is certainly not obvious; on the other hand, a scholar as widely read as Hrabanus is likely to have been acquainted with the treatise.[21] It was certainly known to two other authors of the ninth century. Jonas of Orléans quotes extensively from all three Books in his *De institutione laicali,* while Aeneas of Paris, in his collection of *Sententiae* from the Fathers put together to refute the doctrinal errors of the Greek Church, finds room for Pomerius' definition of the Trinity and the Procession of the Holy Spirit from the Father and the Son.[22]

Almost a century later Atto of Vercellae in the treatise that he composed primarily against the encroachment of the secular on the ecclesiastical authority, quotes a few words from I, 20. In the first half of the twelfth century Gerhoh of Reichersberg also betrays familiarity with our author. He quotes five lines from II, 11 in a letter to Pope Innocent II, and some years later (A.D. 1148) introduces citations from II, 9 and II, 16 into his commentary on the sixty-fourth Psalm.[23] Both Atto and Gerhoh regarded Prosper as the author of the treatise. It is beyond the scope of this article to attempt to trace the use and influence of the *De vita contemplativa* in the Latin authors of the later Middle Ages. Yet there can be no doubt of its continued popularity; this is proved unequivocally by the great number of extant manuscripts as well as by the evidence of medieval library catalogues. True, a cynic, hardened by the mass production of printed books in our own time, might argue that the mere presence of a work in a library is no proof that it was read, but the analogy would be false. In the Middle Ages reproduction of a book was both slow and costly. No treatise for which there was not a steady demand would have been copied and recopied in the medieval *scriptoria,* so that the evidence to which we must now pass is valid.

Surviving manuscripts of the *De vita contemplativa* number over ninety. The list that follows has been compiled mainly from printed catalogues and has been made as complete as possible. Nevertheless, it is probable that it is not exhaustive

---

[21] *MGH: Epist.* V, 515, 13–15; *PL* 110, 1109–1120.
[22] *PL* 121, 716 D–717 A derived from *De vita contemplativa* I, 18–19.
[23] *PL* 134, 83 A; *MGH: Libelli de lite* III, 477, 15–30 and 479, 2–4.

and that other scholars may be able to add to it. Even so, it may prove useful to some future editor of Pomerius, as well as being clear proof of his popularity throughout the medieval period.

Manuscripts of Pomerius' De vita contemplativa

Alençon 146. s. xii, Abbaye de la Trappe.

Berlin, Cod. Elect. 305, foll. 1–82. s. xii, Magdeburg.

Berlin, Cod. Elect. 306, foll. 1 *v*–65. s. xv.

Berlin, Cod. Elect. 426, foll. 67 *v*–70 *v*. s. xv. Apparently only I, 1 to 25.

Bern 107, foll. 71–110 *v*. Mr. F. M. Carey kindly informs me that this Ms was written c. 830 in the scriptorium at Auxerre.

Bern 612, foll. 73 *v*–84 *r*. s. xi. Incomplete.

Bern 685. s. x.

Bologna, Univers. 564. s. xv, Fratres S. Pauli in Monte.

Bologna, Univers. 892. s. xii, Conv. di San Domenico.

Bourges 84, foll. 36–95 *v*. s. xii, St Sulpice de Bourges.

Bruges 117, foll. 134 *v*–162 *r*. s. xiii, Sancta Maria de Dunis.

Burgo de Osma, Rojo 142; l. s. xiv.

Cambrai 204, foll. 69–112. s. x, Cathedral.

Cambridge, Univ. Libr. Ii. 1. 41, foll. 1–82, s. xiii, Christ Church, Canterbury.

Cambridge, Trinity College 19 (B. l. 20), foll. 2–33 *v*. s. xiii.

Charleville 202, vol. 13, item 5. s. xii ex., Signy. Cf. Morin, *S. Caesarii Sermones* I, p. lxxvii.

Chicago, Libr. of Ernst F. Detterer 31. Paper. s. xv, Italian.

Dijon 588, foll. 38 *v*–80 *r*. s. xii, Cîteaux.

Dôle 66–68, pp. 61–205. s. xiv, Collège St Jérome.

Douai 206, foll. 28–85 *v*. s. xii, Anchin. Cf. Morin, *op. cit.*, I, p. xxxiv.

Dublin, Trinity College 517. s. xiv, Merton College, Oxford.

Einsiedeln 282, pp. 1–203. s. x. Book I, 1–4 is missing.

Florence, Bibl. Med.-Laur., Plut. XXIII. 14, pp. 1–67. s. xv.

Florence, Bibl. Med.-Laur., Plut. XVIII, Dext. cod. 8, pp. 13–33, s. xiii.

Florence, Bibl. Med.-Laur., Fesul. LXII, pp. 158–195. s. xv.

Heiligenkreuz 289. s. xiii.

Laon 405. s. ix, St Vincent. The treatise is preceded by Isidore, *De fide catholica;* cf. Beeson, *Isidorstudien,* p. 38.

Liège 124. s. xiii, St Trond.

London, Brit. Mus. Royal 5 C. VI, foll. 109–30. s. xiv, Worcester.

London, Brit. Mus. Royal 5. E. IX, foll. 3–57 *v.* s. xiii, Bristol.

London, Brit. Mus. Royal 5. E. X. s. xii, Rochester.

London, Brit. Mus. Royal 5. F. XI, foll. 4–54. s. xii.

London, Brit. Mus. Royal 5. F. XVI, foll. 99–146. s. xii ex., Merton Priory.

London, Brit. Mus. Royal 6. D. V, foll. 1–45. s. xii ex., Rochester.

London, Brit. Mus. Royal 8. B. XIV, foll. 28–73. s. xiii.

London, Lambeth Pal. 129, foll. 34–56. s. xiv, Lanthony.

Metz 145. s. x, St Arnulf.

Milan, Bibl. Ambros. M. 32 sup. s. x, Bobbio.

Monte Cassino 226, pp. 119–233. s. xi in., Beneventan. For the date see E. A. Lowe, *The Beneventan Script,* p. 346.

Montpellier, École de méd. 218. s. ix.

Montpellier, École de méd. 484. s. ix. The treatise in this and in the preceding manuscript is followed by Prosper's *Epigrammata.*

Munich 18565, foll. 45–149. A.D. 1472, Tegernsee. This is the date given in *Catal. Clm.* II, 3, p. 181. Degenhart (p. 28) says 1412. Presumably this is a misprint.

Munich 18665, foll. 150–228. s. x–xi, Tegernsee. The earlier part of the codex contains Bede on the Apocalypse. Cf. Laistner, *A Handlist of Bede MSS.,* p. 28.

Munich 18609, foll. 1–60. s. xv, Tegernsee.

Munich 26701. A.D. 1398. Not collated by Degenhart.

Naples, Bibl. Naz. VI. B. 12. A.D. 817–35, Beneventan. See E. A. Lowe, *op. cit.,* pp. 77 and 354, with plate in *Scriptura beneventana.*

Orléans 169 (146), pp. 1–299. s. viii–ix, Fleury. For the date see W. M. Lindsay, *Notae latinae,* p. 496. Cuissard, whose dating is notoriously erratic, assigns the codex to the eleventh century!

Oxford, Bodl. Libr., Bodl. 126 (SC 1990), foll. 1–58. c. A.D. 1100, English.

Oxford, Bodl. Libr., Laud. lat. 31, foll. 30–117. s. xii, Eynsham. The manuscript is from Eynsham, not from Evesham, as stated in Coxe's catalogue. See N. R. Ker, *Medieval Libraries of Great Britain,* pp. 43 and 47.

Oxford, Bodl. Libr., Canon. patr. lat. 100. s. xiv.

Oxford, St John's College 199. s. xii.

Paris, Bibl. nat. 2038. s. xiii, Colbertinus.

Paris, Bibl. nat. 2150. s. x, Bigotianus.

Paris, Bibl. nat. 2151. s. xi.

Influence of De vita contemplativa

Paris, Bibl. nat. 2152. s. xii.

Paris, Bibl. nat. 2153. s. xiii, Foucarmont (Colbertinus). Cf. Morin, S. Caesarii Sermones I, p. xxxvi.

Paris, Bibl. nat. 2154. s. xiii, Moissac (Colbertinus).

Paris, Bibl. nat. 2155. s. xiv, Moissac (?) (Colbertinus).

Paris, Bibl. nat. 2770. s. x et xiii, Limoges.

Paris, Bibl. nat. 2771. s. xii, olim Philiberti de la Mare.

Paris, Bibl. nat. 5331. s. xiii, Tellerianus.

Paris, Bibl. nat. 9567. s. xii.

Paris, Bibl. nat. 13400. s. ix, St Germain (Corbie?).

Paris, Bibl. nat. Nouv. acq. 1065, foll. 1–88. s. x, Beauvais.

Paris, Bibl. de l'arsenal 175, foll. 108–28. s. xii, Fontenay. Also Mss 254 (*St Martin*) 272 B (*Grands Augustins*), 499 G (*Célestins*). All s. xv.

Paris, Bibl. Mazarine 982, foll. 16 *v*–36. s. xiii ex.

St. Gall, Stiftsbibl. 186. c. 825–830, St Gall. Cf. A. Bruckner, *Scriptoria medii aevi helvetica: St Gallen* I, p. 68, with Plate XLIII.

St Gall, Stiftsbibl. 187, pp. 164–270. s. ix[1], St Gall. Cf. *ibid*. II, p. 80.

St Omer 213. s. xiii, Clairmarais.

Tortosa, Capit. (Denifle 110). s. xiv.

Toulouse 179, foll. 43–51. s. xii. Incomplete.

Troyes 5, item 8, s. xii, Clairvaux.

Troyes 1921. s. xii, Clairvaux. The treatise is preceded by Augustine, *De vera religione* and followed by the same writer's *Liber de quantitate animae*.

Turin, Bibl. naz. 669 (d. I. 38). s. xiii.

Turin, Bibl. naz. 718 (d. II. 38), foll. 19–49 *v*. s. xiv.

Valencia, Catedr. (Canalda 180; 2). s. xv.

Vatican City, Pal. lat. 238, foll. 4–74. s. viii–ix, Lorsch. For this product of the Lorsch *scriptorium*, see W. M. Lindsay, *Palaeographia latina* III, p. 29 and E. A. Lowe, *Codices latini antiquiores* I, No. 88.

Vatican City, Urbin. lat. 100, foll. 273–309. s. xv.

Vatican City, Vat. lat. 556. s. xi.

Vatican City, Vat. lat. 558, foll. 9–72. s. xii.

Vatican City, Vat. lat. 559, foll. 2–34. A.D. 1447.

Vendôme 142, foll. 1–22. s. xiii.

Vienna, Nationalbibl. 760, foll. 43–89. s. xiv.

Vienna, Nationalbibl. 968, foll. 1–89. s. ix.

Vienna, Nationalbibl. 1047, foll. 1–48 *v.* s. xii. More than half of Book III is missing, the text breaking off at the words, "peccati desideriis serviamus" (Migne 59, 496 C).
Vienna, Nationalbibl. 4390, foll. 92 *v.*–132 *v.* s. xv.
Vitry le François 43, foll. 165–205. s. xii, Cheminon.
Wisbech, Museum (James, No. 189). s. xii, Bury St Edmunds.
Wisbech, Museum (James, No. 190). s. xii, Bury St Edmunds. For these two manuscripts from Bury see M. R. James, *English Historical Review* 41 (1926), p. 257.
Zürich, Stadtbibl. Car C 157, foll. 2–53 *v.* s. xv.

Manuscripts Containing Fragments or Short Extracts

Berlin, Görres 52, fol. 153 *r–v.* s. xiii, Himmerod.
Chartres 80, foll. 53–55. s. ix, Saint Père. This composite manuscript also contains fragments of Isidore's *Etymologiae* and of Bede. Cf. Beeson, *Isidorstudien,* pp. 90, 100–1; Laistner, *A Handlist of Bede MSS.,* pp. 96 and 140.
Munich 18524 *b,* foll. 119–123. s. ix, Tegernsee. Used by Degenhart.
St Gall, Stiftsbibl. 277. c. 850, St Gall. Cf. Bruckner, *op. cit.* II, p. 91.
St Gall, Stiftsbibl. 397. s. ix², St Gall. A fragment from II, 9 (Cf. Steinmeyer-Sievers, *Althochdeutsche Glossen* IV, 450, 42). The same Ms contains Bede's *De natura rerum* and *De temporum ratione* and *computistica* (Laistner, *op. cit.,* pp. 143, 150, 155).
Vatican City, Reg. lat. 66. s. xiv.
Vatican City, Reg. lat. 195. s. ix–x. For the fragments in these two *Reginenses* see Dom. A. Wilmart, *Cat. codd. regin.* I, pp. 146 and 468.
Vienna, Nationalbibl. 1051, foll. 144 *v*–145. s. xii.
Vienna, Nationalbibl. 1488, fol. 8 *r–v.* s. xiii, Salzburg.

Even from the extant manuscripts alone it is clear that copies of the *De vita contemplativa* were diffused early over a great part of the European continent. Codices, varying in date from the end of the eighth to the early tenth century, survive not only from France, Germany, and Switzerland but from both the North and South Italian areas. Nor was the process of diffusion arrested, since manuscripts of the twelfth century and later abound. Besides this, there is the evidence of catalogues from medieval libraries. The work appears in the book-lists of St Vandrille, Murbach, Reichenau, St Gall, Lorsch, Cologne, Oviedo, Pannonholma, Bec, Cluny, Limoges, Maillezais, Pontigny, St Amand, St Pons de Tomières, Tournai, the Sorbonne, Salem, the Neithart library in Ulm, Fulda, Aggsbach, Heiligenkreuz, Klosterneuburg, Zwettl, and Melk.[24] To these libraries we may probably add St Bertin and Corbie (cf. Paris, Bibl. Nat. 13400), although their respective catalogues are not specific but record only "libri Prosperi" without giving any details. The Corbie catalogue of c. 1200 also contains an item, "Iulianus Pomerius. omelie," but this may refer, as we have already seen, to Julian of Toledo's *Prognosticon*.[25] One would wish to know at what date the treatise first was brought to England. I could find no trace of its use in Aldhelm or Bede, but this proves little or nothing. There was no reason why Aldhelm should quote from it in any of his extant works, while Bede's primary interest was Biblical exegesis rather than pastoral theology. In the *Epistle to Egbert* there are two quotations from Gregory the Great and one from Ambrose; for the rest Bede is drawing on his own experience and observation of abuses prevalent in the English Church of his time. That Alcuin, at least at the time when he composed his short *liber de virtutibus et vitiis*, had not read the *De vita contemplativa* is most likely; otherwise one would certainly have expected to find echoes or even direct citations from it in Alcuin's tract. In view of the popularity enjoyed by Pomerius' book on the continent during the ninth century, it is hard to believe that a copy did not reach England at that time; but, in the absence of definite evidence, it must remain an open question whether the book was available in any English library before the Norman Conquest. After that there is no doubt. The medieval home of eleven extant manuscripts, now in England and Ireland, is known; a twelfth (Bodl. 126), though of uncertain provenance, was written in England. From the surviving book-lists it appears that there were also copies at Lindisfarne (A.D. 1095), Whitby and Durham in the twelfth century, Rievaulx in the thirteenth, and Syon in the fifteenth.

[24] The treatise is also listed in an unidentified catalogue of the tenth century (Becker, No. 29, 61). In the catalogue of Maillezais no author's name is given. Melk in 1483 had two copies of the treatise (B 107 and F 19); it is probable that one, if not both, of these manuscripts is still at Melk.

[25] Becker, No. 136, 255.

The demand for the treatise continued even after the invention of printing. The statement found in standard works of reference, however, and repeated by Degenhart and Sister Prendergast, that the *editio princeps* appeared in 1487, is incorrect.[26] The first edition was issued from the press of Peter Drach at Speyer in 1486. Another edition by the same printer followed in the next year.[27] There is a copy of the rare edition of 1486 in the library of Cornell University. It came to the University from the Benno Loewy Bequest. At some earlier date it had belonged to the Cistercian Abbey at Schöntal in Württemberg; for on the title-page above the printed title a former owner has written, "a conventu vallis speciose." Collation of a few passages of the *De vita contemplativa* in this book with the text of Mangeant as reprinted in Migne's *Patrology* shows substantial differences between the two. In the 1486 edition the chapter headings to Book I follow immediately after the first sentence of paragraph 3 in the preface. Then the text reads: "Prologus primi libri. Itaque iubes ut paucis . . . adiuvante tractemus." Similarly, the chapter headings for Books II and III precede the brief prefaces. The same arrangement is found in an eleventh century manuscript now in the Vatican Library (Vat. lat. 556); in another codex (Cambridge, Trinity College 19; s. xiii) the *capitula* of Book I precede the entire preface. It would seem, therefore, that at least in the later manuscripts there was a good deal of variation in the arrangement. The text of the *editio princeps* deviates noticeably from Mangeant's. There are occasional differences in the order of words. At times the text agrees with the manuscript at Cambrai collated for the edition of 1711, for example:

> Migne 59, 416 C *praecipitat*] *praecipitabit*.
> 420 C *typho superbiae*] *tipo superbiae*.
> 422 C *nec maioris meriti sibi aliquid quisque ar-*

---

[26] Degenhart (*op. cit.*, p. 4) says, "erschien als Prospersches Werk separat an unbekanntem Verlagsort"; Sister Prendergast (*op. cit.*, p. 7) names Cologne as the place of publication.

[27] See *Catalogue of books in the fifteenth century, now in the British Museum* (London, 1912), II, pp. 495 and 496 for a full description of both editions.

rogabit] *nec maior meriti sibi aliquid arrogabit.*

Elsewhere, however, the readings diverge from those of the Cambrai codex and, very occasionally, from Mangeant's text and variants all together, for instance:

> 416 C *attexam*] *attingam.*
> 440 C *laciniosae* (Cambrai Ms *lacunosae*)] *lachrymose.*
> 520 A *vernantis eloquii* (with several variants, including *versuta* and *versutis*)] *versutis eloquiis.*

A new edition of the treatise, for which all the early manuscripts and a few of the later had been collated, would probably show that the codex used by Peter Drach for his printed edition belonged to a clearly marked family or group. After 1486–7 the *De vita contemplativa* was frequently reprinted, separately at Cologne in 1536, and, together with the works of Prosper, in 1539 at Lyons, 1577 at Douai, and again at Cologne in 1630. It was also included in the *Magna bibliotheca veterum patrum* (Cologne, 1618) and the greatly enlarged *Maxima bibliotheca* issued at Lyons in 1677.

It is only a select and relatively small number of books for which the demand has continued steadily through a thousand years. There is also a certain irony in the fact that, although no codex of Pomerius is as venerable as the famous Trèves Prosper written in 719 in uncials, nevertheless, to judge by the extant manuscripts and by medieval catalogues, his treatise at least till the sixteenth century enjoyed infinitely more popularity than any of the theological works composed by Prosper himself.

ADDENDUM

Since this article was sent to the printer I have noted the following additional Mss of Pomerius' treatise:

Arras 435 (326), foll. 65–122 *v.* s. xi.
Brussels 1187, foll. 2–60 *v.* A.D. 1460, Corsendonck.
Leipzig, Universitätsbibl. 326, foll. 39–68. s. xv.
Leyden, B. P. L. 85, foll. 33–70. s. ix.

Lisbon LXVII—356. s. xiii, Alcobaça.
Monte Cassino 230, pp. 95–147. s. x ex.
Utrecht 270, foll. 1–74. A.D. 1468, Carthusians.
Utrecht 271, foll. 1–86. s. xv.
Wolfenbüttel, Weiss. 76. s. vii.
Zwettl 328, foll. 2–70. s. xii et xiii.

For some fragments of the treatise elsewhere cf. *Clavis patrum latinorum* No. 998.

4

The Western Church and Astrology during the Early Middle Ages [*][1]

IT IS now nearly forty years ago that two scholars independently drew attention to Ambrosiaster's attacks on the paganism of his age. Cumont in a brilliant article, La polémique de l'Ambrosiaster contre les paiens, analyzed and discussed Quaestio CXIIII, Adversus paganos, and Quaestio CXV, De fato, of the writer whose identity must still be regarded as uncertain.[2] The purpose of Souter's admirable monograph, A study of Ambrosiaster, was quite different. Primarily he was concerned to prove once and for all that the pseudo-Augustinian Quaestiones veteris et novi testamenti CXXVII were composed by the same author as the highly individual commentary on the thirteen epistles of St. Paul included among the works of Ambrose. The common authorship of the two works is now universally accepted. Souter's book was also a preliminary study for his definitive edition of the Quaestiones which appeared some years later in the Vienna Corpus. To prove his main contention he

* Harvard Theological Review, 34 (1941), 251–275. Reprinted by permission of the Harvard University Press.

[1] I wish to thank Professor A. D. Nock for a number of bibliographical hints and Dr. C. W. Jones for his help on computistical matters.

[2] Revue d'hist. et de litt. relig., 8 (1903), 417–440.

instituted a careful comparison of the Biblical citations in the two treatises, of the language, and of the opinions expressed on a great variety of topics. Amongst these last was a strong dislike for astrology and astrologers; this was frequently noticeable in the commentary, but found its fullest expression in Quaestio CXV. Nevertheless most modern investigators who have touched on astrology during the Later Empire have ignored the writings of this unknown contemporary of Jerome and Pope Damasus. The sweeping generalization, however, with which Cumont concluded his article, seems to have been generally approved; at least no serious attempt to test its validity has been made. In 1903 he wrote as follows:

Mais tandis que la magie se perpétua à travers tout le moyen âge, l'Eglise latine réussit à la longue à détruire cette superstition savante. Alors que, dans l'empire byzantin, des empereurs même devenaient ses adeptes, comme Léon le Sage, ou ses défenseurs, comme Manuel Comnène, elle resta à peu près ignorée en Occident depuis l'époque franque jusqu'au XIIe siècle. La *Mathesis* de Firmicus Maternus est le dernier traité théorique sur la matière qui nous ait été conservé, et l'on ne trouve presque aucun manuscrit carolingien où il soit question d'astrologie. Celle-ci ne recommença à se répandre en Europe que sous l'influence des Arabes, et si elle jouit à la Renaissance d'une vogue éphémère elle le dut au prestige que lui prêta la science grecque et le grand nom de Ptolémée.

In the latest edition of his masterly book on the Oriental religions of the Roman Empire, published in 1929, he expresses virtually the same opinion.[3] The primary purpose of this essay is to review the existing evidence for the Latin-speaking West from the time of Constantine to the end of the ninth century. This is the more necessary because most recent writers have tended to concentrate all or most of their attention on astrology in the Eastern Mediterranean World; and, though Cumont and Toutain, for example, have touched on some of the Latin material, not a little of this seems so far to have been entirely ignored. There is, moreover, a certain tendency to dogmatize about the popularity or unpopularity of a given author in the Middle Ages without taking seriously into account the invalu-

[3] Les religions orientales⁴, 290, note 63.

able light often thrown by medieval library catalogues, as well as by the extant manuscripts. Yet these are sometimes the safest guide to truth when the purpose is to ascertain the beginning or the revival of intellectual trends that are altogether new or else have lain dormant for a considerable period of time. That the final conclusions to be drawn from the available data are very different from Cumont's thesis is the conviction of the present writer. It is for his readers to judge whether he has made good his case.

Refutations of 'Scientific' Astrology [4]

One fruitful source of confusion in books and articles dealing with our subject has been a failure to distinguish clearly between 'scientific' and popular astrology. Modern inquirers are not entirely to blame if they have often confused the two; for the line of demarcation between them is sometimes blurred and, in addition, the ancient sources themselves are not always as precise as one could wish.[5] Astrology, the illegitimate sister of astronomy, had become thoroughly acclimatized in the Greek World of the Hellenistic Age. That it came to the Greeks from the Orient is clear, although the contributions made respectively by Babylonia and by Egypt may still be a matter of dis-

[4] The modern literature on ancient astrology is enormous, but it may be helpful to indicate a few works containing ample bibliographical information: Franz Boll, Studien über Claudius Ptolemaeus (Jahrbücher für classische Philologie, Supplementband 21 [1894], especially 181–238); Franz Cumont, Les religions orientales dans le paganisme romain (ed. 4, 1929), ch. VII and 284–292; A. D. Nock, Sallustius, lxx–lxxv; J. Toutain, Les cultes paiens dans l'empire romain II, 179–223; W. Gundel in Pauly-Wissowa's Realencyclopädie, s. v. Heimarmene. The same writer's survey in Bursian's Jahresberichte 243 covers the period from 1907 to 1933. It must, however, be used with caution, as it is not always wholly trustworthy. Thus, for instance, Gundel states (p. 147) that Duhem's discussion extends from pp. 459 to 494 and is devoted to an examination of the Church Fathers' views on astrology and particularly Augustine's at different periods of his life. Actually the astrological part of Duhem's chapter extends only from 454 to 460 and Duhem confines himself almost exclusively to examining the fifth book of the City of God! The reference to Boll's article in Zeitschrift für neutestamentliche Wissenschaft should be vol. 18 (1917–18), not 17 (1916). Gundel also omits to mention J. K. Fotheringham's article in Journ. Theol. Stud. 10 (1909), 116–119.

[5] In particular there is the unfortunate tendency, as we shall see, in both official and unofficial references to astrology to group it with magic, augury, divination, and other pagan rites and superstitions. Cf. below, page 70, also Apostolic Constitutions, 8, 32, 11 (ed. Funk, I, 536, 3–9).

pute.[6] If at that time it met with the strongest opposition from certain philosophical schools, like the Sceptics and the New Academy, some of its doctrines met with approval from the later Stoics, notably from Posidonius. The Jews rejected astrology decisively. Certain passages in the Old Testament, as will appear later, were in due course cited by Christian commentators in their anti-astrological polemic. About the middle of the second century B.C. the Jewish compiler of certain Sibylline oracles spoke in no uncertain voice: [7] 'There is a city down in the land of Ur of the Chaldees, from which comes a race of most righteous men, who ever give themselves up to sound counsel and fair deeds. For they search not out the circling course of the sun or the moon, nor monstrosities beneath the earth, nor the depth of Ocean's shimmering sea, nor portents of sneezes, and birds of augurers, nor wizards, nor magicians, nor enchanters, nor the deceits of ventriloquist's foolish words, nor do they study the predictions of Chaldaean astrology, nor do they astronomize: for all these things are in their nature prone to deceive, such things as witless men are searching out day by day, exercising their souls for a work of no profit.' Philo, besides condemning the pseudo-science in many of his writings, devoted a whole treatise to Providence in which a considerable section is directed against believers in fatalism and star-lore.[8] To the Christian teacher all forms of astrology were from the first abominable, the popular varieties, because they were pagan superstitions with a wide appeal, the 'scientific,' because it sought to substitute for God and the operation of Divine Grace and Providence a fatalistic scheme of the Universe in which the life and fortunes of every man were rigidly predetermined from the moment of birth or even of conception. As long as Christianity was itself a *religio illicita,* Christian authors in general had more pressing tasks than the detailed rebuttal of doctrines whose original home was traditionally believed to be Chaldaea. Here and there a word of condemnation may occur, as in Ter-

[6] Cf. the judicious remarks of A. D. Nock in Gnomon, 15 (1939), 363–364.
[7] R. H. Charles, Apocrypha and Pseudepigrapha of the O. T., II, 382–383.
[8] Cf. numerous references listed by P. Wendland, Philos Schrift über die Vorsehung, 24, note 1.

tullian or Lactantius, but longer disquisitions are still rare. Bardesanes' lost work, however, belonged to the second century, while Hippolytus devoted a section of his Philosophumena to astrology. After expressing strong disapproval of it, he expounds its tenets, taking his material from Sextus Empiricus. The all-embracing mind of Origen, too, had touched on the 'science' of the stars in more than one of his works.⁹ There were also related topics that called forth vigorous protests from the orthodox. Tertullian composed a tract combatting Hermogenes' hypothesis of eternally existent matter, while in the East Methodius sought to controvert Origen's similar contention, συναΐδιον εἶναι τῷ μόνῳ σοφῷ καὶ ἀπροσδεεῖ θεῷ τὸ πᾶν.¹⁰ With the establishment of Christianity as the official religion of the Empire treatises against astrology, like the suppression of various popular superstitions, became a more urgent need, the more so because certain concepts implicit in the pseudo-science found a place also in the speculations of Christian heretics and Gnostics. Thus during the fourth and fifth centuries anti-astrological literature became much more abundant. That there were still pagan opponents also can be seen in Hierocles' treatise on fate and in Sallustius' work on the gods.¹¹ Cyril of Alexandria indulged his finest vein of invective against the victimization of women and common folk by astrological practitioners: 'Dost see these fellows who own the workshops of deceit, the places where they sell their falsehoods? It is they who marvel all the while at shooting stars and now and then for a few pence prate of the mysteries in the heavens. They get women into their clutches, bewitch the minds of the common herd, and make their purses ripe for picking. Nay more, by filching trifling profits they collect for themselves the wages for their quite insipid marvel-mongering. Yet, as says the enemy of truth, they are learning heaven's all-directing destiny (τὴν πάντα κραίνουσαν οὐρανοῦ ψῆφον) in the movement of the stars! We would convict them of being cheats and liars and utterly ignorant of truth.' ¹²

---

⁹ Tertullian, de idol. (CSEL, 20, 38, 3 ff.); Lactantius, Inst. (CSEL, 19, 167, 1 ff.); Hippolytus, PG, 16, 3056C–3090A.

¹⁰ Methodius ap. Photium, PG, 103, 1140C ff.

¹¹ Hierocles ap. Photium, *ibid.*, 702D–703A.   ¹² PG, 76, 1052B.

In general, however, Christian refutations of astrology are either full-dress discourses on fatalism or else they are briefer statements by Biblical commentators called forth by a passage or episode in Scripture. To the former class belong the treatises on fate by Diodorus of Tarsus and by Gregory of Nyssa, Nemesius' discourse on the nature of man, and two notable poems, De providentia, by Gregory of Nazianzus; and in Latin, Ambrosiaster's Quaestio CXV and a series of chapters in the fifth book of Augustine's City of God. To the second group may be assigned extended treatments of the subject in the commentaries of Basil the Great, Procopius of Gaza, and Ambrose, on Genesis, and in the exposition of Job by Julian of Halicarnassus, besides briefer comments in other expositors.

It has been shown long since that the main arguments, as well as much of the illustrative material, set out by these writers had become stereotyped by the Late Imperial Age; for ultimately they go back to the later Hellenistic period, to Carneades and the New Academy, and in some degree to the Stoics. Boll, whose contribution to the subject is most valuable, has pointed out that from the second century B.C. to Byzantine times two main lines of argument against astrological fatalism are elaborated to a greater or less degree by all its critics. In the first place they pose the question, how can it be maintained that the physical and mental peculiarities of a man depend on the position of the stars at the time of his birth or conception, when actually the same bodily and mental characteristics are to a great extent found in all the members of one people? In order to show that the question is not only legitimate but unanswerable by their opponents a great wealth of illustrations is used. Augustine and others discuss fully the case of twins. We feel that Ambrosiaster missed an opportunity when he contented himself with recording Roman forerunners of the Dionne quintuplets, without elaborating the astrological complications attendant on so unusual an occurrence! [13] Diodorus again, so far from confining

---

[13] CSEL, 50, 342, 13–16—*legitur namque cautum in quodam iuris libello aliquando mulierem quinque peperisse: quomodo subreptum est fatis, ut huic soli hoc natura decerneret, quod non erat fati? quod si fati fuisset, aliquantae hac sorte oneratae fuissent.*

himself to human kind, treats at length of animals and plants. Secondly, the Christian writers attack vigorously the doctrine that certain planets or signs of the zodiac influence given geographical areas and determine the manners and customs of those who inhabit them. Rather, it was argued, the particular characteristics of an individual in a certain geographical region prove that his life is determined not by the natal or prenatal influence of a star or constellation, but by his own untrammeled will.[14] Many of the *exempla* used, whether to illustrate national customs or natural phenomena that bring benefits or disaster in their train, occur again and again in our authors. Thus they instance circumcision and the observance of the Mosaic Law as common to all Jews, wherever their place of residence. Certain sexual practices, which Greeks and Romans regarded as incestuous, are characteristic of the Persians, while the Amazons afford an example of a strange social and economic organization.[15] Similarly, general allusions to earthquakes, inundations, war, pestilence, drought, and famine partake of the nature of commonplaces in these writers, although they treat the topic with varying degrees of elaboration. What is of far greater interest is that two, Gregory of Nyssa and Ambrosiaster, enliven the narrative by introducing personal experiences. Gregory recalls a violent manifestation of nature in a way which leaves no doubt that he is speaking as an eye-witness.[16]

Who does not know [he remarks] that such disturbances of the earth arise not merely in its inhabited regions but in those that are uninhabited? Whoever has seen the Sangaean mountain range that lies on the borders of Bithynia, or has heard tell of it by others, will know that I speak truth when I say that the entire mountain ridge has subsided down to the level of the road passing through and affords a terrifying spectacle to the traveller. Similar convulsions have occurred in Paphlagonian territory, and in some places human dwellings have been swallowed up in these chasms. In many regions,

---

[14] Cf. Boll, Studien, 183 ff.

[15] Cf., for example, PG, 103, 864A (Diodorus); PG, 45, 169B–C (Gregory of Nyssa); Rhein. Mus., 55, 332 (Julian of Halicarnassus); PG, 1, 1410B, 1412A, 1414B–C (ps.-Clement); CSEL, 50, 323, 5–9, 324, 17–19, 344, 3–21 (Ambrosiaster); and generally Boll, *op. cit.*, 202 ff., Nock, Sallustius, lxxii and 19.

[16] PG, 45, 168B–C.

when such a calamity happens, we see the area denuded of its inhabitants. And what need is there for me to refer individually to Cyprus, Pisidia, and Achaea, where there are many signs of the disasters that I have named?

A little earlier he had enumerated a number of historical examples from the past and then continued: [17]

But even if we pass all these occurrences by, the events of our own life-time furnish sufficient proof of what has been said. Who does not know that the great capital of Bithynia, numbered amongst the world's outstanding cities, and the broad and spacious land of Thrace were utterly and without warning laid in ruins, the one by an earthquake and fire, the other by war? How many there— children, infants, young and old men, free men and slaves, victors and vanquished, rich and poor, healthy and sick—perished in a moment of time?

On the 21st July, 365, when Gregory was about thirty years of age, a violent earthquake accompanied by tidal waves occurred, which caused great devastation and suffering in various parts of the Eastern Aegean, as well as in Constantinople and the vicinity. Our chief informant about the event is Ammianus, but there are allusions in other authors as well.[18] It seems highly probable, though modern historians of the period seem to have ignored the passages quoted, that Gregory is alluding to this disaster, which may well have affected Pontus where he was at that time residing. As for the utter devastation of Thrace by war, the most likely interpretation would find in this allusion a reference to those Visigothic invasions that culminated in 378 in the battle of Adrianople. If this contention be correct, it also provides a *terminus post quem* for the composition of Gregory's treatise. Ambrosiaster, too, whose writings are diversified by many apt illustrations drawn from his reading or his own experience, makes mention of a contemporary misfortune, when he speaks of the desolation of Pannonia. He doubt-

---

[17] *Ibid.*, 165B.
[18] Ammian., 26, 10, 15–19; cf. Otto Seeck, Geschichte des Untergangs der antiken Welt, V, 79 and 458 with the references there given.

less had in mind the destruction caused by the Quadi and Sarmatians in 374.[19]

Among the poems of Gregory of Nazianzus are two, written respectively in hexameters and in iambic senarii, which are less known than they deserve to be.[20] Both are entitled περὶ προνοίας, and set forth with considerable elegance and not a little poetic imagery the traditional arguments in favor of a Divine Providence. Both in consequence contain passages against fatalism and its 'scientific' justification, astrology. In one there is an allusion to the Star of Bethlehem, and the poet relates how even the Magi were converted, abandoned their craft, and adored Christ. In the other poem five lines of Aristotelian precision deserve to be quoted: [21]

> ἔρροιεν οἱ Πρόνοιαν ἐξηρνηκότες
> ὥσπερ τὸ σώζεσθ' ἐκ θεοῦ δεδοικότες
> ἀλλ' ἢ φορᾷ νέμοντες ἀστάτῳ τὸ πᾶν,
> ἢ καὶ διδόντες ἀστέρων κινήμασι,
> τοῖς πῶς, πόθεν τε, κἀκ τίνος, κινουμένοις·

Substantial as was the anti-astrological literature of the Greek World, most of it remained unknown to the Latin-speaking West. An exception was the novelistic composition of the pseudo-Clement, for the Recognitions were translated by Rufinus; and Ambrose was familiar with both Basil and Origen. Augustine's views, based on Cicero, are expounded most fully in his City of God. Astrology, he there argues, must be rejected not only by Christians, but by pagans who believe in the gods; for to accept it is in effect an admission of atheism. He then embarks on a lengthy argument regarding true twins and twins of opposite sex. In the course of it he reviews the scientific opinions of Hippocrates and the unscientific superstitions of Posidonius and Nigidius Figulus; he also devotes a whole chapter to the twin sons of Isaac, Esau and Jacob. In short the major part of Augustine's attack is levelled against only one part of astrological practice, genethlialogy or the casting of nativities. Subsequently

[19] CSEL, 50, 334, 16–17; cf. generally Cumont in Revue d'hist. et de litt. relig., 8, 419, and Souter, A study of Ambrosiaster, 31 ff.; 168 ff.
[20] PG, 37, 424–429.   [21] Ibid., 430A.

he inveighs against the absurdity of doing certain things only on astrologically favorable days, a form of popular superstition that incurred the contempt of Ambrosiaster also.[22] In the seventh book Augustine derides the folly of identifying certain stars with certain gods, of calling planets after Mars, Venus, and Mercury. And why do constellations or the signs of the zodiac receive no temples or altars? Why are they not at least reckoned as plebeian deities? [23] The briefer discussion of astrology in the commentary on Genesis adds nothing further, but the short letter to Lampadius is of some interest. It is wholly concerned with the danger to morality and human conduct inseparable from adherence to astrology. Implicit belief in fate and fortune undermines all laws and institutions, in short leads to anarchy. Augustine writes with a certain pawky humor and gives us a glimpse of quasi-Oriental manners. The master of the house will correct his wife by blows, if she stares incessantly (*immoderatius*) out of the window instead of attending to her wifely duties. If she exclaims, 'why do you strike me; strike Venus who compels me to act thus,' he will realize how justified his chastisement is.[24] In the ninth book of the Recognitions the discussion is centred mainly on what Boll has called astrological ethnography. If there is little that is new and better stated elsewhere in the book, its influence in the West during the earlier Middle Ages was, as will appear hereafter, quite exceptional. Finally there is a Latin work of the early fifth century which seems to have been generally overlooked, although it throws a remarkable sidelight on our subject. In the Acts of St. Sebastian, once wrongly fathered on Ambrose, we read how the future saint visited the astrological laboratory of Chromatius. It had been built all of glass by Chromatius' father, Tarquinius, at a cost of more than two hundred pounds of gold. The episode appears to be so little known that it deserves quotation: [25]

Tunc ille: habeo, inquit, cubiculum holovitreum, in quo omnis disciplina stellarum ac mathesis mechanica est arte constructa, in cuius fabrica pater meus Tarquinius amplius quam ducenta pondo auri

---

[22] CSEL, 40, 209–221; CSEL, 50, 345, 8–16.   [23] CSEL, 40, 323, 4–324, 9.
[24] Aug., Epist. 246 (CSEL, 57, 583, 17–585, 17).
[25] PL, 17, 1044D–1047B; the passage cited is on 1045A–B.

dignoscitur expendisse. Cui S. Sebastianus dixit: si hoc tu integrum habere volueris, te ipsum frangis. Chromatius dixit: quid enim? Mathesis aut ephemeris aliquo sacrificiorum usu coluntur, cum tantum eis mensium et annorum cursus certo numero per horarum spatia distinguuntur? et lunaris globi plenitudo vel diminutio, digitorum motu, rationis magisterio, et calculi computatione praevidetur? S. Polycarpus presbyter dixit: illic signa Leonis et Capricornii et Sagittarii et Scorpionis et Tauri sunt, illic in Ariete luna, in Cancro hora; in Iove stella, in Mercurio tropica, in Venere Mars, et in omnibus istis monstruosis daemonibus ars Deo inimica cognoscitur.

Sebastian's arguments which follow ultimately prevail with Chromatius. He is converted, *universa idola crystallina et holovitrea et omne opus illud mechanicum* are destroyed, and an angelic messenger appears from heaven. The refutation of astrology is to a great extent based on the ninth book of the Recognitions, even to exact verbal correspondences here and there.

When we pass to certain episodes or quotations in the Bible which bear on our subject, it is natural to begin with the star that guided the Magi to Bethlehem. To the author of the Protevangelium Jacobi and to Ignatius it was a star that outshone all other stars.[26] In the Infancy Gospel it is a guiding angel, a version readily explicable as a contamination of Matthew, 2, 9–10 with Luke, 2, 9–10.[27] The Fathers of the Eastern Church, however, adopted a more mystical explanation, while the fact that they found it necessary to controvert an astrological interpretation proves that this last was widely believed. Basil the Great, for instance, begins his discussion of the phenomenon with the challenging sentence: 'let no one drag in the paraphernalia of astrology (τὴν τῆς ἀστρολογίας κατασκευὴν) to explain the rising of the star.' It was not one of the regular stars, neither was it a comet.[28] Diodorus of Tarsus and John Chrysos-

---

[26] J. A. Fabricius, Codex apocryphus novi testamenti, I, 115—ἀστέρα παμμεγέθη, λάμψαντα ἐν τοῖς ἄστροις τοῦ οὐρανοῦ καὶ ἀμβλύνοντα τοὺς ἄλλους ἀστέρας ὥστε μὴ φαίνεσθαι αὐτούς. Ignatius, Ephes. 19, in Kirsopp Lake, Apostolic Fathers, I, 192— ἀστὴρ ἐν οὐρανῷ ἔλαμψεν ὑπὲρ πάντας τοὺς ἀστέρας, καὶ τὸ φῶς αὐτοῦ ἀνεκλάλητον ἦν, καὶ ξενισμὸν παρεῖχεν ἡ καινότης αὐτοῦ. τὰ δὲ λοιπὰ πάντα ἄστρα ἅμα ἡλίῳ καὶ σελήνῃ χορὸς ἐγένετο τῷ ἀστέρι· αὐτος δὲ ἦν ὑπερβάλλων τὸ φῶς αὐτοῦ ὑπὲρ πάντα.

[27] Fabricius, *op. cit.,* 173.   [28] PG, 31, 1469C ff.

tom describe it in very similar terms as not one of the familiar heavenly bodies, but as a kind of divine power transformed into a star.[29] In a sermon on the Nativity attributed to Gregory of Nyssa the star of Bethlehem, unlike other stars which are either planets or fixed in the firmament, both moved and stood still.[30] It goes without saying that all these commentators strongly reprobate those who would bring the appearance of the star into astrological connection with Christ's birth. Ambrosiaster, like Diodorus, Gregory of Nyssa, and Jerome, makes the Magi familiar with the prophecy of Balaam, son of Beor (Num., 24, 17), and interpret the star, which they understood to be *extra ordinem mundi,* in a Messianic sense.[31] Gregory the Great in a homily on the Epiphany does not discuss the star: nevertheless he takes occasion to introduce an anti-astrological paragraph at this point.[32] Other passages in Scripture bearing directly on star-lore or lending themselves to astronomical or astrological exposition are few. The short dissertation against astrologers of Julian of Halicarnassus is introduced as a comment on Job, 38, 7, but the Latin commentators on this verse did not follow suit. Gregory the Great makes no remark, while in the exposition of the so-called Philippus the stars are identified as so many angels, but only in a tropological sense.[33] Isaiah's contemptuous allusion to 'the astrologers, the star-gazers, the monthly prognosticators' (47, 13–14) and the fate that awaits them is explained by Jerome strictly with reference to the scriptural passage, that is to say, to the augury and star-lore of Babylonia. He is even briefer when he comments on Jeremiah, 10, 2, contenting himself with what is hardly more than a general definition: *proprie adversum eos loquitur qui venerantur caelestia et, quae in signa sunt*

---

[29] Diodorus, PG, 103, 877A—δύναμίν τινα θειοτέραν εἰς ἄστρον μὲν σχηματιζομένην, Chrysostom, PG, 57, 61 ff.—δύναμίς τις ἀόρατος εἰς ταύτην μετασχηματισθεῖσα τὴν ὄψιν.

[30] PG, 46, 1133D. That this is an authentic work by Gregory has been disputed by some, maintained by others. Cf. O. Bardenhewer, Gesch. der altkirchl. Lit., 3, 208. Boll, Zeitschrift für neutest. Wiss., 18, 40–48, scarcely concerns himself with the Eastern Fathers' interpretation of the Star of Bethlehem. The modern rationalism of Fotheringham (Journ. Theol. Stud., 10, 116–119) suggested that the star was Mars.

[31] CSEL, 50, Quaestio LXIII.   [32] See below, page 75.

[33] PL, 26, 619 ff.

*posita annorum, temporum, mensuum et dierum, ab his aesti-
mant regi humanum genus et ex causis caelestium terrena mode-
rari.*[34] Maximin, the Arian, in denouncing pagans who worship
the heavenly bodies and the elements, cites against them St. Paul
(Rom., 1, 20–23) and the Book of Wisdom (13, 1–4).[35] The
passage in Romans also elicits a short criticism from Ambrosiaster: 'for they esteem themselves wise men, because they think
that they have searched out the working of the physical universe *(physicas rationes)*, as they scan the courses of the stars
and the properties of the elements, while scorning the Master of
these. Thus they are foolish; for if these deserve praise, how
much more so their Creator.'[36] Disapproval of astrology, as
Souter long since pointed out, is expressed by this commentator
again and again. If there are relatively few quotations from
Scripture which lent themselves to polemic against astrology,
there were, on the other hand, not a few occurrences which
demonstrated the intervention of God in human affairs. To
Christian authors desirous of disproving the inevitability of
fate such Biblical episodes were welcome material for illustrating their argument. Some are used many times, others are found
only in a single author. Thus, both Gregory of Nyssa and Ambrosiaster group together Noah's preservation at the time of the
Flood, the destruction of Sodom and Gomorrah, and the drown-
ing of Pharaoh's host in the Red Sea. Maximin, to exemplify
the efficacy of prayer, instances the experience of Noah, Moses,
Joshua, Elijah, and Jonah. Joshua and Hezekiah (II Kings, 20,
11) are introduced by Ambrosiaster, while Ambrose describes
the miracle of Jonah, but takes his other examples from the
New Testament—the penitent thief, Peter guided out of prison
by an angel, Paul's blindness and recovery of his sight, his
preservation from shipwreck and from the bite of the viper.[37]

[34] CSEL, 59, 128, 22–25. The two quotations from the prophets occur also in
Diodorus (PG, 103, 876A–B).
[35] Journ. Theol. Stud., 17 (1915–1916), 323, 81 ff. That the Arian bishop Maximin, not Maximus of Turin, was the author of this sermon has been shown by B.
Capelle, Revue bénédictine, 34 (1922), 81 ff.
[36] PL, 17, 58A. A. Souter, A study of Ambrosiaster, 31–33.
[37] PG, 45, 165A; CSEL, 50, 323, 10–18; Journ. Theol. Stud., 17, 329, 262 ff.;
CSEL, 50, 333, 4–19; CSEL, 32, i, 119, 15–120, 2.

The Western Church and Astrology

It is necessary in this section to distinguish as far as possible between official condemnation levelled specifically and exclusively against astrology and the efforts of the Church and its officers and writers to combat various popular and especially rustic superstitions which flourished like hardy perennials. And nothing is more remarkable than the paucity of evidence for the former, and the copious material for the latter. The entire sixteenth book of the Codex Theodosianus is devoted to matters of religion. Orthodoxy is defined, the status of the Church and its ministers is laid down, and a long series of ordinances against Jews and heretics is there collected. The tenth section, moreover, contains enactments against paganism, its temples, its rites and sacrifices; yet there is no mention of astrology. In the ninth book, however, which is concerned with criminal law, there are three brief entries. Two of these aim to suppress various practitioners of superstition, the third, beginning with the incisive words, *cesset mathematicorum tractatus,* is directed solely against astrologers. Finally, in an enactment of April 22, 386, included in the Constitutio Sirmondiana, the emperors grant pardon to divers offenders but exclude those convicted of major crimes—murderers, adulterers, *in astra peccantes,* poisoners, magicians, coiners, and so forth.[38] Astrology was condemned by the Council of Toledo in 400 and by the Council held at Braga betweeen 560 and 565.[39] But the phraseology makes it clear that the anathemas of the assembled bishops were directed specifically against the Priscillianists. This heretical sect is also the object of Leo I's severe condemnation. In a remarkable letter he fulminates against impiety 'which, not content with accepting the false teaching of those who under cover of Christ's name have strayed from the Gospels, has plunged itself into the darkness of heathendom, so that by the profane secrets of magic arts and the empty lies of astrologers (*mathematicorum vana mendacia*) they might place the faith of religion and the reason for their conduct in the power of demons and in the ac-

[38] Cod. Theod. (edd. Mommsen and Meyer), ix, 16, 4; ix, 16, 6; ix, 16, 8; page 913.

[39] Mansi, Concilia, 3, 1004, para. xv; 9, 775, para. ix and x.

tion of the stars.' The result must be a suspension of law and order, the criminal will disclaim responsibility for his acts and blame the stars. The bishop goes on to define astrology somewhat more closely, a passage best cited in the original:

Ad hanc insaniam pertinet prodigiosa illa totius humani corporis per duodecim caeli signa distinctio ut diversis partibus diversae praesideant potestates; et creatura quam deus ad imaginem suam fecit, in tanta sit obligatione siderum in quanta est connexione membrorum. Merito patres nostri, sub quorum temporibus haeresis haec nefanda prorupit, per totum mundum instanter egere ut impius furor ab universa ecclesia pelleretur.

Here we have a very definite allusion to 'scientific' astrology with its doctrine of the regional influence of the stars; the last sentence shows that Leo is still thinking of the Priscillianists alone.[40] He reverts once more to astrology later in this letter and calls it the eleventh blasphemy of these heretics 'whereby they deem that men's souls and bodies are bound fast (*obstringi*) by the fatal stars.' In one of his sermons he denounces sunworship at some length and in another there is a passing allusion to fatalism.[41] The second redaction of Dionysius Exiguus' first collection and translation of Church Canons was formally adopted for use by the Roman Church and consequently attained prime importance for the Latin-speaking world. In this work there is only one direct mention of astrology and its exponents, where Dionysius quotes from the acts of the Council of Laodicea, held in 365: [42]

quod non oportet sacerdotes aut clericos, magos aut incantatores esse, vel mathematicos vel astrologos aut facere quae dicuntur phylacteria, quae quidem sunt animarum ipsarum vincula.

Other citations allude only to divination and magic, while the somewhat later collections of Ferrandus and Cresconius add nothing further.[43]

In contrast to this scarcity of official condemnations of astrology there is abundant evidence to show how the Western Church struggled unceasingly to suppress rustic superstitions,

[40] PL, 54, 679A–B.   [41] *Ibid.*, 685C; 218B–C; 434A.   [42] PL, 67, 74B.
[43] *Ibid.*, 54B; 156A–B; 168C; Ferrandus, *ibid.*, 955C; Cresconius, PL, 88, 876C.

fortune-telling, spells, and similar pagan abominations. Preachers like Maximus of Turin in the fifth or Caesarius of Arles and Martin of Braga in the sixth century inveighed against these practices, and their denunciations were echoed in later ages and sometimes in identical language by Eligius, Pirmin, and others. George, bishop of Ostia, writing to Pope Hadrian I in 786 mentions British synods that he had attended, where he had counselled the British bishops to proceed against augury and other such heathen survivals.[44] Prohibition of magic, augury, and other superstitious customs and beliefs is found frequently in the penitential literature.[45] Yet astrology and astrologers as such are mentioned infrequently. Caesarius, who in his sermons thunders again and again at his hearers for relapsing into all manner of pagan usages, alludes only twice to *mathematici,* in one case coupling them with the Manicheans and condemning the familiar irresponsibility argument of the fatalists.[46] In a third sermon he disapproves the pagan names of the week and instructs his congregation to say *prima, secunda, tertia feria* instead of *dies Martis, dies Mercurii, dies Iovis.*[47] In the Penitentials the *mathematicus* is described only twice and in almost identical words: 'if any one is a *mathematicus,* that is, if he takes away the mind of a man by the invocation of demons, he shall do penance for five years, one year on bread and water.' Thus, at least in the Penitentials the word *mathematicus* has lost its

[44] Maximus, PL, 57, 483C; Caesarius, see the indexes in Morin's edition of the sermons; Martin, De correctione rusticorum (ed. C. P. Caspari), passim; M. L. W. Laistner, Harv. Theol. Rev., 31 (1938), 270–271 with references there given [below, pages 173–174]; MGH, Epist., IV, 21, 33–34.

[45] J. T. McNeill and Helena M. Gamer, Medieval Handbooks of Penance, 198; 228–229; 276–277; 288; 331.

[46] Sermo XVIII (ed. Morin, 82, 15) and LIX (249, 8 ff.)—*Dicit homini serpens ille per mathematicos et Manicheos, ne confiteatur homo peccatum. Per mathematicos sic loquitur: Numquid homo peccat? stellae sic sunt positae; necesse est ut faciat homo peccatum. Dicit ergo per mathematicos, quia stella facit ut homo peccet; nam ipse non peccat. Sic blasphemias convertit in deum: creator enim stellarum deus est.*

[47] Sermo CXCIII (744, 31–34). Yet in the second century a Christian apologist had used the pagan names of the week without demur. Justin Martyr (Apol., I, 67), speaking of the Passion, wrote: τῇ γὰρ πρὸ τῆς κρονικῆς ἐσταύρωσαν αὐτὸν καὶ τῇ μετὰ τὴν κρονικήν, ἥτις ἐστιν ἡλίου ἡμέρα, φανεὶς τοῖς ἀποστόλοις αὐτοῦ καὶ μαθηταῖς ἐδίδαξε κτλ. No example of ἡ κρονικὴ in this sense is given in the new edition of Liddell and Scott.

original meaning; he is a sorcerer, not an exponent of star-lore.[48] Perhaps, however, the most significant circumstance of all is this: Dr. Charles W. Jones, who, as the result of prolonged acquaintance with the extant manuscripts, is thoroughly familiar with the computistical literature of the earlier Middle Ages, has assured the present writer that there is a complete absence of astrological material in the *computi* down to the end of the ninth century. And though, as will appear hereafter, astrological literature began to circulate again in that century, it scarcely affected the *computi* until the tenth. But in the later compilations of the eleventh and twelfth centuries the addition of frankly astrological lore to computistical works is not unusual.

The chief authors from the sixth to the eighth centuries have little to say about our subject beyond generalities. Gregory of Tours in his little astronomical treatise, which in any case does not seem to have enjoyed more than local success, adheres strictly to scientific astronomy and disclaims expressly any astrological purpose, *quia non in his mathesim doceo neque futura praescrutare praemoneo.*[49] Cassiodorus, after pointing out the practical value of astronomy for navigators and farmers, proceeds:

cetera vero quae se ad cognitionem siderum coniungunt, id est ad notitiam fatorum, et fidei nostrae sine dubitatione contraria sunt, sic ignorari debent, ut nec scripta esse videantur.

He reinforces his condemnation by appealing to the authority of Basil and Augustine.[50] There is also a brief mention in his commentary on the Psalms; it shows how he was aware that astrology had had its pagan opponents too.[51] Isidore of Seville,

---

[48] McNeill and Gamer, *op. cit.,* 277 and 306.

[49] MGH, Script. Merov., I, 863, 12–15; and cf. generally M. L. W. Laistner, Thought and Letters in Western Europe [2], 130. It is significant that only one manuscript containing the whole of Gregory's treatise survives, though the introductory section on human and divine Wonders was copied frequently.

[50] Cassiod., Inst. (ed. Mynors), 156, 23–157, 2. The Augustine reference is to the De doctrina Christiana (PL, 34, 57), where the African Father expresses the opinion that astronomy is harmless, but of little value for the study of Scripture. It is best avoided because astrology is related to it.

[51] Pl., 70, 505B—*astrologiam . . . quam etiam nobilium philosophorum iudicia damnaverunt.*

as might be expected of an encyclopedist, provides a variety of information. Its significance is obvious in view of the immense popularity that his works enjoyed in the earlier medieval period. He expresses the usual disapproval of astrology that befitted a sound Churchman. Astronomy is natural (*naturalis*), whereas astrology is partly natural, partly superstitious—*superstitiosa vero est quam mathematici sequuntur qui in stellis augurantur.*[52] Yet he is not wholly untainted by its tenets when he speaks approvingly of those who would associate bodily changes with the qualities of the stars.[53] He devotes a lengthy chapter, entitled De magis, to every kind of hocus-pocus and its exponents; in the course of it he provides his readers with definitions of *astrologi, genethliaci, geneses, mathematici, horoscopi,* but adds the face-saving observation:[54]

cuius artis (i.e. astrology) scientia usque ad evangelium fuit concessa ut Christo edito nemo exinde nativitatem alicuius de caelo interpretaretur.

[52] Etym., 3, 27, 1–2. One possible source of confusion, it is well to remind oneself, is to be found in the words *astrologia, astrologus* themselves. In classical Latin these had been used invariably both for the science and the pseudo-science and their exponents. *Astronomia, astronomus* came into use only in the Silver Latin Age and later (cf. Thes. linguae latinae, s. v.). Now, although *astronomia, astronomus* became more and more common, the older words continued to be used in both senses even by one and the same writer. Bede, for example, employs *astronomia* in E.H., 4, 2, but in his commentary on the six days of Creation, in the sentence *stellae quas planetas, id est, errantes, vocant astrologi,* the last word obviously signifies astronomers. Similarly, in D.T.R., 36, a passage derived from the Latin Josephus, *astrologia* and *geometria* are coupled and described as *gloriosae utilitatis.* More than a century later John the Scot consistently writes *astrologia* and its derivatives, when he means astronomy; cf. PL, 122, 866B; 869C—*astrologiam cuius maxima vis est motus siderum per loca et tempora considerare;* and in 716C he speaks of *astrologica supputatio,* astronomical reckoning. In the earliest library catalogues the work of Hyginus and sometimes the Latin Aratus are described as *liber astrologiae,* and this title is found side by side with *liber astronomiae* as late as the fifteenth century. Hyginus himself had of course employed *astrologia* consistently to mean astronomy, but it is easy to see how the uninitiated student in the Middle Ages might be led astray by the survival of this earlier Latin usage. For the popularity of Hyginus and the Latin Aratus in the Middle Ages cf. Max Manitius, Handschriften antiker Autoren in mittelalterlichen Bibliothekskatalogen, 80–82, who lists 43 manuscripts varying in date from the early ninth to the sixteenth century.

[53] Etym., 4, 3, 4.   [54] Ibid., 8, 9.

Finally, in another of his writings he classifies philosophy into seven kinds, the four which the Middle Ages grouped together as the *quadrivium* with the addition of astrology, mechanics, and medicine. This classification reappears in Aldhelm and again in the ninth century.[55]

In Gregory the Great we meet with two highly characteristic utterances. He sneers at the names of the constellations which go back to the empty tales of Hesiod, Aratus, and Callimachus. Job (9, 9) did not follow their stories about Arcturus or Orion, but Scripture uses the terms invented by students of secular wisdom, because they have become part of the common parlance.[56] More important for our purpose is the excursus on astrology that he introduced into his Homily on the Epiphany. He begins with a reference to the Priscillianists who to him, as to Leo I, seem to have been the main exponents of the pseudo-science and its doctrine of fate. He alludes briefly to the twins, Esau and Jacob, and then speaks scornfully of the supposed natal influence of the stars. Anyone born in the sign of Aquarius will become a fisherman. But Gaetulia is said to have none such. Who is to say that no one there is born under Aquarius, when there is not a single fisherman in that country? Those born under the sign of Libra are to become financiers (*trapezitae*). But in many districts there are no such persons at all. The astrologers must admit either that in those parts no one is born under the Balance or else that fate plays no part in their birth. Those of royal and of servile stock, though born under the same star, nevertheless live and end their lives as princes or slaves respectively. The pope ends impatiently—*haec de stella breviter diximus, ne mathematicorum stultitiam indiscussam praeterisse videamur.* Alas! Much that sounds impressive when declaimed passionately and with well-rounded lips from pulpit or platform becomes singularly flat and unconvincing when seen in writing or in print.[57] Aldhelm, who follows Isidore in including astrology among the seven kinds of philosophy, de-

---

[55] Liber numerorum (PL, 83, 188B) also in Diff. II (PL 83, 94B); for the seven *genera* in Aldhelm see MGH, Auct. Ant., XV, 71, 23 and 277, 5. Cf. also below, page 79.

[56] PL, 75, 865C.   [57] PL, 76, 1110A–1114B.

nounces the ridiculous stupidity of its devotees with their doctrines of fate and natal influence.[58] Of much greater interest is a solitary passage in Bede, which deserves to be quoted in full:

Attamen mathematici in explorandis hominum genituris ad atomum usque pervenire contendunt, dum zodiacum circulum in XII signa, signa singula in partes XXX, partes item singulas in punctos XII, punctos singulos in momenta XL, momenta singula in ostenta LX distribuunt, ut considerata diligentius positione stellarum, fatum eius qui nascitur quasi absque errore deprehendant. Quae quia vana et a nostra fide aliena est observatio, neglecta ea videamus, potius quo apostolus ad celeritatem resurrectionis intimandam huiusmodi temporis vocabulo utitur, dicens: 'omnes quidem resurgemus, sed non omnes immutabimur, in atomo, in ictu oculi, in novissima tuba.' (I Cor., 15, 51–52)

In the earlier part of the chapter from which this quotation is taken Bede, whose purpose was to explain the divisions of the sun-dial, gave an account of the various subdivisions of time, ending with the smallest which is indivisible and which he called atom. He adds that others have employed the terms *punctus* or *momentum*. So far he had followed the so-called Irish computus; but then, with a passage in Ambrose in mind, he points out that the method of dividing up the heavens used by astrologers is closely analogous.[59]

The student of the earlier Middle Ages would fall into serious error if, in appraising the extent to which superstitions in general and those connected with the stars in particular had currency, he were to assume that such beliefs were confined to

---

[58] In MGH, Auct. Ant., XV, 73, 6–10, he mentions the signs of the zodiac, *unde mathematici fatum, fortunam, vel genesim aut suprema Parcarum fila . . . se divinare et praenoscere posse ridiculosa stoliditate arbitrantur.* There is a similar passage on 269, 5–7.

[59] Bede, D.T.R., 3 (PL, 90, 302 ff.); Irish computus, *ibid.*, 653B; Ambrose, Hex., 4, 4, 14 (CSEL, 32, i, 121, 13–122, 10). As Ambrose's discussion closely resembles that of Procopius of Gaza, Wendland (Philos Schrift über die Vorsehung, 35, note 2) not unreasonably assumed that both writers were indebted to a lost work by Origen. Origen's exposition as given by Eusebius (Praep. evang., 6, 10, 74) is divergent. The words *in atomo* in Bede's quotation from I Corinthians are no doubt taken from Ambrose, who also cites this passage of Scripture. For this translation of the Vetus Latina, which is found also in Tertullian and Augustine, Jerome's Vulgate reads *in momento*.

the uneducated masses. Rather it would be true to say that such notions were universally entertained; for what other conclusion is possible, when we find them among educated Churchmen from the fifth to the ninth century? Sidonius relates a curious tale of a murdered man whose fate was foretold by astrologers. After expressing disapproval of such superstition, he weakens and adds: 'it must be admitted that in the present case there was neither appearance of mere conjecture nor deliberate ambiguity; death enmeshed our reckless inquirer into the future exactly when and as it had been foretold; all his shifts to evade it were in vain.' [60] Gregory of Tours, who in his astronomical tract reprobates astrology, nevertheless in his History of the Franks mentions without disapproval many portents connected with the stars. We have just seen that Bede condemned astrology. Yet in a chapter headed De effectiva lunae potentia, he, like Basil and Ambrose before him, accepts certain superstitions regarding lunar influence on the growth of animals and plants and respecting the right and wrong time in the month to perform agricultural operations. Elsewhere he speaks of comets that portend a change of reign, pestilence, wars, or winds and tides.[61] Finally Servatus Lupus, the most cultured man of his age, perhaps with the passage of Bede in mind, wrote to his friend Altuin: [62]

De cometis qui visi sunt timendum quam disserendum videtur. Et quia de his nil usquam divina loquitur auctoritas, id opinari, immo metuere possumus quod gentiles illis apparentibus usu deprehenderunt. Hii portendere cometas pestilentiam vel famem vel bella tradiderunt.

Surely the significant words here are *timendum* and *metuere*, coupled with an acceptance of pagan notions. He goes on to quote Virgil, Josephus, and Justin, and his further remarks show that he was also scientifically interested in this comet, which is

[60] Sidonius, Epist. (tr. Dalton), 8, 11, 9 ff.
[61] D.T.R., 28; D.N.R., 24. That the moon influences the growth of plants and animals is an opinion found in an agricultural writer like Palladius (cf. De la Ville de Mirmont, Rev. des études anciennes, 8 [1906], 155 ff.). Yet Palladius was one of the authors recommended by Cassiodorus to his monks (Inst., ed. Mynors, 72, 11).
[62] Lupus, Epist., 8 (ed. L. Levillain, I, 68).

mentioned by other contemporary writers and which was visible in April, 837.[63]

The Carolingian Age

The ninth century was of crucial importance. In the main a knowledge of astrology, or rather of the commoner arguments against it, was still being disseminated through the wide use in monastic circles of three or four Patristic works. There is no doubt which was the most popular of all. The pseudo-Clementine Recognitions were easy to read and to assimilate. Apart from the fact that their Clementine authorship was not questioned, so that they enjoyed all the authority due to a book composed in the sub-Apostolic age, they contained a good, and at times exciting, story and they did not make the stern demands on their readers' intelligence that were called for by the more philosophical arguments of an Ambrose or an Augustine. The Recognitions were used by Aldhelm and Bede. They appear frequently in medieval library catalogues and are usually called there *S. Clementis liber* or *S. Clementis historia,* the title of the book being much more rarely given.[64] Extant manuscripts, moreover, are exceedingly numerous. E. C. Richardson listed no less than seventy-eight, but made no mention of codices in Einsiedeln, Tours, and Namur. And there are probably others, especially in the smaller uncatalogued collections.[65] More advanced students would become familiar with the arguments of Ambrose and Augustine. The popularity of the Hexameron and of the City of God needs no demonstration, but it

[63] Another comet appeared in 842 and was visible for several months. Nithard (ed. Ph. Lauer, 108) relates that it could be seen at the time that Louis the German and Charles the Bald signed their famous pact.

[64] Cf. the index of G. Becker, Catalogi bibliothecarum antiqui.

[65] See E. C. Richardson in A. von Harnack, Gesch. der altchrist. Literatur, I, 229 ff. The Einsiedeln manuscript (264) was copied partly in the ninth, partly in the tenth century (G. Meier, Cat. codd. mss. qui in bibl. mon. Einsidl. servantur and W. M. Lindsay, Notae latinae, 455). For Turonensis 267 (late 10th c.) see E. K. Rand, Manuscripts of Tours, I, no. 197 with Plate CLXXXVIII, 1, reproducing the end of Book 1 and the beginning of Book 2. For the Namur manuscript (Grand Séminaire, 37; 11th c.) see P. Faider, Catalogue des MSS. conservés à Namur, I, 462. This codex is in one respect unique; it alone preserves the early Latin version of I Clement. This was published by G. Morin in Anecdota Maredsolana, II, where a detailed description will be found (iii–v).

is worth recalling to mind that, although the oldest manuscripts of the City of God are incomplete, one of the sixth century and one of the seventh contain Book V. In addition Hoffmann used one of the eighth and one of the ninth century. Similarly, Ambrose's commentary has survived in several manuscripts of the eighth and ninth centuries, besides many of later date, while the Orléans library still possesses a few folios of a codex copied in the seventh. Ambrosiaster's Quaestiones were evidently to be found in many libraries and extant manuscripts of the commentary on the Thirteen Epistles are numerous.[66]

There is, on the other hand, indubitable evidence for a slow revival of interest in 'scientific' astrology during the Carolingian Age. In proof of this one can point to a long letter by an anonymous author containing an astronomical discussion, but with definitely astrological additions.[67] Again, among the works wrongly attributed to Bede is a ninth century compilation which Charles Jones has called a 'brilliant exposition of the teaching of the rational school of the ninth century.'[68] The treatise is based on various earlier sources, as Jones has rightly stressed, but he has overlooked the fact that the addition of astrology and medicine to the four subjects of the *quadrivium* goes back to Isidore. And in the section entitled, De planetarum ordine et designatione, the unknown author has recourse to the Recognitions, as when he explains the evil influence of Mars and Saturn:[69]

---

[66] For his text of the revised version of the Quaestiones Souter used four MSS of the ninth, three of the tenth, and one of the thirteenth century, and there are others. But as his *stemma codicum* (CSEL, 50, xxxii) shows, these extant MSS presuppose many earlier ones now lost. The MSS of the commentary are listed in Souter's The earliest Latin commentaries on the Epistles of St Paul (Clarendon Press, 1927), 56–59; but a definitive edition of this work is still to seek owing to the death of successive editors (cf. Souter's recent comment in Journ. Theol. Stud., 41 [1940], 304).

[67] MGH. Epist., VI, 198, 36 ff.

[68] C. W. Jones, Bedae Pseudepigrapha, 83–84.

[69] Cf. Recogn. (PG, I, 1408A): *Denique cum Mars centrum tenens in domo sua ex tetragono respexerit Saturnum cum Mercurio ad centrum, luna veniente super eum plena, in genesi diurna, efficit homicidas et gladio casuros, sanguinarios, ebriosos,* etc. These passages and also Acta Sebast. (PL, 17, 1045)—*quod tempus tuum a malitioso Marte susceptum est aut Saturnus apocatasticus fuit*—may be added to the long list of examples, mostly from Greek writers, collected by A. D.

Mars positus in centro mundi, si Saturnum ex tetragono respexerit, si proximo loco post eum Mercurius cum plena luna idem tetigerit centrum, qui nascuntur in illa diurna genesi efficiuntur homicidae, gladio casuri, sanguinarii consilio vel facto, libidinosi, ebriosi, demoniosi, scrutatores secretorum, necromantici, malefici, sacrilegi, praecipue si nulla prospera impediverit.[70]

Furthermore, Van de Vyver has recently shown that the Latin versions of the so-called Letter of Petosiris and of the *ratio spherae Pythagoricae* were known already in the ninth century in important monastic centres, like Fleury, Chartres, and Corbie.[71] The astrological section in the Acta Sebastiani was also receiving a good deal of attention at this time. In the Scholica of Martin of Laon we find definitions of *apocatasticus, climacterica, diametrum, ephemeris, horoscopus, mathesis,* and *syndeton,* and in the case of three of these we are specifically told that the explanations given are those employed by the *mathematici.*[72] That some, if not all, of these definitions explain words in the Acta Sebastiani is made certain by comparison with some Glossae collectae contained in Ms. Vatic. lat. 1469 (Fol. 83r.–83v.) copied in 908. These glosses, as W. M. Lindsay has shown, presuppose a copy of the Acta with marginal annotations on such words as *diametrum, climacterica, synditus (sic), ephymeris (sic),* and *mathesis.*[73] That the commentator was not always entirely clear about his text is obvious from the following glosses:

mathesis centrum: id est disciplinalis punctus quo circulus volvitur
mathesis centrum: id est disciplinalis punctus circuli

The close relationship, however, between the Glossae and the Scholica is self evident.

Nock, Sallustius, lxxiii, note 54, to illustrate the malign activities of Mars and Saturn.

[70] PL, 90, 898A.

[71] A. Van de Vyver, Les plus anciennes traductions latines médiévales (Xe–XIe siècles) de traités d'astronomie et d'astrologie, in Osiris, I (1936), 658–691.

[72] M. L. W. Laistner, Bulletin of the J. Rylands Library, 7 (1923), 421–456. See A80, C12, D11, E13, H1, M3, S25. The alternative definition given for *ephemeris— annalis computatio continens seriem totius anni descriptam*—almost certainly refers, as Dr. Jones kindly informs me, to lists of solar and lunar letters, such as are frequently found in computistical manuscripts.

[73] W. M. Lindsay, Class. Quart., 15 (1921), 38–40.

The two authoritative presentations of 'scientific' astrology composed in Latin were the poem of Manilius and the treatise, Matheseos libri VIII, by Firmicus Maternus. No writer down to the end of the ninth century appears to show any acquaintance with either. In the medieval library catalogues Manilius appears but once, in a fifteenth century catalogue at Urbino. Firmicus' book, a copy of which may have existed in the tenth century at Regensburg, was to be found c. 1200 at St. Maur des Fossés and in Bamberg somewhat later; it is also recorded in three fifteenth and in one sixteenth century book-list.[74] Extant manuscripts of Firmicus are fairly numerous, but none is older than the eleventh century. Kroll and Skutsch, however, point out that the manuscripts of one group, though they go back to the same archetype as their main manuscripts (MVR), have been corrected by reference to other codices now lost. This second recension was already current in the eleventh century; the editors are, moreover, of the opinion that a manuscript existed in the Carolingian Age more complete than surviving manuscripts of the eleventh century. The end of Book 4 and Books 5 to 8 survive only in manuscripts of the fifteenth and sixteenth centuries, but their text, as Kroll and Skutsch believe, goes back ultimately to this Carolingian exemplar. The case of Manilius' poem is somewhat similar. No extant manuscript of it is earlier than the eleventh century and Housman has observed that the archetype need not have been older than the tenth. But he also admits the likelihood of the text having passed through an Insular stage.[75] Thus it is obvious that at least one manuscript of Manilius and only one of Maternus must have survived from pre-Carolingian times. Yet these authors had clearly been forgotten long since and only began to be rediscovered in the course of the ninth century.[76] But the mul-

---

[74] For the solitary mention of Manilius cf. Max Manitius, HSS antiker Autoren in mittelalterlichen Bibliothekskatalogen, 72–73; for Firmicus Maternus, *ibid.*, 172–173. The manuscript once at St. Maur des Fossés may be, according to Sittl, the extant codex, Paris. Bibl. nat. lat., 7311 (cf. W. Kroll and F. Skutsch in their edition of Firmicus, II, vii). Manitius assumed that the Regensburg manuscript was a copy of Firmicus. But is this certain, seeing that no author's name is given in the catalogue, but only the title, De creatione vel super mathesin?

[75] Manilius, ed. Housman, V, xviii.

[76] Or possibly in the eighth century. But if the Insular Manilius was copied in

tiplication of manuscripts was evidently very slow, and the absence of references to either Manilius or Firmicus in writers of the ninth century is also significant.

From the material which has been presented above certain conclusions would seem to emerge. The Latin-speaking West was acquainted with no book on 'scientific' astrology before the ninth or the tenth century. What little it did know about the subject was gleaned from a few Patristic works of small originality, in which were repeated arguments and illustrations that had become traditional in the course of centuries. Ambrosiaster alone diverged somewhat from the beaten track when he chose uncommon illustrations drawn from his own experience or from his varied reading. The attitude of the Church and of its leaders was indeed never in doubt. They tried constantly, but unsuccessfully, to root out all manner of superstitions of which popular astrology was one. Yet it would seem from the extant evidence that this was less of a menace to faith and morals than sorcery and other heathen practices. As for 'scientific' astrology, there is no adequate ground for asserting that it disappeared in the West because it was suppressed by authority. Had that been the case, some unambiguous proof of the fact would surely have survived. But the only clear example of official action was the attempted suppression not of astrologers as such, but of a heretic sect, one of whose heresies was believed to be an addiction to astrology. Not persecution or prosecution, but the lack of proper manuals caused the disappearance of 'scientific' astrology in the West for four or five centuries after Firmicus composed his astrologers' handbook.

---

the British Isles, it need not have been older than the ninth, since the Insular script survived there long after it had disappeared on the continent in Insular centres.

⟨ 5 ⟩

Ernst Robert Curtius'

Europäische Literatur und

*Lateinisches Mittelalter**

ERNST ROBERT CURTIUS, *Europäische Literatur und lateinisches Mittelalter*. Bern: A. Francke AG Verlag, 1948. Pp. 601. 44 Swiss francs.

THIS book is the fruit of sixteen years of study and reflection. Its high quality will surprise no one familiar with the many preliminary articles—twenty-five are listed on page 568—published by the author between 1932 and 1944. He now addresses himself not only to specialists but to educated readers interested in literature as literature. Regarded in one way, the book is a reasoned protest against the practice, that still predominates in Higher Education, of studying the vernacular literatures of western Europe in isolation, and of ignoring, or at best underrating, their debt to the Latin literature of the Middle Ages, which itself was rooted partly in pagan, partly in Christian antiquity. After some preliminary pages that contrast the ancient, the mediaeval, and the modern world, Mr. Curtius passes on methodically to mediaeval education, and from there to a more detailed consideration of rhetoric. Separate chapters are assigned

* *Speculum*, 24 (1949), 259–263. Reprinted by permission of the Mediaeval Academy of America.

83

to various rhetorical *topica,* to the use of metaphor, and to the treatment of larger themes—e.g., *Helden und Herrscher, Ideallandschaft.* Two chapters are devoted respectively to the relation of poetry to philosophy and to theology in the thought of the Middle Ages. Discussion of the Muses, the meaning of the term 'classical' together with the growth of literary canons, literary mannerisms, and symbolism derived from the book and the tools that go to its making bring the reader to the final chapter on Dante, the greatest figure in mediaeval literature. Throughout the text the argument is supported and justified by abundant quotations from ancient, mediaeval, and modern literature. There follow no less than twenty-five appendixes (pp. 409–564) in which questions too technical for the main narrative are investigated in detail. They range all the way from the metaphorical use of rhetorical terms or humor in the Middle Ages to Calderón's theory of art, and reminiscences of Virgil, Horace, and Ovid, in Diderot and Montesquieu. A work traversing so extended a field and so copiously documented might easily have become unreadable—a work of erudition suitable only for reference. But Mr. Curtius writes admirably and has a pretty wit. Moreover, he is always urbane—a *vir humanus*—even when he is indulging in polemic. See, for instance, his remarks on historians of art (pp. 22–24), or the disastrous effect on French literature of a narrow 'classicism' (pp. 272–274), or his discussion of Ehrismann's theories about the knightly virtues (pp. 508–523), or the gentle irony with which, at the end of his chapter on the relation between poetry and theology, he alludes (pp. 231–232) to the Neothomist school of thinkers.

Fully to review this book in all its aspects would require many pages and is a task beyond the competence of your reviewer. Hence the remarks that follow are confined to matters of which he can claim to have some knowledge and also offer additional illustrations or minor criticisms that seem to him to be pertinent. In the section on Greek rhetoric (p. 72) the author, like so many other scholars, all but ignores Isocrates. It is not the least of the many merits of H. I. Marrou's recent book, *Histoire de l'éducation dans l'antiquité,* that he has given credit where credit is due. Isocrates, not Plato nor yet Aristotle, was the father of higher education, that is to say, rhetoric in its ancient sense, as practised in the Hellenistic and the Graeco-Roman world. The truth is that, where Mr. Curtius is concerned as he is through the greater part of the book, with specific influences of earlier on later writers as shown in word or thought, his treatment is masterly and often all but exhaustive. But where the question at issue is the general influence of an author and the degree to which he was read at all at different times, his method is defective because he has disregarded an important part of the evidence. This fault is most apparent in his discussion of school-authors (cf. pp. 56 ff., 72 ff.) particularly those of pagan antiquity, read in the Middle Ages. In the first place it seems very doubtful whether one can assume anything approaching a uniform practice even as late as the twelfth century; for, in the last analysis, the authors studied were primarily those available in the nearest monastic or cathedral library, and only in a much less degree those that could be borrowed from other collections. Again, the copying of manuscripts was both laborious and, in view of the high cost of parchment, expensive; so that, when we find a book copied in a scriptorium, we can assume, especially if it was a pagan Latin author, that it was of direct interest to some teacher who in turn would bring it to the attention of his brighter pupils. Thirdly, Mr. Curtius is too brief on the Carolingian Age and says little about schools in the tenth and eleventh centuries. Thus, referring to a twelfth-century list of authors, he remarks (p. 57): 'Die Cicero-Auswahl wird erweitert durch *De oratore,* die "Tusculanen," die *Paradoxa stoicorum* und *De officiis.* Dazu kommen Symmachus, die Erdbeschreibung des Solinus. . . .' Again, when describing the authors familiar to Hugo of Trimberg and John of Salisbury, he leaves the impression on the reader's mind that certain authors, e.g., Macrobius, Gellius, Valerius Maximus, were only then coming into their own. The whole picture is badly out of focus because the author completely neglects both the catalogues of mediaeval libraries and the extant manuscripts. There are three early manuscripts of *De oratore,* one of which was written throughout by Servatus Lupus (who is nowhere mentioned!). Among the dozen extant manuscripts annotated by him one contains Valerius Maximus (Bern 366), another, Symmachus' *Letters* (Paris, B.N. 8623), another, Aulus Gellius (Vatican City, Reg. lat. 597). Lupus had also heard of a copy of Macrobius that he was anxious to see (*Epist.* 21, ed. Levillain, I, p. 110), and Manitius (*HSS antiker Autoren in mittelalterlichen Bibliothekskatalogen*, pp. 227 ff.) records two other libraries in the ninth, one in the tenth, and eleven in the eleventh century where this author was to be found. There were copies of Solinus in the ninth century at Lorsch, Murbach, St. Gall, and Reichenau, and among the codices used by Mommsen for his edition one was written in the ninth and four in the tenth century. As for Cicero, all the philosophical works, except *De finibus*, the second recension of the *Academica*, and the fragments of *De republica* were known in those same two centuries, as is clear from the combined testimony of Lupus, Hadoard, and the surviving manuscripts. Mr. Curtius asserts that the speeches were little studied; mediaeval catalogues and extant codices suggest the contrary. Three of these last (Paris, B.N. 7774A and 7794; Vatican City, Basilicanus H 25) of the ninth century are basic for any modern text of the speeches that they respectively contain; and, while few libraries before the twelfth century had a large collection of Cicero's *Orations*, a goodly number owned one or several: See Manitius, *op. cit.*, pp. 19 ff., and his lists are by no means complete. Zielinski's well-known monograph is useless for the mediaeval period and, as Mr. Curtius himself suggests, a book on Cicero in the Middle Ages still remains to be written. Meanwhile a beginning has been made by C. H. Beeson in *Classical Philology* 40 (1945), pp. 201–222, with a superb article on the *Collectaneum* of Hadoard.

The author is rather sparing of examples illustrating metaphors from food and eating. More famous than the boast of Pindar to which he alludes (p. 142) is the saying attributed to Aeschylus (Athenaeus 8, 347E) that his plays were 'slices from the big banquets of Homer.' Similarly, as can be seen in the *Thesaurus linguae latinae*, the word *epulae* was employed metaphorically—a feast for the eyes, the senses, the mind—by writers from Plautus to Cassiodorus. Then there is the vivid metaphor which Ignatius, anticipating his martyrdom in the arena, used in his *Letter to the Romans* (4, 1): 'I am the wheat of God and I shall be ground by the teeth of wild beasts that I may be found to be the pure bread of Christ.' These words were transmitted to the West by Jerome (*De viris illustribus,* 16) and reappear in mediaeval writers, like Bede (Giles, XII, 422) and Christian of Stavelot (Migne, *P.L.,* CVI, 1294A–B). The *prosimetrum* (p. 159) had its roots farther back than in the *Spätantike.* Mr. Curtius has forgotten Menippus of Gadara and especially the Menippean Satires of Varro, medleys of prose and verse on a great variety of topics. It is there that we meet with the story of the ten-year-old boy who slept till he was sixty and then looked out on a changed world, a remote ancestor of Rip van Winkle. To the meanings of *laus* and *laudes* (pp. 163 ff.) should be added the liturgical use of the word in connection with royal coronations and episcopal enthronements. See Ernst Kantorowicz, *Laudes regiae* (Berkeley, 1946). A parallel to the type of laudation, which consisted in elevating a poet above all his predecessors (p. 170), occurs also in panegyrics on saints. Thus, Gregory of Nazianzus at the beginning of his oration on Athanasius introduces a list of patriarchs, prophets, and kings in the Old Testament, and then continues: 'With some of these Athanasius vied, by some he was slightly excelled, and others, if it is not bold to say so, he surpassed' (*Library of Nicene and Post-Nicene Fathers;* Second series, VII, p. 270). Similarly, Bede in his metrical *Life of St. Cuthbert* (lines 11–24) lists eight saints in different regions of the world who have been illumined by the Light of Christ—Peter and Paul in Rome, John in Asia, Bartholomew in India, and so forth—before passing to Cuthbert in Britain.

The *nomina Christi* (p. 231, note 1) had become a *locus theologicus* long before Isidore's time. They had been treated briefly by Gregory of Elvira (Migne, *P.L.* xx, 42–43) and more fully by Niceta of Remesiana (A. E. Burn, *Niceta of Remesiana,* pp. 1–5). As the author admits (p. 217, note 3), the passages that he and Kollwitz have collected to illustrate the concept of Christian doctrine as Christian philosophy are all inconclusive. The unequivocal formulation of the concept is due to Augustine. When refuting the Pelagian, Julian of Aeclanum, he exclaims

(Migne, *P.L.* xliv, 774): 'obsecro te, non sit honestior philosophia gentium quam nostra Christiana, quae una est vera philosophia, quandoquidem studium vel amor sapientiae significatur hoc nomine.' Mr. Curtius refers (p. 314) to the teacher stabbed to death with the pens of his angry pupils and immortalized in a poem by Prudentius (*Peristeph.*, ix). Centuries later this tale was utilized by William of Malmesbury, when he invented a similar end at the hands of his students for John Scotus.

Mr. Curtius quotes a number of passages (p. 423) to show how the Fathers counseled gravity and avoidance of laughter, but he has missed Jerome's letter of condolence to Heliodorus on the death of his nephew, Nepotian. Throughout the Middle Ages this was one of the most admired of Jerome's epistles, and in it he says of the deceased (*Epist.* 60, 10, 6): 'gravitatem morum hilaritate frontis temperabat. Gaudium risu, non cachinno, intelligeres,' which one may call a sensible mean between two extremes. The study of Priscian (cf. p. 441) in the eleventh and twelfth centuries forms the subject of a valuable article by R. W. Hunt in *Mediaeval and Renaissance Studies*, 1 (1943), pp. 194 ff. It may be right to call Cassiodorus' use of the phrase *catholici autores* 'eigenartig.' Yet this meaning of *catholicus* is perhaps foreshadowed in Vincent of Lérins (*Commonitorium* 2, 2–3) who, just before giving his famous definition of the Catholic Church, observes: 'multum necesse est . . . ut propheticae et apostolicae interpretationis linea secundum ecclesiastici et catholici sensus normam dirigatur.' The proposed emendation of Sergius to Servius (p. 461 top) is unnecessary. As the position of the name next to Donatus and Priscian shows, Aimeric meant the treatise on Donatus' grammar going under the name of Sergius (Keil, *Gramm. lat.*, iv). It is listed in a ninth-century catalogue of St. Gall, and it had been used by Bede and by the anonymous Irishman whose own exposition of Donatus survives in *MS Ambrosianus L 22 supra* (cf. Sabbadini in *Studi italiani di filologia classica* 11, 1903, pp. 165 ff.). P. 463: here a reference would have been in order to Lucretius' well-known invocation of Epicurus—'te sequor . . . inque tuis nunc ficta pedum pono pressis vestigia signis'—a passage that may have been in Statius' mind when he wrote the lines quoted by Mr. Curtius. He follows Winterfeld in assuming (p. 490 with note 1) that *Isia* in Abbo's poem on the siege of Paris is an invention of the poet's. But the latest editor, Henri Waquet (*Les classiques de l'histoire de France au moyen âge,* xx, p. 13), since Abbo in the same passage refers to the Argolid, would identify *Isia* with Hysiae. As Hysiae is mentioned by the elder Pliny (*N.H.* 4, 12), a fact which Waquet has overlooked, the suggestion is plausible.

Among the founders of modern classical scholarship (p. 508) one misses the name of Richard Bentley. He was not, as so many persist in believing, merely a textual critic. His consummate familiarity with every phase of classical antiquity, and his conviction that the proper understanding of its literature calls for a knowledge of history and archaeology, are seen most fully in *Phalaris;* but the same wide grasp is shown also in his letters and in his *Reply* to Collins' *Discourse of Free-Thinking.* And was there any other scholar of or near his time who pointed out, with copious illustrations, the value of studying not hexameter or elegiac verse, but the iambic and trochaic metres of Latin comedy, in order to help a proper comprehension of the metres employed in vernacular poetry? 'Quo magis est dolendum atque indignandum,' he writes (*P. Terenti Afri Comoediae,* London, 1726, p. x), 'jam a literis renatis pueros ingenuos ad Dactylica, quod genus patria lingua non recipit, ediscenda, ferula scuticaque cogi: Terentiana vero metra, quae domi tamen et in triviis inscientes ipsi cantitant, Magistrorum culpa penitus ignorare.' It was not only Isidore (p. 512) to whom mediaeval readers could turn for information about the four cardinal virtues of pagan philosophy. They had been discussed by Pomerius towards the end of his *De vita contemplativa,* a book which had an immense vogue right down to the sixteenth century.[1]

The book is admirably printed and produced. Three small *errata* deserve mention: The last sentence in note 2 on page 29, especially in view of the cross-reference to page 32, note 1, does not seem to make sense. Presumably *nicht* has inadver-

---

[1] See M. L. W. Laistner in *Miscellanea Giovanni Mercati,* II, pp. 344–358 [No. 3 in this volume].

tently been omitted before *berührt*. On page 241, note 4, for 'Saager' read 'Jaager,' and on page 276 *divisas* should be *divisam*. The comparative study of literature as an academic subject is still young. It is one on which many look askance because what often passes under its name in our universities is base metal, not the genuine gold. But in the hands of a master it is a fascinating, if rigorous, discipline leading to a true understanding of the past. We cannot do better than to let the author of this notable book have the last word (pp. 23–24):

Die akademische Organisation der philologischen und literarischen Studien entspricht dem geisteswissenschaftlichen Aspekt von 1850. Dieser Aspekt ist von 1950 aus gesehen ebenso veraltet wie das Eisenbahnsystem von 1850. Die Eisenbahnen haben wir modernisiert, das System der Traditionsübermittlung nicht. Wie das zu geschehen hätte, kann hier nicht erörtert werden. Aber eines darf gesagt werden: ohne ein modernisiertes Studium der europäischen Literatur gibt es keine Pflege der europäischen Tradition.

The Venerable Bede

6

Bede as a Classical and
a Patristic Scholar * ¹

AMONG the many and complex problems with which the history of Europe in the Middle Ages—and especially the earlier period of the Middle Ages—teems is the character of the intellectual heritage transmitted to medieval men from classical and later Roman imperial times. The topic has engaged the attention of many scholars, amongst them men of the greatest eminence, so that much which fifty years ago was still dark and uncertain is now clear and beyond dispute. Yet the old notions and misconceptions die hard, especially in books approximating to the textbook class. In a recently published volume on the Middle Ages intended for university freshmen there is much that is excellent and abreast of the most recent investigations; but the sections on early medieval education and scholarship seem to show that the author has never read anything on that subject later than Mullinger's *Schools of Charles the Great*. Even in larger works it is not uncommon to find the author merely repeating what the last man before

* Read May 11, 1933. Published in the *Transactions* of the Royal Historical Society, 4th series, 16 (1933), 69–94. Reprinted by permission of the Royal Historical Society.

¹ The following abbreviation has been used throughout: *MGH A.A.* = *Monumenta Germaniae Historica: Auctores antiquissimi,* cited by volume and page.

him has said, without inquiring into controversial matters for himself. Years ago Ludwig Traube pointed the way to a correct estimate of Greek studies in Western Europe during the earlier Middle Ages, and subsequent research, while it has greatly added to the evidence collected by him, has only fortified his general conclusions. Nevertheless one still finds Alcuin or Hrabanus Maurus listed amongst those who knew Greek, on the strength of a few words or phrases that, as a very little research shows, were taken over by them from Jerome. What is now needed is not striking generalisations, but a patient accumulation of *data*, not brilliant reinterpretations, but critical editions of the many texts that are still only available in antiquated and faulty publications. It is the purpose of this paper to examine the work of only a single author—to consider, without any claim to have studied all his writings, the extent of the Venerable Bede's reading and method of work. Since his activity as an author extended over about forty years, it may also prove possible to gain here and there some little insight into the growth of his mind. In taking Bede as the subject of our inquiry we are, moreover, considering a man not only unique in himself, but the most important forerunner of the Carolingian Revival, indeed one of the outstanding figures of the whole medieval period. His example shows us what could be done to revive humane and theological studies; but we must not fall into the error of believing that there were many besides him who did it. In actual fact there were but few men who came within measurable distance of his achievement, and fewer still who accomplished more.

When Bede was born neither of the two monastic houses with which his name is so closely linked was yet founded; only four or five years had passed since Theodore of Tarsus landed in England. On the other hand, much civilising work had been carried on for the past half-century in the northern parts of England by Paulinus, Wilfrith, and their associates, and by the Irish from Iona. These last laid the foundations of Northumbrian scholarship and gave to the English a script which they transmuted into a national hand. The monastery of Wearmouth was founded in 674 by Benedict Biscop. To the care of its abbot

Bede as a Scholar

and teachers the boy Bede was entrusted at the age of seven. When he was nine or ten, another religious house was established near-by at Jarrow. Wearmouth and Jarrow were indeed intended to form a single monastery. But political and ecclesiastical affairs often demanded Benedict Biscop's presence elsewhere, so that in practice each house had its own permanent head. Bede appears to have been transferred to Jarrow at, or soon after, its foundation; at all events, if the identification of him with the small choirboy, who aided Abbot Ceolfrith to carry on the services of the Church during the awful visitation of the plague in 686, is correct, he was established by that year in the surroundings where he was to pass the remainder of his life. There is but little information about the schools at Wearmouth and Jarrow. The picture which modern writers have been apt to draw, by using in the main the evidence of the Carolingian schools, is likely to be more misleading than helpful. Two facts, however, stand out: Benedict Biscop had brought many books to the north and Abbot Ceolfrith added greatly to them.[2] In the second place, even the earliest works of Bede, though they may show little originality, make it abundantly clear that he had already then read widely, doubtless far more widely than any of his school-fellows. It is well to remind oneself, moreover, in order properly to appraise the magnitude of Bede's achievement, that Latin was a foreign language to the people of England. Bede's mastery over Latin idiom, like the German Einhard's a century later, is the more astounding.

Bede's earliest treatises—*De arte metrica, De schematibus et tropis, De orthographia*[3]—were intended for school use. They prove that he was brought up on, and, when he became himself a teacher, adapted and excerpted such writers as Donatus, Charisius, Audax, Caper, and other grammarians of the later Roman imperial age. Wide reading from the first in the Old and New Testament, doubtless accompanied by much

---

[2] Bede, *Historia abbatum*, 4, 6, 9, 11, 15.

[3] The *De arte metrica* and *De orthographia* should be consulted in volume 7 of Keil's *Grammatici Latini*: the *De schematibus et tropis* in Halm's *Rhetores Latini Minores*.

memorisation, gave Bede an unrivalled knowledge of the Bible text. In all his works Biblical citations from every part of the Sacred Writings abound; but from no book does the former choirboy quote more frequently than from the Psalms.

The attitude of leading churchmen to pagan literature had varied from age to age, and continued to vary after Bede's time. Amongst the Fathers, Basil the Great and Jerome adopted the most liberal, Gregory I the most hostile, position.[4] In England during the seventh century the two tendencies are well represented by Aldhelm and Bede. Aldhelm's poetry is steeped in Virgil, and in his prose writings he parades the tortuous and artificial conceits of the late imperial rhetorical schools. Bede, as we might expect from a profound admirer of Gregory I, in his early works makes very sparing use of illustrations from pagan authors. The *De schematibus et tropis* contains but one non-Biblical citation, and in the other two treatises also examples from the Bible and from Christian authors preponderate. Still, there is a fair array of quotations from classical sources which can easily lead the unwary astray. We must not be misled by the occurrence of single lines from Terence, Lucretius, Varro, Lucilius, the *ars poetica* of Horace, Martial, or Sallust; for, if we look a little further, we find the identical quotations in the grammarians used by Bede or else in the *Etymologies* of Isidore.[5] Then, too, a tersely expressed sentiment, particularly if it were in verse and in conformity with Christian teaching, might become part of the teacher's stock-in-trade, and its original source be forgotten. The line of Juvenal,

> Crescit amor nummi, quantum ipsa pecunia crescit [6]

was cited by Isidore; it is used by Bede, and it reappears in three places in Christian of Stavelot's commentary on Matthew.[7] Neither Bede nor Christian seems to have known the

---

[4] For a fuller discussion of this topic, cf. my *Thought and Letters in Western Europe*[2], pp. 44, 109–110, 208.

[5] Line 763 from Terence's *Eunuchus*, cited in *De orthographia* (291, 22), doubtless comes from a grammarian, though it is not found elsewhere in Keil.

[6] Juvenal, 14, 139.

[7] Bede, *PL*, 91, 1025A. For Christian, see my article in *Harvard Theological Review* 20 (1927), p. 137, note 30 [below, p. 224].

author of the line. In fact, the one poet of the classical period whom Bede can be safely said to have known at first hand was Virgil. True, many of the Virgilian quotations are found in the grammarians, but there is a good sprinkling of those that do not appear to come from an intermediate source. Furthermore, Virgil was a favourite author of the Irish, and his works were certainly in England before Bede's time. Their extensive use by Aldhelm is sufficient proof of this. Bede refers in different ways to the poet. Sometimes it is directly by name. *Lege in Virgilio,* he writes in his commentary on Samuel,

> Loricam consertam hamis auroque trilicem.[8]

Or again, in the commentary on the General Epistles: *iuxta illud Maronis,*

> Dat sine mente sonum.[9]

At other times the allusion is more vague. *Cui simillimum est illud etiam saecularium litterarum:*

> Qui candore nives anteirent, cursibus auras.[10]

Unde poeta dicit [11] is yet another turn, while sometimes a citation is introduced without any preparation at all.[12] In one such case Bede's memory failed badly; for the line in the *Second Eclogue,*

> Lac mihi non aestate novum, non frigore defit,

appears thus:

> Nec tibi lac aestate novum nec frigore desit.[13]

There are two quotations from Ovid's *Metamorphoses* in the commentary on Genesis; but the former—three lines from Book 1—is to be found in Isidore of Seville.[14] The other—a single line from Book 4—I have not been able to trace in any intermediate source,[15] yet it seems very doubtful whether Bede

---

[8] *Aen.,* 3, 467 in *PL,* 91, 611D.   [9] *Aen.,* 10, 640 in *PL,* 93, 74A.
[10] *Aen.,* 12, 84 in *PL,* 91, 721A.
[11] *PL,* 91, 745D, introducing *Aen.,* 3, 126–127.
[12] E.g., *PL,* 91, 400D and 1019C.   [13] *Ecl.,* 2, 22 in *PL,* 91, 1019C.
[14] Ovid, *Met.,* 1, 84–86 in Isid., *Etym.,* 11, 1, 5.
[15] Ovid, *Met.,* 4, 58 in *PL,* 91, 126C.

had read the poem, a doubt which applies to Aldhelm also.[16] A few other Ovidian tags in Bede's early treatises are all to be found in the grammarians. The evidence for some acquaintance with Lucan is stronger, though not conclusive. Bede quotes six lines from the *exordium* of the *Pharsalia,* introducing them with the remark, "an ancient poet being about to describe the battles of Caesar and Pompey begins thus." [17] In one of his scientific treatises Bede cites twelve lines of Ausonius, but it is questionable whether he knew the poet's name.[18] The classical prose-writers, with one exception, have left little discoverable trace. In the *De orthographia* we light upon a few words from Cicero's *Pro Cluentio* not quoted by extant grammarians, and a sentence attributed to Cicero but still unidentified.[19] In one of the Biblical commentaries Bede reproduces the famous sentence from Suetonius' *Life of Claudius; Claudius Iudaeos, impulsore Christo assiduo tumultuantes, Roma expulit.*[20] But although the citation does not appear in Rufinus' translation of Eusebius' *Ecclesiastical History,* a work constantly used by Bede in this and other commentaries, its character is such that we can safely assume a Patristic author to have been the intermediate source. The one exception to which I have just referred is the *Natural History* of Pliny the Elder. The Second Book of this work was used extensively by Bede in his scientific treatises; he seems also to have known Books 4, 5, 6, 13, and 16, but there is nothing to show that he knew the later books of the *Natural History.*[21] Of the Christian poets there was evidently a large

[16] The only evidence given by Ehwald in his edition of Aldhelm (*MGH A.A.,* 15) is that two of the riddles exhibit similarities to two passages of the *Metamorphoses.*

[17] Keil, *Gramm. Lat.,* 7, 245, 9 ff.

[18] *De temporum ratione,* ch. 16. I owe this reference to the thesis of C. W. Jones named below, p. 100, note 24.

[19] Keil, *op. cit.,* 7, 267, 18 and 269, 2–3. The second citation—*solis innocens acclamationibus punitus est*—is not in the *Thesaurus* (s.v. *acclamatio*). A possible allusion to Livy appears in Keil, *op. cit.,* 7, 292, 18.

[20] Suet. *Claud.,* 43 in *PL,* 92, 981B. All the Bede manuscripts that I have seen read *Christo,* not *Chresto.*

[21] Cf. below, pp. 101 and 108. In *PL,* 92, 1023D–1024A Bede transcribes a sentence from Pliny, *N.H.,* 16, 9. Jones in his thesis (cf. below, p. 100) is justified in arguing that it is inconceivable that Bede knew Book 18, else he could not have failed to use it when writing the *De temporum ratione.* That there was in Bede's

selection at Jarrow, and Bede studied and loved them. Not only did he use them for purposes of illustration in his early school-treatises in preference to classical poets, but he constantly quotes from them in his later works. Ambrose, Juvencus, Prudentius, Paulinus of Nola, Sedulius, Prosper, the *De virginitate* and some other poems by Fortunatus, and Arator [22] are all represented. Less known than any of these is Cyprianus Gallus, from whose epic on the Pentateuch Bede quotes fifteen lines. The epic is in hexameters, but there are several insertions in lyric metres. One of these serves Bede as an example of the Phalaecian.[23] It is an interesting fact that the same poet was known also to Bede's older contemporary, Aldhelm.

If one views Bede's work as a whole, one must say that his attention to theology, and especially to exegesis, came first and never waned throughout his life. But his scientific attainments, particularly for the age in which he lived, were far from negligible. The practical application of mathematics to chronological problems was of absorbing attraction to him and bore fruit in the early work, *De temporibus,* and in the more elaborate composition of his mature years, the *De temporum ratione,* finished in 725. Between these two he composed the brief cosmological treatise, *De natura rerum.* For his special interest in chronology there was a general and a particular reason. A satisfactory chronological system applicable to world history— a chronological framework into which all historic events since the creation of the world could be fitted—seemed essential to one with as strong a historical sense as Bede. For it may be observed in passing that, apart from the *Ecclesiastical History,* which by universal consent is the supreme example of Bede's genius, the interest in historical occurrences and in chronology

---

time a complete manuscript of the *Natural History* in England can, I think, be ruled out. Extant manuscripts of Pliny, it is true, number over 200, but those of the earlier group contain only small portions of the whole, while even in the later group very few manuscripts are approximately complete.

[22] Bede used Arator especially when writing his commentary on Acts. One of the earliest manuscripts of the latter (Paris, Bibl. Nat., *lat.* 12284; saec. ix) also contains Arator's poem. At Manchester, MS. Rylands 107 contains Bede's commentary amplified by many citations from Arator, to illustrate passages in Acts not elucidated by Bede.

[23] Keil, *Gramm. Lat.,* 7, 254, 16–30.

meets one at every turn in his numerous Biblical commentaries. A more special reason for the chronological treatises is the practical application of time-reckoning to the Easter question, which, as is well known, was a matter of hot dispute between the Roman and Celtic Churches before and during Bede's day. A most competent investigation by a young American scholar, Dr. Charles W. Jones, has demonstrated, amongst other things, that Bede's library on Easter calculation or the Paschal Question was by 725 astonishingly complete. It comprised not only the better known Patristic writings in which this question was discussed, but special treatises like those of Dionysius Exiguus, Victor of Capua, and Polemius Silvius.[24]

Bede's historical library was serviceable, though not specially remarkable, comprising Josephus, Jerome's translation of Eusebius' *Chronicle,* Rufinus' version of Eusebius' *Ecclesiastical History,* Orosius, Eutropius, a good selection of chronicles, including that by Marcellinus Comes,[25] and, for literary history, Jerome's *De viris illustribus* with Gennadius' continuation. To this list may be added the *Liber Pontificalis* and the chronological treatises referred to in connection with Bede's scientific books, and finally Gildas. However, since the sources for the *Ecclesiastical History* have been investigated by Plummer, we may turn at once to the commentaries. Bede's use of Rufinus, and of the historical information scattered through the many works of Jerome with which, as will be seen, he was familiar, needs no further discussion; but a word or two about two passages from Marcellinus and about Josephus will not be out of place. Bede's commentary on Mark contains a long story about the finding of John the Baptist's head and the chapter of accidents by which this precious relic came to be buried at Edessa.[26] The whole of this narrative is adapted from Marcellinus. Bede also referred to that author in his commentary on the Catholic Epistles, but

---

[24] Charles W. Jones, *Materials for an edition of Bede's De temporum ratione,* a thesis presented for the degree of Doctor of Philosophy in June, 1932. Two typewritten copies of the work are in the library of Cornell University.

[25] For the sources of Bede's *Chronicle,* cf. Mommsen's edition in *MGH: Chronica Minora,* 3.

[26] *PL,* 92, 192D–193A; Marcellinus in *MGH A.A.,* 11, 84–85.

apparently cited from memory with unfortunate results. In commenting on the words, "for every kind of beasts, and of birds, and of serpents, and of things in the sea, is tamed and hath been tamed of mankind," [27] he gives two illustrations. One he attributes to Pliny, the other to Marcellinus; both attributions appear to be wrong. The tale, said to be from Pliny, of an Egyptian asp, which was tamed by the father of a family and came regularly every day from its lair to get its food-allowance (*annona!*), does not seem to be in the *Natural History*. The story from Marcellinus is to the effect that the emperor Anastasius received from India a present of a tame tiger. Actually Marcellinus relates that in A.D. 496 "India sent to the emperor Anastasius as a gift an elephant, which our poet Plautus calls *lucabus,* and two giraffes." [28] There is not a word concerning tigers; but, on the other hand, a tame tiger was, according to Pliny, one of the sights when the theatre of Marcellus was formally dedicated in 11 B.C.[29] While I hesitate to ascribe to Bede a confusion of Marcellus with Marcellinus, there is not any doubt that he confused his references. The source of the asp-story has so far eluded me.

Bede's acquaintance with the writings of Josephus is a matter of considerable complexity. If, for example, we take the commentary on Acts, we find that five out of six passages in which Josephus is mentioned by name come not directly from him, but from Rufinus' version of Eusebius. The sixth passage refers to an Old Testament episode in Josephus, but it is not clear whether Bede was using a Latin translation of the *Antiquities,* or an intermediate source, or the Greek original. The same is true in the case of a reference found in Bede's *Retractation.* But, indeed, appeals to the authority of Josephus are exceedingly numerous in our author, particularly in the commentaries devoted to the historical books of the Old Testament.[30] In his *Epistle to Plegwin* Bede quotes *verbatim* a passage from the treatise against Apion; nevertheless comparison makes it evident that he did not use the Cassiodorean version.[31] So much

[27] James, 3, 7; *PL,* 93, 28A–B.   [28] *MGH A.A.,* 11, 72.
[29] Pliny, *N.H.,* 8, 65.   [30] E.g., *PL,* 91, 547C, 721C, 722A, 848A, 859B, 876D.
[31] See Boysen's edition in *CSEL,* 37 [see below, pp. 127–128].

is certain: some of Bede's citations or adaptations from Josephus were made directly from that historian, while others were taken over from Rufinus or perhaps from Jerome. But whether Bede read Josephus in the original Greek must remain undecided still. It seems by no means impossible that he did. I cannot leave the subject of Bede's historical studies without pointing out that he quotes in one place some lines from his great predecessor in the art of historical composition, Gregory of Tours.[32] It is also interesting to find that the oldest manuscript of the *Retractation*—headed by one written in the first half of the ninth century [33]—gives the name of the author cited as *Georgius*, not *Gregorius*. Georgius Florentius was the name of the historian of the Franks, who adopted that of Gregory in memory of his maternal great-grandfather.

It is, however, only when we investigate the Patristic authors known to Bede that we get a full insight into the breadth of his studies, and, incidentally, into the remarkable richness of the library or libraries to which he had access. I propose to speak in some detail of Bede's two commentaries on Acts, and then to supplement this by some reference to his other exegetical works. The *Commentary* and the *Retractation on Acts* are especially instructive for our purpose, because, while they seek to elucidate the same book of the New Testament, they were written by Bede at different times of his life. The one was composed some time between 709 and 716, the other not till after 731.[34] In 1896 the late Charles Plummer remarked in his edition of the *Ecclesiastical History:* "a really critical edition of Bede which should show exactly how much he borrowed and how much is original is a great desideratum; 'necdum illud merui videre.'"[35] In 1933 the stigma still attaches to England

[32] *PL*, 92, 1032B; Greg. Turon, *H.F.*, 5, 26 (34), a description of a severe epidemic that visited Gaul in A.D. 580.

[33] Karlsruhe, *Augiensis* LXXVII. For a full description of this manuscript, which contains both the Acts commentaries, see A. Holder, *Die Reichenauer Handschriften.*

[34] The *Retractation* is not included in Bede's own list of his writings appended to the *Ecclesiastical History* (5, 34) and was therefore written after that work. The interesting reference in the *Retractation* (*PL*, 92, 1027D) to a living Pope must accordingly be to Gregory III, who became Pope in 731.

[35] *Hist. Eccles.*, 1, p. xxiii, note 3.

and to English scholarship that all but one of the works composed by one of the greatest of her scholars must be read in an edition which, even for the time when it was published, was a disgrace, or else in the slightly emended reprint of Giles' text reproduced in Migne's *Patrologia Latina.* It is difficult to believe that, had Bede been a native of France or Germany, he would have suffered such long neglect in the country of his birth. It may here be further remarked that a proper understanding of Bede's methods as a commentator will help to illuminate the general practice of the medieval scholar, save that, at least in the earlier centuries, few approached within measurable distance of his standards.

The truth is that modern critics are still far too vague in their treatment of such questions. Medieval scholars commonly did not indicate at all the works from which they borrowed, or, if they did, usually thought it sufficient to give the author's name. If that author was a *vir unius libri,* no great trouble ensues; but a general reference to Augustine or Jerome or Gregory the Great is a very different matter. To say, as has often been done, that this or that medieval writer knew or used Augustine, really tells one nothing in view of the African Father's enormous literary output. Bede himself seems to follow no consistent practice. Not infrequently he gives a writer's name and no more; occasionally—but considering how much he wrote, it is not often—he names the work as well.[36] Far more commonly, however, there is no indication in the text that a phrase, or a sentence, or even a paragraph has been taken over from a previous writer. To every one quotation attributed by name to Gregory the Great one can find ten or a dozen in Bede's works that are outwardly indistinguishable from Bede's own comments. Bede's own usage, it is true, was also to indicate in the margin the sources from which he borrowed, and he requested his copyists not to omit these signs. Until very recently it was universally assumed that all medieval scribes had ignored his request. But in 1926 Father Sutcliffe pointed out that two extant manuscripts of Bede's commentary on Mark

---

[36] For instance, *Cyprianus in libro de habitu virginum (PL,* 93, 46D) or *Hieronymus in historia beatae Paulae,* that is to say, *Epistle* 108 *(PL,* 92, 958A).

preserve these source-indications for the borrowed material from the four Doctors of the Church. More recently the present writer has found similar source-marks, wholly or partially preserved, in sixteen other manuscripts of the same commentary, and, besides this, *marginalia* of a like character in nine manuscripts of the commentary on Luke.[37] Even so the modern editor is still far from his goal, if he only knows that such and such a quotation was taken by Bede from one of these Fathers. Moreover, if we would reach a proper estimate of what the English libraries in Bede's time contained, we must seek to ascertain not merely what authors, but what works by those authors, were then available in our island. For example, a copy of Augustine's *Retractations* in the Mayence library about the middle of the ninth century had all those works by Augustine marked which were then in that collection. While the list numbers forty-eight items, the *De doctrina Christiana* and other notable works are absent.[38] Even the cathedral library at Lyons, which in the time of Deacon Florus possessed a magnificent body of Augustinian writings, probably did not own all his works.[39] These examples of rich collections, however, belong to a time when, under the influence of the Carolingian Revival, *scriptoria* had greatly multiplied, and many of these kept working at full pressure for years. How much more restricted, then, must the resources of Wearmouth-Jarrow, of York, and even of Canterbury have been at the beginning of the eighth century, notwithstanding the scholarly zeal of Theodore and Hadrian in the south and of Benedict Biscop and Ceolfrith in the north of England.

The following sources, so far as I have been able to trace them, were consulted by Bede in writing his commentary on Acts:[40] of Gregory the Great the *Homilies on Ezekiel* and *on the Gospels*, the *Pastoral Rule*, and the *Moralia*. Ambrose is

---

[37] E. J. Sutcliffe, S.J., in *Biblica*, 7 (1926), pp. 428–439; M. L. W. Laistner in *Journal of Theological Studies* for October, 1933.

[38] W. M. Lindsay and P. Lehmann in *Palaeographia Latina*, 4 (1925), p. 37.

[39] On the Lyons *scriptorium*, see S. Tafel in *Palaeographia Latina*, 4 (1925), pp. 40 ff.

[40] Full indications of Bede's sources will be given in my forthcoming edition of the *Commentary* and *Retractation on Acts*.

represented by the treatise, *De Spiritu Sancto,* Augustine by the *De consensu evangelistarum. Quaestiones in Heptateuchum,* and the *De Genesi ad litteram.* Arator's poetic version of Acts is mentioned in general terms by Bede in his preface and is cited ten times in the commentary itself. But the author to whom Bede in this work is most constantly indebted is Jerome. Thus, he knew and used the commentaries of Jerome on Isaiah, Jonah, Ezekiel, Matthew, Galatians, and probably that on Amos. Further, he was familiar with Letters 53, 71, 108, and 112,[41] with the treatise against Helvidius, and with that on Hebrew names and places; he also quotes several times from the *De viris illustribus.* Near the end of the commentary a lengthy quotation is rounded off with the statement: *haec de beati Didymi libris excerpta hunc in nostris opusculis teneant locum.* Actually Bede used Jerome's translation of Didymus' treatise, *De Spiritu Sancto;* he had already cited from it without acknowledgement in an earlier chapter of his commentary.[42] But the most surprising discovery is that Bede knew and cited— again without any reference to the author—the short commentary of Jerome on the Psalms which, long believed to be lost, was only recovered and published in 1895 by that eminent Benedictine scholar, Dom Germain Morin.[43] There are fourteen places in the Acts commentary where Isidore's *Etymologies* have been consulted, and about a dozen in which Bede either quotes verbally or else adapts passages in Rufinus' *Ecclesiastical History.* He also refers his readers in one place to the *Shepherd* of Hermas, calling it *Liber Pastoris,* if they wished for further information concerning guardian angels. The passage that Bede presumably had in mind was Vision 5 in that work. The Greek original of the *Shepherd* was only recovered in the middle of last century, but the book was well known to the Middle Ages

---

[41] As with Pliny's *Natural History,* so here it is unlikely that Bede had access to a complete collection of Jerome's correspondence. For, as Hilberg (*CSEL,* 54, p. v) points out: *inter codices qui alicuius pretii habendi sunt, ne unus quidem omnes epistulas conplectitur.*

[42] *PL,* 92, 994A–B quoting from *PL,* 23, 129A, 129B, 105C–106A. The earlier quotation will be found in *PL,* 92, 954D and comes from *PL,* 23, 151A and B.

[43] Published in *Anecdota Maredsolana,* III, part 1. Bede cites from these *Commentarioli* five times.

in translation. Two Latin versions survive, of which one, called the *versio vulgata,* is preserved in many manuscripts; it was undoubtedly this rendering to which Bede had access. In the second chapter he copies without acknowledgement a whole paragraph from Rufinus' translation of the oration on Pentecost by Gregory of Nazianzus. Years afterwards he referred to this quotation in the *Retractation,* because he had been criticised for the views expressed on the miracle of tongues. He silenced his detractors by an appeal to the authority of the "holy and in every way irreproachable master, Gregory of Nazianzus." [44] Lastly it would appear that Bede had seen the Latin translation, made by Evagrius, of Athanasius' *Life of St. Antony.* The words, "and after three months we departed in a ship of Alexandria, which had wintered in the isle, whose sign was Castor and Pollux," [45] stimulated Bede to explain to his readers who Castor and Pollux were. He adds a word concerning the sailor's superstition that, if one of Gemini is seen at the mast-head, the passage will be stormy; if both appear, the ship will enjoy a fair voyage. From the explanation of Castor and Pollux, which is based on Isidore,[46] Bede passes on to their mother, Leda, whom he calls the wife of Theseus, and to her gallant adventure with Jupiter disguised as a swan. From this union Helen was born. Hence, he adds, the saying: *iste modulatus ales Ledaeos petivit amplexus.* These words are taken from the *Life of St. Antony.*[47] Now this biography is also mentioned by Aldhelm in a general way, although there is nothing to show that he knew more than the name. The fact that Bede cited from this book shows that at least one copy of it existed in England. Had Aldhelm's latest editor, Ehwald, known this evidence, he would perhaps have been more ready to believe that Aldhelm had read Evagrius' translation.[48]

In the *Retractation on Acts,* which the oldest extant manuscript calls *liber secundus expositionis in actus apostolorum,*

[44] *PL,* 92, 947B–D = *CSEL,* 46, 160, 17–161, 11. Reference to Gregory: *ibid.,* 999D.

[45] Acts xxviii. 11. [46] Isid., *Etym.,* 15, 1, 40.

[47] *PG,* 26, 75 (= *Acta Sanctorum,* 2, 97). These texts read *expetivit.*

[48] In *MGH A.A.,* 15, 265, note 1, Ehwald observes: *num Evagrii versionem noverit Aldhelmus, ex eis quae dicit, parum constat.*

Bede's primary interest is in textual criticism, and particularly in comparing the Greek original with the Latin versions of the Bible text that were at his disposal. The sources that I have been able to trace are: Jerome's commentary on Ezekiel, the treatise on Hebrew names, and Letters 71, 108, and 112; Rufinus; two quotations from Hilary's *Tractate on the Second Psalm*, and one each from Cyprian's *Liber Testimoniorum* and Fulgentius' anti-Arian dissertation addressed to the Vandal king, Thrasamund. There are also single references by name to Eusebius' *Chronicle*, Josephus—a passage not taken from Rufinus—and Hippocrates *in Aphorismis*—that is, one of the medical treatises in Latin passing under Hippocrates' name in the Middle Ages. Augustine is represented by the *De consensu evangelistarum;* but there are some other Augustinian quotations that so far I have been unable to trace. To the passage from Gregory of Tours allusion has been made in another context. Lastly there are two works of a hagiographical character which, it may be suspected from the length of the citations and the interest they clearly aroused in Bede, had only recently come into his hands. The first was the *De transitu Beatae Virginis,* falsely attributed to Melito, bishop of Sardes.[49] Bede was quite aware that it was a later forgery, and criticised it severely because its evidence conflicts with the testimony of St. Luke on a point of chronology. The second was Avitus of Bracara's Latin version of Lucian of Caphar Gamala. This last-named writer in A.D. 415 had published an account of the miraculous discovery of St. Stephen's relics. From this curious narrative Bede copied a whole page into that part of his commentary which elucidated the martyrdom and subsequent burial of the saint.[50]

[49] Bede does not exactly give this title, but describes the author as, *librum exponens de obitu beatae genitricis Dei.* See *PL,* 92, 1014C.

[50] There is a clear allusion to the same narrative in the *Comm. on the Epist. of James (PL,* 93, 24D). Now, while we know from Bede himself *(PL,* 92, 940B) that his commentary on the Epistles of John was sent to Acca at the same time as that on Acts, it is inconceivable that, if Bede had at that time known Avitus' translation, he would not have used it for chapters 7 and 8 of Acts. Thus we must assume, what is inherently probable, that Bede's expositions of the Seven Catholic Epistles were composed at different times. When all had been written, he added a general preface, and issued them as a single work, although

One of the objects that Bede kept steadily in view when he composed the *Retractation* was to correct errors in his earlier commentary. References to two examples must suffice, both, as it happens, bearing on his acquaintance with pagan rather than Christian writers. In the *Commentary* he had explained the word *scapha*, a small boat, by a quotation from Isidore. In the *Retractation* he remarks that he had since perused the writings of others and had discovered that the true definition of *scapha* was not that given by Isidore, but a kind of canoe hollowed out of a single log. C. W. Jones has quite lately published the interesting discovery that by "other writers" is meant Vegetius' pamphlet on military tactics, from which Bede had already extracted information for his *De temporum ratione* and the *Ecclesiastical History*.[51] My second instance shows how Bede, good scholar though he was, nevertheless, like Homer, occasionally dozed. In Acts xx. 14 we read: "and when he met with us at Assos we took him in and came to Mytilene." On this verse Bede remarks:

in my first book, following Plinius Secundus, I wrote that Mytilene is an island opposite Asia; but the same Pliny also writes in another place that Mytilene is a town in the island of Cyprus. We may believe both these statements to be true, but nevertheless that Paul and his companions on this occasion came not to the island of Cyprus but to the Asiatic island. For it is attested that much later, and after he had travelled through many districts, he appeared off Cyprus but did not land there.[52]

The last allusion is to Acts xxvii. 4, when Paul was on his way as a prisoner to Rome: "and when we had launched from thence, we sailed under Cyprus, because the winds were contrary." The original information from Pliny may be found in the fifth Book of the *Natural History* (5, 139), where a list of Lesbian towns, including Mytilene, is given. But the supposed additional information—that there was also a Mytilene in Cyprus—is a myth; for Bede, I regret to say, misunderstood his authority. In the thirteenth Book (13, 10) Pliny discusses

privileged friends like Acca had already seen the separate parts as they first appeared.

[51] See *Classical Review*, 46 (1932), pp. 248–249.   [52] *PL*, 92, 1028B.

various drugs and says of one: *optimum hoc in Cypro, Mytilenis, ubi plurima sampsuchus.* Pliny has indulged his rather common habit of *asyndeton*, but Bede, not realising this, has construed *Mytilenis* in apposition to *Cypro.* Yet this, and perhaps some other trifling errors, must not blind us to the mature excellences of the *Retractation.* The book seems to me to be on a different plane to the other commentaries. Bede's judgment in his textual criticism is sound, his handling of quotations from the original Greek shows that his knowledge of that language near the end of his life was substantial, not superficial, and all through there appear to be much more of Bede's own thought and far greater independence of authorities than in his other exegetical works. In short, the *Retractation* is worthy to be set beside the *Ecclesiastical History* as an achievement of ripe scholarship.

It is not possible to give more than a short survey, which makes no claim to being complete, of the source material from the Fathers found in Bede's other commentaries. Gregory the Great's works are constantly used, but it is often laborious to locate passages from them in Bede. The modern editor is helped to some extent by two collections of excerpts from Gregory's work made respectively by Paterius, a contemporary of that Pope, and by Alulfus, monk and librarian of St. Martin at Tournai in the first half of the twelfth century. Both collections are printed as an *addendum* to Gregory's works in Migne, and precise references to the place whence each extract is taken are added. Paterius' *Liber Testimoniorum* provides a briefer selection, but the extracts illustrate Gregory's exposition of both the Old and the New Testament. Alulfus takes only Gregory's exegesis of the New Testament into account, but, within these limits, gives a much fuller selection than his predecessor.[53] It may be said at once that Bede did not use Paterius. For one thing, there are many citations from Gregory in Bede that are not found in the *Liber Testimoniorum.* Besides this we have Bede's own expression of regret that he could not obtain Paterius. He had heard that this man, a disciple of Gregory, had made a collection in one volume of Gregory's

[53] Both *florilegia* in *PL.,* 79.

utterances on the whole of Sacred Scripture. "If I had this work in my hands," he continues, "I could more easily and more completely carry out what I wish." [54] Two extracts from Cyprian's *De habitu virginum* and one from the same author's *De zelo et livore* find a place in the commentary on the Catholic Epistles.[55] Father Sutcliffe has shown that in the commentary on Mark the following works of Augustine were used by Bede: the *De consensu evangelistarum, Quaestiones in evangelium, Enarrationes in psalmos,* and some sermons. We have already seen that the first of these treatises was used in both the commentaries on Acts; more remarkable still is Bede's indebtedness to it in his long preface to the commentary on Luke, two-thirds of which is copied verbally from Augustine.[56] Bede himself acknowledges in a general way his obligation to Augustine's *Tractates* on the First Epistle of John,[57] and he groups together, as aids to the interpretation of Genesis, the *De Genesi ad litteram* and *De Genesi contra Manichaeos,* the *Confessions,* and also "the admirable compositions written against the enemy of the Law and Prophets." [58] This last can only mean the treatise, *Contra Faustum,* the main purpose of which was to defend the Old Testament against the attacks of the Manichaean bishop. It is known, moreover, that Bede was familiar with it, since he cites from it in the *De temporum ratione.* Elsewhere he quotes from the *De sancta virginitate* [59] and refers his readers to a book which he calls *Liber de mendacii generibus octo.* As he does not appear to give extracts from it, it is not clear which of two Augustinian tracts, *De mendacio* or *Contra mendacium,* he means.[60] His *Letter to Plegwin* contains passages from Augustine's fifty-sixth letter, from the *Tractate on Psalm 6,* and from the fifteenth Book of the *City of God.*[61] However, Bede's

[54] *PL*, 91, 1223B.

[55] *PL*, 93, 46D = *CSEL*, 3, 192, 2–11; 55A = 193, 27–194, 4; 66C = 420, 1–18. There appears to be an allusion to Cyprian's *De lapsis* in *PL*, 91, 434D. The same work is quoted in Bede's *Martyrology* (for 22 May), but as Bede's share in this compilation is uncertain, this evidence must not be pressed.

[56] *PL*, 92, 305–306 = *CSEL*, 43, 4, 4–5; 6, 3–7, 3; 9, 3–10, 14.

[57] *PL*, 92, 940B.   [58] *PL*, 91, 9–10A [see below, p. 131, note 41].

[59] *PL*, 93, 173D–174A = *CSEL*, 41, 263, 7–264, 4; 264, 17–19.

[60] *PL*, 91, 650B. Both treatises of Augustine will be found in *CSEL*, 41 [see below, p. 132, note 42].

[61] *PL*, 94, 672C–673A; 673C–D; 674C–D.

debt to Augustine cannot be finally determined until all Bede's works have been critically edited; it is enough here to add one more to the list of Augustinian books known to our author. Bede, himself a great teacher, was familiar, one is glad to know, with that greatest of Christian educational treatises, the *De doctrina Christiana*. To his commentary on the Apocalypse he prefixed a long introduction in which he devoted much space to a summary of Tyconius' seven rules of Scriptural interpretation. This long disquisition, including some Biblical quotations, is transcribed *verbatim* from Augustine's fuller summary of the Donatist teacher, introduced at the end of Book 3 of the *De doctrina Christiana*.[62] Here it may be observed that the degree of Bede's indebtedness to Tyconius' exposition of the Apocalypse still awaits investigation; indeed, it may be doubted whether a final estimate will ever be possible, because Tyconius' book has not survived and its contents are only recoverable from contemporary critics or subsequent commentators.[63]

Of Ambrose, besides the short *De Spiritu Sancto,* Bede had certainly read the *Hexameron,* the briefer *De Noe et arca,* and the commentary on Luke.[64] To the list of Hieronymic writings already given above can be added the diatribe against Jovinian, the commentary on Daniel, and the Martyrology.[65] Other Bible commentaries utilised with or without acknowledgement by Bede were Cassiodorus' book on the Psalms, itself largely culled

[62] *PL,* 93, 129D–134A, abbreviated from *PL,* 34, 82–90.

[63] As Bede in his commentary on the Apocalypse names Tyconius no less than ten times, the quotations thus introduced may prove to be all that he borrowed. The care taken to indicate the source in the text, and not merely in the margin, was probably due to the fact that Tyconius was a heretical writer.

[64] Bede himself wrote commentaries on Genesis and on Luke, and he refers to his great predecessor by name in this connection. Cf. *PL,* 91, 10A. *De Noe et arca,* as Jones has shown, was also used for the *De temporum ratione.*

[65] There are two citations in the *Comm. on the Cath. Epist.* from the *adv. Iovinianum,* viz., *PL,* 93, 14B–C (cf. *PL,* 23, 286D–287A) and 79B–C (cf. *PL,* 23, 287C). The *Comm. on Daniel* is cited in Bede on the Apocalypse—*PL,* 93, 154C (cf. *PL,* 25, 579B). The *Martyrology* is described briefly in Bede's *Comm. on Mark* (*PL,* 92, 192D): *in Martyrologio quod Eusebii et Hieronymi vocabulis insignitum est.* In his later *Retractation* he writes as though anxious to correct erroneous notions about that work: *liber martyrologii qui beati Hieronymi nomine ac praefatione adtitulatur; quamvis idem Hieronymus libri illius non auctor sed interpres, Eusebius autem auctor extitisse narretur.* A new edition of Jerome's *Martyrology,* with a most valuable introduction by Delehaye, was published in 1931 in *Acta Sanctorum,* November II, pars 2.

from Augustine, and Primasius on the Apocalypse; [66] and in the *De temporum ratione* he borrows in two places from a commentary on Job by a Philippus. This writer is believed to be identical with a priest of the same name who was a pupil of Jerome. The commentary attributed to him exists in a shorter and a longer version, and it is from the latter that Bede quotes.[67]

It would not be proper to conclude this survey of Bede's sources without some mention of the Greek Fathers. Only a few observations can be offered because the problem is a very intricate one and calls for separate investigation. If we except certain short, technical treatises consulted by our author on the Easter reckoning, the number of Greek theologians whom he names is not large. Origen is criticised several times as a heretical writer, or else a biographical detail about him is given. In the commentary on Genesis there is an appeal to his authority on the structure of Noah's ark. Origen's homilies on Genesis, as well as on some other books of the Bible, were, however, translated by Rufinus. It was probably from this version of the Second Homily that Bede took his information, but he does not cite it *verbatim*.[68] In his preface to the same commentary Bede makes a general acknowledgement to Basil the Great's *Hexameron*, adding the useful information that this book had been rendered into Latin by Eustathius. Later, in the commentary itself, Bede proceeds to quote at length from the Latin version.[69] Again, he mentions Clement of Alexandria eight times. One of these passages contains a biographical item. The remaining seven are citations, but four of them are taken word for word from Rufinus' *Ecclesiastical History*.[70] It is safe to assume that the other three were also borrowed by Bede from an intermediate source. A citation from Evagrius' translation

---

[66] On Bede and Cassiodorus cf. Lehmann, *Philologus*, 74 (1917), pp. 359–360 and my *Thought and Letters*², p. 102, note 1. For Primasius, cf. *ibid.*, p. 85, note 1.

[67] The identification of Philippus rests on Gennadius' authority, *De viris illustribus*, 62.

[68] *PL*, 91, 91A–C; cf. *PG*, 12, 161–175.

[69] *PL*, 91, 16B–C = *PG*, 30, 887B–C.

[70] *PL*, 92, 131D–132D reproduces Rufinus, H.E. (*ed.* Mommsen), I, p. 141, 1–19. The other identified passages occur in the Acts commentary.

of Athanasius' *Life of St. Antony* has already engaged our attention. In Bede's commentary on Nehemiah the redoubtable champion of orthodoxy in the Eastern Church is named in a general way together with Ambrose, Hilary, and Augustine.[71] In the preface to the commentary on the Catholic Epistles Athanasius' authority is quoted for the belief that the First Epistle of John was addressed to the Parthians.[72] I have been unable to find verification for this in Athanasius; on the other hand, it may be noted that an eminent Patristic scholar of our own time has stated that the words "to the Parthians" in the title of this Epistle first appear in Augustine.[73] The third mention in Bede of Athanasius introduces what is more probably a quotation than a paraphrase, but it is still unidentified.[74] Bede advised his readers to become acquainted with the "treatise of John Chrysostom on the theme that no one can be harmed by any one save himself." [75] In several other places he alludes to John of Constantinople. Plummer was uncertain how this designation was to be understood.[76] There is no doubt, however, that Chrysostom is meant; for in his commentary on Luke Bede reproduces and attributes to John of Constantinople certain chronological observations connected with the conception of St. Elizabeth and the dumbness of Zacharias, which are adapted from Chrysostom's homily on the Nativity.[77] The use by Bede of Rufinus' translation of Gregory of Nazianzus has been illustrated in an earlier part of this essay.

We thus reach two general conclusions: only some of the material from the Greek Fathers came to Bede from the works themselves, and, even when this was so, it was a Latin translation, not the Greek original that he consulted. I do not know a single passage on whose evidence one could say with certainty that Bede had read a particular homily or treatise in the Greek. On the other hand, the number of cases where he demonstrably employed a translation is substantial. This is highly significant.

The information presented in the preceding pages is not

---

[71] *PL*, 91, 912C.   [72] *PL*, 93, 9B–10A.

[73] O. Bardenhewer, *Geschichte der altkirchlichen Literatur*, 4, p. 486, note 1.

[74] *PL*, 93, 58B.   [75] *PL*, 93, 56D.

[76] *Hist. Eccles.*, 1, note on p. li.   [77] *PL*, 92, 314B–C; cf. *PG*, 49, 357–358.

meant to be exhaustive; nevertheless it will have achieved its purpose if it has placed Bede's attainments as a scholar in a clearer light. Bede's own statement in the famous biographical notice appended to the *Ecclesiastical History* is to the effect that he spent his whole life from the age of seven at Jarrow.[78] This must not be taken too literally, since it is clear from allusions elsewhere that he visited Lindisfarne and York.[79] One wonders whether he did not at some time visit Canterbury as well; for we have seen that certain rare, or at least unusual, books were known to both Aldhelm and Bede. Alternatively we must suppose that the loaning of manuscripts by one library to another, for purposes of collation or copying *in toto,* was already as fully developed as in Alcuin's day. Certainly Bede's working library, whether composed entirely or only in part of manuscripts owned by Wearmouth-Jarrow, was astonishingly large and diversified for that age. And he made the best use of it, even though it did not very greatly stimulate his own originality; for to be a scholar meant in his day, and for many years to come, being a traditionalist. Bede's importance lies not in his original ideas, but in the selfless devotion with which he digested much of the learning and doctrine of the Fathers and passed it on in a simpler and more intelligible form to his own people and to later generations. The manner in which, in a comment of moderate length on a Scriptural passage, he will fuse into an organic whole quotations and adaptations from several authorities together with some observations of his own proves him a clear thinker and an admirable teacher.[80] What he set out to do and succeeded in doing was to some extent analogous to the aims of Caesarius of Arles and Gregory the Great. Both had, so to say, popularised a large portion of Augustinian doctrine for the men of their own time; even so Bede's contemporaries and subsequent ages received from him Patristic teaching, especially from Jerome and Gregory I, in a form better suited to their capacities than were the original

---

[78] *Hist. Eccles.,* 5, 24.   [79] See Plummer's edition, 1, p. xvi.

[80] The reader will find a good example in the Acts commentary (*PL,* 92, 942D–943C), where, in a discussion of the identity of James, son of Alpheus, passages from Jerome, Rufinus, and Isidore are combined with remarks of Bede himself.

works. It is not too much to say that Bede's authority, after
his time, grew to be little inferior to that of the Four Doctors
of the Latin Church. The immense popularity of his exegetical
writings is proved by the survival in the European collections
of innumerable manuscripts. There are seventy-seven extant
manuscripts of the commentary on Acts, no less than fourteen
of these having been copied before A.D. 900.[81] Even the *Retractation,* in spite of the advanced and somewhat specialised
nature of the contents, survives in twenty-four *codices.* Jones,
in an admittedly incomplete list, enumerates sixty-one complete
manuscripts of the *De temporum ratione* and another twenty
containing important sections from that treatise. In the summary lists of manuscripts in the Bibliothèque Nationale, published in the *Bibliothèque de l'école des chartes* from 1862 to
the present time, will be found no less than forty *codices* of
Bede. And this figure is for a single library and takes no account
of Bede manuscripts bearing press-marks between 1 and 9,000.
Evidence like this cannot be gainsaid. For seven centuries men
turned to Bede the scholar for enlightenment and spiritual
guidance. Can we doubt that not a few also were inspired by
the single purpose and unswerving devotion to a noble cause of
Bede the man? A great poet has drawn the moral of Bede's life
for all time in moving words: [82]

> But what if One, through grove or flowery mead,
> Indulging thus at will the creeping feet
> Of a voluptuous indolence, should meet
> Thy hovering shade, O venerable Bede!
> The saint, the scholar, from a circle freed
> Of toil stupendous, in a hallowed seat,
> Of learning, where thou heard'st the billows beat

[81] Yet it may be accounted remarkable that there is not a single early manuscript in Great Britain. Of five manuscripts in the British Museum, eight at
Oxford, and one in Glasgow, only one (Bodl. canon. pat. lat. 222) is as early as
the tenth century. Of the fourteen ninth-century manuscripts one, Paris, B.N.
Nouv. Acq. 1630, contains only a few fragments. The manuscripts, Dijon 153,
Oxford. Bodl. Laud. misc., 312 and 268, are not included in the figures given in
the text. They contain different attempts to abbreviate the Acts commentary and
to conflate it with portions from the *Retractation.* Nor is Manchester, Rylands
107 (cf. above, p. 99, note 22) reckoned herein.

[82] Wordsworth, *Ecclesiastical Sonnets,* Part 1, no. 23.

On a wild coast, rough monitors to feed
Perpetual industry. Sublime Recluse!
The recreant soul, that dares to shun the debt
Imposed on human kind, must first forget
Thy diligence, thy unrelaxing use
Of a long life; and, in the hour of death,
The last dear service of thy passing breath!

7

The Library of the
Venerable Bede*

EVERY student interested in the intellectual history of the Early Middle Ages must regret that, in contrast to the substantial information available for the continent of western Europe, so little is known of the state of English libraries during the same period. Early catalogues of the collections at Fulda, Würzburg, Reichenau, St. Gallen, Fleury, not to mention many smaller religious houses, still survive; and, even when they have been preserved only in part, they throw an invaluable light on that state of learning in France and Germany during the late eighth and the ninth centuries. No such book-lists exist of the monastic and cathedral libraries in contemporary England. The concluding section of Alcuin's poem on the see and bishops of York is but a poor substitute for an official inventory of what was regarded in his day as an unusually rich collection of books, sacred and profane. Alcuin's list is marred by two serious defects, both inseparable from the metrical form in which the information is imparted to the reader. The poet names only the authors and not their writings, so that, unless

* *Bede: His Life, Times, and Writings*, ed. A. H. Thompson (Oxford: Clarendon Press, 1935), 237–266. Reprinted by permission of the Oxford University Press.

one is prepared to maintain the entirely untenable thesis that all the works of so prolific a scholar as Augustine were to be found at York, the occurrence of Augustine's name is not very helpful. Again, it is certain that exigencies of metre compelled Alcuin to omit the names of writers who were certainly represented to some extent in the library, for example, Isidore of Seville. Thus, in order to reconstruct as far as possible a catalogue of the books to which Bede had access more than half a century before, one must have recourse to his own statements and to a comparison of his works with earlier commentators. The task is made more difficult by the fact that a careful examination of Bede's authorities has been carried out for very few of his writings. Plummer has tracked down the sources of the *Ecclesiastical History* and Mommsen has done the same for the *Chronicle*. Father Sutcliffe has listed the borrowings from the Four Doctors of the Latin Church in the commentary on Mark, in so far as they are indicated by marginal letters in the two manuscripts that he used. But the list is incomplete even for those four authors and takes no account of the other authorities. The present attempt to determine the contents of Bede's working library does not claim to be final. Completeness will not be attainable until the entire *corpus* of Bede's works can be read in editions answering to the demands of modern scholarship.

It would be unjustifiable to assume that all the books consulted by Bede throughout a long life devoted to scholarship were actually to be found in his day in the libraries of Wearmouth and Jarrow. Just as friends and admirers in different parts of the country supplied him with biographical *data* or local traditions which he utilized in the composition of the *Ecclesiastical History,* so it may be supposed that books not to be found in the twin monasteries were occasionally borrowed from centres like Lindisfarne or Canterbury for consultation or copying. Indeed, when one observes that both Aldhelm and Bede show familiarity with some relatively rare work or one by a little known author, for instance, Cyprianus Gallus' epic on the Pentateuch, Evagrius' translation of Athanasius' Life of St. Antony, or even the pseudo-Clementine *Recognitiones,* although they had a wider appeal, it is a reasonable deduction that single examples of such works existed in the south of England, presumably at Canterbury, before Bede's time and in due course were borrowed by him. If time and circumstance allowed, the copy might be duplicated by him or under his direction. Unhappily Bede, although he has much to tell about the early years of the two monasteries with which his name is inseparably linked and about their first abbots, makes only very general statements when he alludes to the libraries. Benedict Biscop brought back many treasures to Northumbria after his several journeys to the Continent, and amongst them were many manuscripts. The language used by the historian makes it clear that there was a preponderance of theological works.[1] How large 'the most noble and abundant library' may have been on Benedict's death it is impossible to estimate. Besides, Bede's phraseology is a little rhetorical, since he uses almost the identical words to describe the library collected by Bishop Acca at Hexham.[2] Ceolfrid during his abbacy enlarged the library of Wearmouth-Jarrow still further ; indeed, if Bede's account is to be taken literally, he doubled its resources.[3] Amongst these additional books were three copies of the Vulgate. One of them, which Ceolfrid later set out to take to Rome as a gift to Gregory II, still survives, the so-called *Codex Amiatinus* in the Laurentian library at Florence.

But if Bede is vague about the twin libraries to which he had access, he fortunately was so modest about his own remarkable erudition that he was impelled to inform his readers in many places of the authorities on which his own works were based. In the introduction to his edition of the *Ecclesiastical History* the late Charles Plummer drew up a list of writers named in Bede.[4] Plummer himself was well aware that his catalogue of

---

[1] The books brought back by Benedict Biscop from his fourth and sixth journeys were theological (*H.A.* 4, 9). From his fifth journey to Rome he returned with a more diversified selection, *innumerabilem librorum omnis generis copiam* (*ibid.* 6).

[2] Cf. *H.A.* 11 and *H.E.* v. 20.

[3] *H.A.* 15, *bibliothecam utriusque monasterii . . . ipse non minori geminavit industria.* The author of *H.A. An.* (xx) more cautiously writes, *nobiliter ampliavit.*

[4] Plummer, i, pp. l–li.

some 130 authors was only tentative. If it has to be pointed out here that the list needs correction in three ways, no adverse criticism is implied of that scholar. The more students of Bede use Plummer's introduction and commentary, the more they will be impressed by his profound knowledge both of Bede's life and work and of the times in which he lived. In the first place, many of the quotations from authors listed by Plummer were obtained by Bede at second hand, and consequently they cannot be used as evidence for his direct acquaintance with those writers. This, as will be seen, is especially the case with citations from classical Latin authors. For this reason some thirty names can be eliminated from Plummer's catalogue. Again, the same editor has included a good many 'phantom' authorities, for instance, Jovinianus and Helvidius, although the allusion implied by Bede is to Jerome's treatises against these two advocates of heterodoxy; or Ignatius and Polycarp, about whom Bede merely relates some biographical item.[5] Finally there are a few authors whom Bede never mentions by name; yet he can be shown to have consulted, or even copied from, their writings, for example, Victorinus of Pettau and Salonius.

In his theological treatises Bede points out over and over again that he is but following the footsteps of the Fathers.[6] Not infrequently he adds valuable particulars, as in his preface to the commentary on Genesis where he groups together as his main authorities the *Hexaemeron* of Basil and of Ambrose and several treatises by Augustine. Or again, in the introduction to his exposition of Ezra and Nehemiah he informs his readers that he has consulted Jerome's commentaries on those prophets of the Old Testament who had foretold the events narrated in the two historical books.[7] In the commentaries themselves

---

[5] The story about Ignatius (*PL* xciii. 187 B) is derived from Jerome, *De viris illustribus*, that about Polycarp (*PL* xciii. 122 B) from Rufinus' translation of Eusebius.

[6] E.g. *PL* xci. 758 A, *sequens magnorum vestigia tractatorum; ibid.* 1077 B, *seduli patrum vestigia sequentes; PL* xcii. 134 A, *maxime quae in patrum venerabilium exemplis invenimus, hinc inde collecta ponere curabimus.* Cf. also *H.E.* 5, 24; *PL* xcii. 304 D.

[7] Cf. *PL* xci. 9 A–11 A, 808 B.

Bede's practice varied and he appears to follow no consistent usage. Often he merely gives an earlier writer's name as authority for a certain statement or interpretation. Less frequently the reference is more precise and indicates not only the author but the treatise cited. But far more commonly there is nothing in Bede's text to show that he has borrowed from a predecessor. His debt, for example, to Gregory the Great can be traced in all his commentaries; yet the occasions on which he names that pope are a very small percentage of the places where he cites him at greater or shorter length. In justice to Bede, however, it must be pointed out that in the prefaces to his commentaries on Luke and on Mark he expressly states that he had indicated his indebtedness to others by signs in the margins of his manuscript. Father Sutcliffe was the first to draw attention to two extant *codices* of the commentary on Mark now in the Vatican Library in which these source-marks for material taken from the Four Doctors of the Church are still preserved. More recently the present writer has been able to add other manuscripts of this work in which similar *marginalia* survive wholly or in part, and, in addition, to list some surviving *codices* of the commentary on Luke in which a similar procedure was followed.[8] Quite probably Bede adopted the same device to show what he had borrowed in his other expository works, but he does not allude to it save in the two passages named. Consequently his copyists appear to have reproduced the source-marks only in the two commentaries for which he left explicit directions and to have ignored them in others.[9] In any case the commentaries on Luke and on Mark are very closely linked. Karl Werner long ago pointed out that the commentary on Mark, which is considerably later in date than the other, reproduces many passages from the earlier work.[10] But his brief statement hardly gives a complete picture of the facts; for a

---

[8] E. J. Sutcliffe in *Biblica*, vii (1926), 428–439; M. L. W. Laistner in *Journ. Theol. Stud.* xxxiv (1933), 350–355.

[9] The two passages will be found in *PL* xcii, 134 A and 304 D. The judgment that I have ventured to express above is, of course, provisional; for the fifty odd manuscripts of various Bede commentaries, other than those on Luke and Mark, that I have seen, are but a fraction of what survives.

[10] K. Werner, *Beda der Ehrwürdige,* 195.

careful comparison of the two treatises shows that nearly one-third of the commentary on Mark is copied word for word from the commentary on Luke. As much of this duplicated material is borrowed, any future editor of the commentary on Luke will derive great help from studying the sources identified by Father Sutcliffe for the Mark commentary.

Such evidence as can be gleaned to demonstrate Bede's acquaintance with pagan Latin writers is to be found mainly in the three school-treatises, *De arte metrica, De schematibus et tropis, De orthographia.* Although only the first can be approximately dated—it was composed while Bede was still a deacon, that is, before 703—it is likely that all three were early works, just as their contents suggest that they were all put together by Bede for the use of his own pupils. The *De schematibus et tropis,* moreover, is not so much a separate work as an appendix to the *De arte metrica.* This last-named work and the *De orthographia* are compiled from grammarians of the later Roman imperial age. It is surprising how many of these were available in England at the end of the seventh century, namely: Donatus, Charisius, Diomedes, Pompeius, Sergius, Audax, Victorinus, Mallius Theodorus, Servius, Agroecius, Caper, and possibly Dositheus. The framework of the *De schematibus et tropis* is derived from two chapters of Isidore's *Etymologies* (1, 36–37); for not only is the order in which the terms are defined almost identical, but many of the definitions are the same, or nearly so. In one respect, however, Bede diverges from his predecessors. All the illustratory quotations in the *De schematibus et tropis* are taken from the Bible with one exception, and that comes from the Christian poet Sedulius. In the *De arte metrica* and *De orthographia* more examples are drawn from the Bible and Christian writers than from pagan sources. But the citations from poets and prose writers of the classical period nearly all occur in the grammarians used by Bede or in the *Etymologies* of Isidore. They cannot therefore be used as proof of direct acquaintance with these ancient authors.[11] In his later works quotations from pagan literature other than Virgil are exceedingly rare. A tag from Sallust in the commentary on Mark—*concordia parvae res crescunt*—is taken with the rest of the passage in

[11] For further particulars see *T.R.H.S.* 72–74 [above, pp. 96–98].

which it occurs from Jerome.[12] The fable of the crow who tried to masquerade as a peacock in Bede's version differs from that in Phaedrus.[13] A line from Horace is not enough to prove that Bede had read the *Epistles*.[14] Virgil, however, Bede seems to have known at first hand; for he reproduces enough verses from the poet to warrant this assumption. Virgil was, moreover, a favourite with the Irish and the existence of his works in England before Bede's time is made certain by Aldhelm's intimate familiarity with the poems. In his later years Bede, when he introduced citations, appears to have relied on what he had learnt of the poet in his youth; for in no less than three instances he misquotes the poet, once so badly that he introduces false quantities.[15]

If Bede's knowledge of classical authors was slight and mostly acquired through intermediate sources, he had read widely in the Christian poets. Besides taking many illustrations from them for his early school-treatises, he inserted suitable passages from time to time in his later works.[16] Thus the range of his reading included Ambrose, Juvencus, Prudentius, Paulinus of Nola, whose versified *Life of Felix* Bede also turned into prose, Sedulius, Prosper, Fortunatus, Arator, and Cyprianus Gallus. Cyprianus' epic on the Pentateuch, though far less known than the other Christian poems, also figured in Aldhelm's library. A

[12] *PL* xcii. 163 C from *PL* xxvi. 79 C.
[13] Bede (*PL* xci. 489 B) calls the bird *cornix* and says that the irate peacocks robbed him of his false plumage and his life. The *graculus* in Phaedrus (i. 3), though stripped of his finery, does not die. Jerome in a letter (*Epist.* cviii. 15) with which Bede was familiar alludes to the fable in a general way.
[14] Horace, *Epist.* I. ii. 69–70 in *PL* xci. 1002 D. The Horace citations in Bede's school-treatises are all found in the grammarians.
[15] The examples are: *Ecl.* ii. 22 in *PL* xci. 1019 C (cf. *T.R.H.S.* 74); *PL* xci. 1101 A, where he makes three errors in two lines from the *Georgics* (iii. 414–415); and *PL* xci. 1189 C, where, in citing *Aen.* i. 723–724, he begins the second line in such a way as to scan *crateras* as an anapaest. It is barely possible that the printed editions, based as they are on late manuscripts, misrepresent what Bede actually wrote. But it is improbable; for the last of three lines of Arator cited by Bede in his commentary on Acts (*PL* xcii. 945 B) is misquoted, so that it will not scan, in nine manuscripts that I have collated. Two of these were written at the end of the eighth century, the other seven in the ninth. Another example of misquotation by Bede will be found below, p. 126, note 23.
[16] E.g. Sedulius is cited in *PL* xci. 733 D; xcii. 615 D; xcii. 480 B; Paulinus in xcii. 398 D; Fortunatus in xciii. 138 and *H.E.* i. 7; Prosper in *H.E.* i. 10; Arator frequently in the commentary on Acts and also in *PL* xciii. 200 A.

few reminiscences in the *Life of St. Cuthbert* and in certain shorter poems attributed to Bede suggest that perhaps Petrus Petricoriensis, Dracontius, and Alcimus Avitus may be added to the list, although the evidence is not strong.[17]

Bede's interest in scientific subjects, and especially in questions of chronology, persisted throughout his life. Earliest in date of the works to which he turned for guidance was the *Natural History* of Pliny. He used Book ii extensively in his three scientific treatises and also in the *Ecclesiastical History*. Occasional quotations demonstrate his use of Books iv, v, vi, xiii, and xvi. In his commentary on the Song of Songs he offers an apology for introducing disquisitions on trees and aromatic shrubs derived from 'the books of the ancients'; for he, and others born and bred in a northern island, could not learn anything about the *flora* of Arabia, India, Judaea, and Egypt save from authors familiar with those regions.[18] The ancient source proves to be Book xii of the *Natural History* from which he inserts excerpts of considerable length into his commentary.[19] With the possible exception of Book xxxvii, the later part of Pliny's encyclopaedia appears to have remained unknown to Bede. Book xviii, for example, would have been invaluable to him when he wrote his *De temporum ratione,* and the absence of all citations from it is convincing proof that it was not in Bede's library. Besides, extant manuscripts of Pliny, though very numerous, are rarely complete, and none of those belonging to the earlier group contains more than a small portion of the work. As for Book xxxvii, Bede, in commenting on the twenty-first chapter of Revelation, discourses at some length on the various gems there mentioned. Although his main guide was Isidore and, in one case, Cassiodorus, his phraseology makes

---

[17] Cf. M. Manitius in *Sitzungsberichte,* Vienna Academy, philol.-hist. Klasse, cxii (1886), 616 ff. I have omitted Symphosius from the list in the text, as the work from which Manitius (*op. cit.* 614–617) takes his examples is probably not by Bede himself.

[18] *PL* xci. 1077 B.

[19] E.g. *PL* xci. 1098 A *Arbores balsami* to 1098 B *minima ligno,* abbreviated from Pliny, *N.H.* xii. 112–118. 1143 D *Arbor est* to 1144 A *nuncupamus,* abbreviated from *N.H.* xii. 58–62. 1144 A *Regio* to 1144 B *nitrosis,* from *N.H.* xii. 52–53. 1146 A *Cyprus,* cf. *N.H.* xii. 109. 1148 A *Est autem myrrha* to *accepit myrrha,* from *N.H.* xii. 67.

it likely that he knew that book of Pliny. The assumption that there was a manuscript of Book xxxvii in England is greatly strengthened by the fact that Aldhelm also makes some brief citations from it.[20] Bede in the *De temporibus* and *De natura rerum* inserted much from Isidore's *Etymologies* and *De natura rerum*. His use of Macrobius' *Saturnalia* in the *De temporibus* and *De temporum ratione* is also beyond dispute. A close examination of the last-named treatise, the maturest fruit of Bede's scientific studies, reveals remarkably wide reading in the specialized literature bearing on chronology and the Paschal question. When one remembers how bitter were the disagreements between the adherents of the Irish and the Roman usage in the matter of the Easter celebration, one can well understand why Benedict Biscop, Ceolfrid, and perhaps some others should have taken special pains to acquire as complete a collection of relevant books as possible. Thus Bede was able to peruse, besides patristic works in which these topics were touched upon incidentally, several tracts by Dionysius Exiguus, Victor of Capua, Victorius of Aquitaine, Polemius Silvius, a Latin version of Theophilus' letter to Theodosius I, the so-called Irish forgeries, and perhaps some other treatises or letters.[21]

Bede's historical library has engaged the attention of Mommsen and of Plummer. With the exception of Josephus, his authorities belong to the later Roman imperial or the early medieval period. Jerome's translation of Eusebius' *Chronicle* and Rufinus' version of Eusebius' *Ecclesiastical History* were of basic importance. More occasional use was made of Solinus, Orosius, Eutropius' *Breviarium,* Cassiodorus' *Tripartite History;* the *Chronicles* of Prosper, Marcellinus, Marius of Avenches, and Isidore of Seville; Jerome's *De viris illustribus* with Gennadius' continuation, the *Liber Pontificalis* and

---

[20] Cf. the index of authors in Ehwald's edition (*MGH. Auct. Antiq.* xv). His evidence that Aldhelm knew *N.H.* xxxii is quite unconvincing.

[21] No attempt has been made here to consider the source of Bede's scientific writings in detail. I have derived great help from the dissertation of C. W. Jones (cf. *T.R.H.S.* 76, note 1), who is preparing a critical text and detailed commentary of the *De temporum ratione*. Cf. also his article in *Speculum,* ix (1934), 50–56, on Bede and Polemius Silvius.

Gildas; also three noteworthy biographies, to wit, Paulinus' *Life of Ambrose*, Possidius' biography of Augustine, and the *Life of Germanus of Auxerre* by Constantius. The little tract, *De locis sanctis*, contains extracts from the *De situ Iudaeae* which bears the name of Eucherius of Lyons but is probably not by him. However, proof of Bede's acquaintance with these various compositions does not rest merely on the evidence of the *Chronicle* and *Ecclesiastical History*. Often valuable confirmation of his thorough familiarity with these historical authorities is found in his exegetical works. Thus, a long description of the Caspian Sea is repeated verbally from Orosius. Marcellinus is the source from which Bede transcribes the discovery of John the Baptist's head and the translation of the precious relic to Edessa. Another tradition regarding John's burial and later exhumation appears to be based on the *Tripartite History* of Cassiodorus.[22] Many biographical details about the apostles, evangelists, and other notable persons in the early centuries of the Christian era are taken from Rufinus' translation of Eusebius or from Jerome's *De viris illustribus*. In discussing the vice of slander or backbiting Bede, without naming his source, reinforces his point by repeating a tale from Possidius' Life of Augustine. According to this Augustine's dining-table bore an inscription bidding slanderers begone: [23]

Quisquis amat dictis absentum rodere vitam
Hanc mensam indignam noverit esse sibi.

To the list of historians already given two additions must be made, Gregory of Tours and Vegetius. In his *Retractation on Acts* Bede, in the course of commenting on the sickness of Publius (Acts xxviii. 8), transcribes part of Gregory's description of the epidemic which wrought great havoc in Gaul in A.D. 580.[24] That towards the end of his life he obtained or

---

[22] Orosius 1, 2, 48–50 in *PL* xci. 868 D; Marcellinus (*MGH. Auct. Ant.* xi. 84–85) in *PL* xcii. 192 D–193 A; Cassiod. *Hist. Trip.* vi. 15 and ix. 27–28 used for *PL* xcii. 190 D. [This last attribution was made in error. Bede here relies on Rufinus, as W. Levison (*England and the Continent in the Eighth Century*, 141, note 1) has shown.]

[23] Possidius, 22. Bede quotes the lines (*PL* xci. 1010 A–B) inaccurately.

[24] *PL* xcii. 1032 B from Greg. Tur. *Hist. Franc.* v. 26 (34).

borrowed a copy of Vegetius' *Epitoma rei militaris* has been demonstrated by C. W. Jones.[25]

Bede's use of Josephus is a matter of some interest and not without complexity because he does not seem to adhere to any uniform practice. There are passages where the context shows clearly that he is citing Josephus from an intermediate source, for instance, Rufinus or Jerome. In one or two places he indicates this method himself, as when he introduces a quotation with the words, *quia Eusebius Iosephum secutus,* or, *Hieronymus ex Iosepho scribit.*[26] Elsewhere the subject-matter is derived from the Jewish historian but the actual words are Bede's own. In the third place, Bede sometimes transcribes shorter or longer excerpts word for word from the old Latin version of Josephus which had been made at Vivarium at the instance of Cassiodorus. In Bede's commentary on Acts, five out of six citations attributed to Josephus are taken, as the context shows, from Rufinus' translation of Eusebius. The sixth refers to an episode in the Old Testament and therefore the original source was the *Jewish Antiquities* of Josephus, not the *Jewish Wars.* A passage from the treatise against Apion is introduced by Bede into his *Epistle to Plegwin,* but the phraseology of the extract does not correspond to the Cassiodorian version. It is in his commentaries on the Old Testament that Bede most often appeals to the authority of Josephus, especially in his *De tabernaculo,* an exposition of Exodus xxiv–xxx, and in the *De templo Salomonis,* a commentary on I Kings v. In these two works the longest excerpts from the Cassiodorian version of Josephus occur.[27] From Bede's *De locis sanctis* it is clear that he had at his disposal a copy of Hegesippus' abbreviated Latin

---

[25] See *Class. Rev.* xlvi (1932), 248–249. Sir George Macdonald published a slight correction in the same journal, xlvii (1933), 124.

[26] *PL* xcii. 1022 C and *PL* xci. 482 C.

[27] For example, *PL* xci. 413 B–C, 440 D–441 A from *Antiq.* iii. 7; 481 B–D from *Antiq.* iii. 8; 746 A, 774 D–775 A from *Antiq.* viii. 3. The quotation in xci. 413 C was also used by Bede in his commentary on *Samuel* (*PL* xci. 653 A) and in part in the commentary on Luke (*PL* xcii. 394 A). The Cassiodorian version of the *Antiquities,* pending its publication in *CSEL,* is not easily procured, as the Latin translations published since the first half of the seventeenth century are all modern (cf. E. Schürer in Herzog-Hauck, *Realencyklopädie für protestantische Theologie und Kirche,* ix. 385). I have used an incunabulum in the Cornell Uni-

version of Josephus' *Jewish Wars*. Thus, to sum up the somewhat confusing evidence, it would seem that Bede had the Cassiodorian version of the *Antiquities* only. For the *Jewish Wars* he appears to have depended primarily on intermediate sources like Rufinus and Jerome; he does not apparently quote verbally from Hegesippus in any of his commentaries on the New Testament. Unfortunately there is nothing to show whether, in addition, he had access to, or used, a text of Josephus in the original Greek. There are many passages where he appeals to the authority of the *Antiquities,* and yet comparison of the two authors shows no close verbal resemblance.[28] He would be a bold man who would decide whether Bede in these cases paraphrased the Cassiodorian translation or the Greek original.

Without doubt the most considerable portion of Bede's library was composed of theological works, especially those of an exegetical character. When referring in general terms, as he so frequently did, to the authority of the Fathers, he was thinking primarily of the four greatest, Ambrose, Jerome, Augustine, and Gregory I. It is therefore convenient to consider first his debt to them, rather than to follow a strictly chronological order. Of the four, Ambrose was the least well represented at Wearmouth-Jarrow and possibly in the other English libraries during Bede's lifetime. The *Hexaemeron* and the *Commentary on Luke* were certainly at Bede's elbow when he composed his own treatises on Genesis and the Third Gospel.[29] The treatise *De Noe et arca* was used in the *De temporum ratione,* a citation from the *De paradiso* occurs in Bede's exposition of Genesis, *De fide* is used in the commentary on Mark, and the *De Spiritu Sancto* is quoted more than once in his commentary on Acts. There is an allusion to the *De virginitate* in the *Epistle to Ecgberct* (5). To these Ambrosian works may probably be added the *De Abraham* and the *De poenitentia*. The explanation in

---

versity Library (Hain, *Repertorium Bibliographicum,* no. 9449). My remarks in *T.R.H.S.* 78 need correction in the light of the additional evidence given above.

[28] E.g. *PL* xci. 46 A (*Antiq.* i. 6), 72 B and 76 B (*Antiq.* i. 3), 178 C–D (*Antiq.* i. 11), 427 C (*Antiq.* iii. 6), 775 D (*Antiq.* viii. 3).

[29] There is also a substantial quotation from the *Hexaemeron* (*CSEL* xxxii. 1, 92, 7–11) in *PL* xci. 1218 B.

the former treatise of the number 318 (T I H) corresponds to that in Bede.[30] In another place he quotes Ambrose's sentiment in the *De poenitentia* on the sinfulness of mankind: *omnes homines sub peccato nascimur quorum ipse ortus in vitio est.*[31] It cannot, however, be denied that this is the kind of epigrammatic utterance which Bede might have found cited in an intermediate source. One tract by Ambrose one can feel certain that he had not read, the *De Isaac vel anima;* for this, as Cassiodorus well knew (*Instit.* i. 6), contains an allegorical exposition of certain passages in the Song of Songs, which Bede would assuredly have studied eagerly, if he could, before composing his own lengthy commentary on that book of the Old Testament.

Bede's profound admiration for Gregory I is shown by his constant indebtedness to the pope's writings and by an eloquent appraisal of his life and work in the *Ecclesiastical History* (ii. I). His library was stocked with all Gregory's genuine works except the *Letters.* There are innumerable quotations in Bede from the *Moralia,* the *Homilies* on Ezekiel and on the Gospels, and the *Regula pastoralis;* and the seventh book of Bede's commentary on the Song of Songs is nothing more than a *florilegium* from Gregory. The *Dialogues* are cited in the *De orthographia* and in the historical works. A few of the pope's letters, which had a direct bearing on the conversion of the English and were valuable contemporary documents, were treasured in England in Bede's time and inserted by him in the *Ecclesiastical History.* But, although Gregory had himself taken steps to have a collected edition of his voluminous correspondence made, this seems to have disappeared early. The largest of the existing collections was not assembled till Carolingian times and two smaller collections are a little older.[32] Again, there is not the least doubt that the great majority of Jerome's

---

[30] With *PL* xci. 149 B–C compare *CSEL* xxxii. 1, 513, 10–15; it should also be noted that Bede's explanation is not found in Jerome's *Quaestiones Hebraicae* which Bede used extensively elsewhere.

[31] *PL* xciii. 119 C; Ambr. *De poen.* (*PL* xvi. 470 C).

[32] The present state of the problem involved in the transmission of Gregory's *Registrum* is admirably summarized by O. Bardenhewer, *Geschichte der altkirchlichen Literatur,* v (1932), 288–290.

writings were accessible to Bede. In the first place he includes in the list of his own works the following compilation: 'in Isaiam, Danihelem, duodecim prophetas, et partem Hieremiae, distinctiones capitulorum ex tractatu beati Hieronimi excerptas';[33] second, there is the evidence of actual citations from Jerome—and they are very numerous—in Bede's extant commentaries.[34] In fact, the only exegetical works that appear to be ignored by, or unknown to, Bede are the commentaries on Ephesians and on Philemon. Of other Hieronymic writings he was familiar with the treatises against Helvidius and against Jovinian, with the *Apology against Rufinus,* and possibly with the *Dialogus adversus Pelagianos.* He certainly knew of the existence of this late and scathing pamphlet from Jerome's pen, but there is nothing to show that he had seen or read it.[35] The treatise on Hebrew names and the *De situ et nominibus* were his main authority for Palestinian geography and the allegorical interpretation of proper names in the Scriptures. He alludes twice to the *Martyrology* but is aware of the doubts surrounding its authorship.[36] He also quotes from *Epistles* liii, lxxi, cvii, cviii, and cxii and from Jerome's translation of the *De Spiritu Sancto* by Didymus the Blind. Bede may, of course, have had other letters by Jerome; but the evidence of the earlier extant manuscripts of Jerome's correspondence, none of which contain more than a small part of the whole collection, makes it exceedingly improbable that more than a fraction of the letters had reached England by the eighth century.[37]

Next to Gregory the Great, Bede's deepest veneration was reserved for Augustine. A noteworthy instance of his attitude of mind is to be seen in Bede's discussion of the four beasts

[33] *H.E.* v. 24.

[34] It is impossible here to list all the passages that the present writer has noted, but the commentaries of Jerome on the following books of the Old and New Testament are represented: Genesis (*Quaestiones Hebraicae*), Ecclesiastes, Isaiah, Ezekiel, Daniel, Amos, Jonah, Micah, Habakkuk, Zephaniah, Haggai, Zechariah, Malachi, Matthew, Galatians, and Titus; also the rare *commentarioli in Psalmos* first edited by Dom Morin (*Anecdota Maredsolana,* iii. I).

[35] He calls it by its sub-title, *dialogus Attici et Critobuli* (*PL* xci. 1073 C).

[36] See *T.R.H.S.* 89, note 4 [above, p. 111, note 65].

[37] Aldhelm appears to have known *Letters* xxii and lxiv, also the short *Lives of Hilarion, Malchus,* and *Paul.*

in Revelation iv. 6–9.[38] He reproduces Augustine's interpretation according to which the lion represents Matthew and the beast 'which had a face as a man' is Mark; and, though he knew Jerome's commentary on Matthew intimately, he suppresses all reference to its preface where Jerome discussed the passage in the Apocalypse. According to Jerome the lion is equivalent to Mark and the beast with human features to Matthew.[39] This was in fact the more usual interpretation and the one that ultimately prevailed. Bede's loyalty to Augustine in this instance aroused protests to which Bishop Acca drew his attention. Thereupon Bede defended himself against his critics by quoting at great length from Augustine, *De consensu evangelistarum*.[40]

Although Bede frequently mentions the African Father by name, he does not often specify the particular treatise of which he is thinking or from which he is borrowing at the time. In view of Augustine's enormous literary output it is at present impossible to speak with finality of Bede's debt to his great predecessor in exegesis; and consequently only a tentative list of Augustinian works at Wearmouth-Jarrow can be drawn up. Only when Bede's theological writings have been newly edited, and borrowed material in them traced to their source, will that important section in Bede's library be fully known. But even the provisional list here offered, which is based, as usual, on the quotations from Augustine that it has been possible to track down, is impressive in scope. In the earlier part of Bede's commentary on Genesis will be found nearly thirty passages transcribed from Augustine's *De Genesi ad litteram*. Some of these excerpts extend to more than a page in the Vienna edition of Augustine. The same book is also quoted more than once in the commentary on Acts. In addition, there are in the Genesis commentary of Bede citations from *De Genesi contra Manichaeos*, the treatise against Faustus, and the briefer tract, *Contra adversarium legis et prophetarum*.[41] Passages from the *Quaes-*

---

[38] *PL* xciii. 144 A, based on Aug. *Tract. in Ioann. Evang.* xxxvi (*PL* xxxv. 1666).

[39] *PL* xxvi. 19 B.

[40] *PL* xcii. 305–306, reproducing *CSEL* xliii. 4, ll. 4–5; 6, ll. 3–73; 9, ll. 3–10, 14.

[41] Through inadvertence Bede's reference to the *Contra adversarium legis et prophetarum* was wrongly interpreted by me (*T.R.H.S.* 88) as an allusion to

tiones in Heptateuchum occur in several of Bede's commentaries. In his expositions of books of the New Testament he had recourse to the *Enarrationes in Psalmos, Quaestiones Evangeliorum,* the Tractates on the fourth Gospel and on the First Epistle of John, the *De consensu Evangelistarum,* and several sermons. The end of Book iii of the *De doctrina Christiana* is transcribed by Bede in a somewhat abbreviated form in the long introduction to his commentary on the Apocalypse. Furthermore, he knew the *Confessions,* and quotes or paraphrases passages from Books xv, xvi, and xx of the *De civitate Dei.* Of the shorter Augustinian works we find the *De sancta virginitate,* the *Enchiridion,* and the *De mendacio* represented in Bede's library,[42] and he quotes substantial passages from Epistles cxlvii, clxvii, and ccv. It should, however, be observed that each of these so-called letters is in reality a treatise on some doctrinal question. The first of the three was described by Augustine himself as *Liber de videndo Deo.*[43] The four oldest extant manuscripts of it contain no other Augustinian letters. Epistle clxvii, addressed to Jerome, discusses a passage in the General Epistle of James. The correspondence between the two great contemporaries, as early *codices* show, was regarded as a special work, distinct from their other letters, and may have been in England by the eighth century. *Epistle* ccv, written for Consentius, is a disquisition *de corpore Domini post resurrectionem.* The oldest manuscript containing it has only nine Augustinian letters in all. It is a ninth-century *codex,* now at Boulogne, written in Anglo-Saxon script.[44] It is not, then, legitimate to assume from the presence of these three *Epistles* in Bede's library that he had access to the whole, or even the bulk, of Augustine's correspondence. Finally, the manner in which Bede refers to Augustine's *Retractations* rather suggests that he knew the book only by hearsay, although he adopted

the *Contra Faustum.* Bede knew both works and used the latter also in the *De temporum ratione.*

[42] I would take this opportunity of correcting a further error in *T.R.H.S.* 88. Bede's allusion in *PL* xci. 650 B is to *De mendacio,* xiv. 25 (*CSEL* xli. 444–445).

[43] *Retractationes,* ii. 41.

[44] For this *codex Bononiensis,* cf. A. Goldbacher in *CSEL* lviii. xxxv.

the title for his own revision of his Acts commentary.[45]

The list of theological works consulted by Bede, other than those written by the Four Doctors of the Church, is not specially long, but contains some unusual items. Amongst the more widely known treatises were the tractate on the second Psalm by Hilary of Poitiers, Cyprian's *Liber Testimoniorum*, *De habitu virginum*, *De zelo et livore*, and perhaps *De lapsis*; a commentary on Job attributed to Philippus; Fulgentius' anti-Arian dissertation addressed to King Thrasamund and some other treatise or letter by the same author now no longer extant;[46] and Cassiodorus' vast commentary on the Psalter. The authority of the pseudo-Clementine *Recognitiones* is invoked several times and Bede appears to have regarded them as the genuine work of Clement of Rome.[47] How intimate Bede's acquaintance with John Cassian may have been, it is difficult to determine. He never names him, but there is one unequivocal allusion to *Collatio* xvii.[48] Moreover, this author's writings, in spite of his semi-Pelagian taint, enjoyed a wide popularity in the Middle Ages; and, in view of Benedict Biscop's connexions with the monasteries of southern France, they are likely to have been included amongst the books which he brought back from one or other of his continental journeys. Bede's familiarity with Benedict's Rule might have been tacitly assumed, but confirmatory evidence is not lacking; for, besides several general allusions, he refers his readers specifically to chapter vii in that book.[49] The first book of Bede's commentary on the Song of Songs is an attempted refutation of the Pelagian Julian of Eclanum, in which he cites verbal extracts from that heresiarch's book *De amore*, and mentions another of his treatises, *De bono constantiae*. The contention of Bruckner, in his interesting

[45] *PL* xcii. 995 B.

[46] *PL* xciii. 54 A. Commenting on 1 Peter ii, 18, Bede remarks: *Fulgentius in opusculis suis sic ponit: servientes cum timore non tantum bonis et modestis sed etiam difficilioribus.* I have failed to trace this citation in Fulgentius.

[47] See *PL* xci. 19 D–20 A; xcii. 1011 C.   C. W. Jones included the *Recognitiones* among the sources of the *De temporum ratione*.

[48] PL xci. 961 C. Aldhelm knew both the *Institutiones* and *Collationes* of Cassian.

[49] *PL* xci. 892 B, a passage that Plummer seems to have overlooked. The general allusions to the Rule will be found in *H.A.* i, vii, xi, xvi.

study of this champion of Pelagianism, that the *De amore* was in reality the introductory part of Julian's commentary on the Song of Songs, carries conviction.[50] Another heretical work named by Bede in the same commentary is Pelagius' *Epistola ad Demetriadem de institutione virginis*. Neither Bede nor Aldhelm was aware of Pelagius' authorship. Aldhelm, not directly but by implication, attributed the letter to Jerome.[51] This view Bede expressly repudiates, and one is tempted to see in his use of the word *nostri* a covert allusion to the abbot of Malmesbury.[52] But he himself errs in attributing the epistle to Julian of Eclanum. In two places Bede quoted from Aponius' exposition of the Song of Songs, but as a whole this piece of exegesis does not seem to have found favour in his eyes; for his own allegorical interpretation diverges from that of the older commentator. Aponius' work was, however, a rarity. A century after Bede's time it was studied by Angelomus of Luxeuil.[53] It would be interesting to know whether the manuscript used by him was a copy of that existing in England in the eighth century.

What is probably the earliest of Bede's theological works presents some curious features to the student of his sources. The commentary on the Apocalypse probably contains far less of Bede's own ideas than do some of his later works. Moreover, in expounding the last book of the New Testament canon, which lent itself so particularly to allegorical interpretation, he had had many predecessors. Three of these were certainly by his side when he wrote his own treatise. Primasius is actually named but once; yet a very large number of Bede's comments are copied word for word from him. Tyconius, on the other hand, is mentioned no less than ten times by name, so that one is inclined to suppose that Bede acknowledged every one of

[50] A. Bruckner, *Julian von Eclanum*, 9, note 5, and 72, note 5. Bede's quotations from Julian have been collected by Bruckner on pp. 74–75.

[51] Cf. *MGH. Auct. Ant.* xv. 303, 15, with Ehwald's note 3.

[52] *PL* xci. 1073 C.

[53] On the use of Aponius by Bede and Angelomus see J. Witte, *Der Kommentar des Aponius zum Hohenliede* (Dissert. Erlangen, 1903). The two citations in Bede occur in *PL* xci. 1112 A (= Aponius, ed. Bottino and Martini, 80) and 1162 C–D (= *ibid.* 155).

his borrowings from that commentary, which unfortunately is no longer extant, because Tyconius was more than a little tinged with heresy. In the third place, Bede appears to have procured the short commentary of Victorinus of Pettau as rehandled and enlarged by Jerome. This book was also used by Primasius, and there are some eight excerpts which Bede took not directly from Victorinus but from Primasius. Two examples will illustrate this:

Victorinus	*Primasius and Bede*
(*CSEL* xlix. 8–10)	(*PL* lxviii. 801 B, and *PL* xciii. 136 B)
Et in capillis albis albatorum est multitudo lanae similis propter oves, similis nivi propter innumerabilem turbam candidatorum de caelo datorum.	. . . propter oves ad dexteram futuras, instar lanae, et propter dealbatorum innumerabilem turbam et electorum a coelo datorum, instar nivis effulgent.
(*Ibid.* 19, 13–15)	(*PL* lxviii. 798 D and *PL* xciii. 135 A)
Qui primo in suscepto homine venit occultus, post paululum in maiestate et gloria veniet ad iudicandum manifestus.	Qui iudicandus primo venit occultus, tunc iudicaturus veniet manifestus.

But there are two passages where Bede follows Victorinus and Primasius does not. The similarities of the following comments on Apocalypse 15, are too close to be accidental:

Victorinus	*Bede*
(*CSEL* xlix. 137, 6–8)	(*PL* xciii. 177 c)
Semper enim ira Dei percutit populum contumacem septem plagis— id est perfecte ut in Levitico dicit— quae in ultimo futurae sunt, cum ecclesia de medio exierit.	Quia semper ira Dei populum percutit contumacem septem plagis, id est perfectis, sicut frequenter in Levitico: 'et percutiam', inquit, 'vos septem plagis'. Quae novissimae futurae sunt, cum ecclesia de medio eius exierit.

The second passage is one where Bede deals rather fully with the number 666.[54] He begins with the word, *Teitan,* whose letters with their numerical values in the Greek alphabet add up to the mystic number. He then passes on to Primasius'

[54] Cf. *Bede: His Life, Times, and Writings,* p. 178.

similar calculation of the word, *Antemos,* and it is on this occasion that he refers to Primasius by name. Now the calculation of *Antemos* was taken over by Primasius from Victorinus-Jerome, but *Teitan* and its numerical computation are found only in the two later redactions of the Victorinus-Jerome commentary, to which the most recent editor, Haussleiter, has assigned the symbols Φ and S.[55] Incidentally Bede's comment on the passage shows that his library contained one or other of these versions and not the pure Victorinus-Jerome text.

Two relatively little known commentators of the fifth century who figure among Bede's authorities are Arnobius the Younger and Salonius. There is a direct citation from Arnobius' brief exposition of the Psalms in the *De temporum ratione.*[56] Dom Morin, who does not refer to this passage, has, however, pointed out an allusion to Arnobius in Bede's *explanatio* to Psalm lxxxiii, prefixed to a later commentary which he attributes to Manegold of Lauterbach.[57] A third piece of evidence is provided by a glossary that is made up chiefly of citations from Cassiodorus' commentary on the Psalms, but also contains two extracts from Arnobius. Though not by Bede himself, the glossary was in all likelihood compiled from Bede's works and not from the earlier writers; for the combination of authors used in the glossary would be hard to explain on any other hypothesis, seeing how rare two out of the three were in the Middle Ages. The gloss on *sela* is, in fact, taken from Jerome's *Commentarioli in Psalmos,* a treatise from which Bede reproduces four or five excerpts in his commentary on Acts.[58]

Salonius, bishop of Geneva and son of Eucherius of Lyons, was a prelate highly esteemed by his contemporaries. To him Salvian dedicated his treatise, *On the governance of God.* But his importance as an author seems to have been slight. The only certain work from his hand now extant is an allegorical inter-

[55] See Haussleiter's Introduction in *CSEL* xlix.
[56] *PL* xc. 525 C–526 A; *PL* liii. 481 A–B.
[57] G. Morin, *Anecdota Maredsolana,* 2e sér. i (1913), 73 and 349.
[58] For the glossary see my note in *Speculum,* v (1930), 217–221. The gloss, *sela,* is copied exactly from Jerome's *Commentarioli (Anecdota Maredsolana,* iii. I, ii, 10–18). This reference replaces those given in my article for that gloss.

pretation, of no great length and cast in dialogue form, of Proverbs and Ecclesiastes. Its success or influence seems to have been negligible, so that it is all the more remarkable that the book found its way into Bede's hands.[59] Bede ignored the dialogue form, but, for the rest, constantly borrowed from it throughout his own fuller commentary on Proverbs, yet without mentioning his source by name. Although he often recasts Salonius' sentences and adds material of his own, his dependence on him is not open to question. Bede's method may be illustrated by examples taken from the opening, middle, and end of his commentary:

Salonius

(PL liii. 970 A)

Per caput designantur principes Iudaeorum. In capite turbarum clamitabat, quia principibus Iudaeorum, homicidium quod in eum patraverant, palam per apostolos ad memoriam reducebat et eosdem ad poenitentiae remedium vocabat.

Bede

(PL xci. 942 D)

In capite turbarum clamitabat, quia etiam principibus qui sibi ei praevaluisse, ut crucifigeretur, videbantur, reatum homicidii, quod perpetrarunt, palam reducebat ad memoriam eosque ad poenitentiae remedium vocabat.

975 D–976 A

Quomodo circulum aureum si infixeris in naribus suis, id est, in naribus porci, ille dum pergit terram vertere ac fodere naso, immergit circulum aureum in volutabrum luti, et tunc perdit circulus aureus decorem quem habuit. Similiter mulier fatua, si habet pulchritudinem vultus, vel si accipiat ornamenta inaurium, monilium, simul et vestimentorum, sordidat pulchritudinem suam et amittit decorem, si se coeno libidinis coinquinare diligit et adulteriis corrumpit.

972 D–973 A

Circulum aureum si in naribus suis infixeris, nihilominus illa terram vertere naso, et volutabro luti properat immergi; ita mulier fatua, si pulchritudinem vultus vel habitus acceperit, suam tamen faciem ad infima declinare, suam speciositatem ad evertendos ubique castitatis flosculos circumferre, seque coeno voluptatis inquinare diligit.

[59] J. A. Endres, *Honorius von Augustodunum,* 74, has shown that Honorius' commentary on Proverbs is merely an abbreviated version of Salonius. He would attribute to Salonius also two nameless commentaries on John and Matthew which are found in the same manuscript and are written in dialogue form.

137

992 A–B

Istae filiae quas divitias congregaverunt? Orationes, ieiunia, eleemosynas, afflictionem et castimoniam carnis, linguae refrenationem, meditationem Scripturarum, et ceterorum bonorum operum divitias: quae verae divitiae sunt, si spirituali fiant intentione, videlicet propter regni coelestis retributionem: aliter nihil prosunt agentibus. Unde filiae, videlicet haereticorum aut malorum catholicorum turbae, frustra congregaverunt sibi divitias; quia vel in fide erraverunt, vel certe huiusmodi bona opera non spirituali fecerunt intentione, de quibus in evangelio Dominus:

1039 C–1040 A

Quae congregaverunt divitias, videlicet bonorum operum operationes, ieiunia, eleemosynas, afflictionem et castimoniam carnis, continentiam linguae, meditationem Scripturarum, et cetera huiusmodi. Quae verae sunt divitiae spiritus, ubi pura mentis sinceritate geruntur; ubi autem sine fide quae per dilectionem operatur fiunt, nihil agentibus prosunt. Sed et illae filiae frustra congregaverunt divitias, de quibus Dominus ait:

Here both commentators quote Matthew vii. 22–23.

Sancta vero ecclesia catholica supergressa est: hoc est, transcendit omnes illas, quia quidquid agit, in fide tantum recta et spirituali operatur intentione.

Sed omnis istiusmodi filias ecclesia catholica supergreditur, quae fide casta, et opere perfecta Redemptoris sui vestigia sectatur.

It is in the highest degree probable that some at least of Isidore's theological works were in Bede's collection. But it is a curious fact, noted by more than one critic but still unexplained, that Bede, whose sense of literary property was in general so unusually high, especially during an age when plagiarism ordinarily was not felt to be improper, treats Isidore with more freedom or less respect than his other authorities. He names him only three times at all, in each case only to controvert him.[60] Yet the *Etymologies* was the handy encyclopedia to which he regularly turned for enlightenment on miscellaneous topics. As often as not, when he does derive his information from that source, he reproduces it, wholly or in part, in his own words. If, as has already been shown, he occasionally treats Josephus in the same way, that is less surprising; for

[60] The three passages are *PL* xcii. 997 C and 1031 C; *De temporum ratione*, xxxv. In the first of these Bede's criticism is not confined to Isidore.

Josephus, though highly valued, had not been a leading figure in the Catholic Church. Bede's usual, though not invariable, practice of citing verbally from his theological forerunners makes the tracking down of his sources feasible, if laborious. Again, indebtedness to Isidore's *Etymologies,* even if the information is given in Bede's own words, is, owing to the nature of that work, not as a rule difficult to establish. But with Isidore's theological writings the case is different; for, whereas many of the sources used in the compilation of the *Etymologies* were not accessible in Bede's time, the authorities consulted by Isidore when he composed his exegetical or homiletic works were all or mostly in Bede's library also. Mere similarity in thought between Bede and Isidore is therefore not enough to prove borrowing of the one from the other, seeing that many of Bede's ideas will have been formed or influenced by direct study of the same Fathers whom Isidore followed. While, then, one may agree with Karl Werner that Bede was acquainted with the bishop of Seville's *Quaestiones in Vetus Testamentum* —and, it might be added, probably with other theological works by the same author—the general similarities between the two writers on which the German scholar laid so much stress really do not prove his case.[61]

Bede's Greek sources were not numerous and can be disposed of more briefly. In addition to the *Vulgate* and one or more versions of the *Vetus Latina* he had at his disposal a Greek text of Acts. This manuscript still survives, for the identity of *codex Laudianus Graecus* 35 in the Bodleian Library, which contains the Greek and Latin text of Acts side by side with the copy collated by Bede for his earlier commentary, and especially for the *Retractation,* is now generally accepted.[62] The chief argument for the identification of the manuscripts is the large number of Biblical readings—over seventy—in which the two concur. Even this considerable number may prove to be an under-estimate. Statistics made from the printed text of Bede

[61] K. Werner, *op. cit.,* 167 ff.
[62] Cf. Plummer, i, p. liv, and particularly the article by E. A. Lowe in *Speculum,* iii (1928), 1–15, with the references there given. The manuscript in question is known to Biblical scholars as *E.*

are unreliable because it is based on the authority of late manuscripts and early printed editions. But in some of the earlier *codices* of Bede's commentary on Acts are found additional cases where the citations from Acts coincide with *E*.[63] If Bede's use of a Greek copy of Acts is beyond dispute, the question whether there were in Wearmouth-Jarrow other parts of the New Testament in Greek, and, further, a copy of the Septuagint, is more problematic. In his other commentaries on the New Testament Bede, in strong contrast to his practice in the commentary on Acts and the *Retractation*, rarely touches on questions of textual criticism. The occasions on which he refers to, or quotes, the original are few, yet in most of these passages he does not appear to be relying on his authorities.[64] As for the Septuagint, the balance of probability that he at times used it directly is even stronger. He pays far more attention to textual variations in his commentary on Genesis than in any of his other works on the Old Testament. Many of the citations from LXX, like all those from the Hebrew original, were taken over from Jerome or occasionally from Augustine.[65] But the residue of passages where Bede appears to owe nothing to his predecessors is appreciable; and, as some of them at least contain a phrase or even a sentence, not only a single word, from LXX, the mere use of a Biblical glossary is ruled out.

Of the Greek theologians, Origen is criticized several times as a heretical writer, or else a biographical detail about him is given. Bede appears to have used his second homily on Genesis, probably in Rufinus' Latin version.[66] Basil's *Hexaemeron* in

[63] Two examples may be given: in Acts. ii, 13 MS. Bibl. Nat. lat. 12283 (saec. ix) and 12284, which was probably copied from it a little later in the same century, read with *E, quia musto repleti sunt*. In Acts xix, 29 *M(urbacensis)*, now Geneva, MS. lat. 21 (saec. viii ex.) and *Sangallensis*, 259 (saec. viii–ix), called *A* in my forthcoming edition, read with *E, unanimo*, for *uno animo*.

[64] E.g. *PL* xcii. 322 B, 369 A; *PL* xciii. 33 C, 40 D, 47 A, 100 A–B. *PL* xcii. 213 D, on the other hand, is repeated verbally from Jerome, *in Matth.* (*PL* xxvi. 119 B).

[65] E.g. *PL* xci. 79 C from Aug. *Quaest. in Heptat.* (*CSEL* xxviii. ii, 4, 25–27); 116 D–117 A from Jerome, *Quaest. Hebr.* (*PL* xxiii. 952 A–952 B–953 A) and *Comm. in Ezech.* (*PL* xxv. 259 D); 161 B and 163 D from Jerome, *Quaest. Hebr.* (*PL* xxiii. 963 B and 964 B).

[66] *PL* xci. 91 A–C; cf. *PG* xxx. 887 B–C. On the other hand, the reference to Origen's views in the next column (*PL* xci. 92 A–B) was reproduced by Bede from Aug., *Quaest. in Heptat.* (*CSEL* xxviii. ii, 5, 25–26, 4).

Eustathius' translation is mentioned in a general way and also quoted verbally or paraphrased on several occasions. There are several references to John Chrysostom, whom Bede usually calls John of Constantinople, and his tract on the topic, *quod nemo laeditur nisi a se ipso,* is recommended for study. Bede also consulted Chrysostom's homily on the Nativity when he wrote the first chapter of his commentary on Luke. Some of the Greek Father's works reached the West early in Latin dress, and it is in this form rather than in the original text that we may suppose them to have come into Bede's hands.[67] Of eight allusions to Clement of Alexandria in Bede one is a biographical item; five others are derived from Rufinus, so that the remaining two may also be assumed to have been taken by Bede from an intermediate source.[68] Besides two allusions of a general nature to Athanasius, Bede quotes or paraphrases him when discussing I Peter iii. 18.[69] Rufinus' translation of sundry orations by Gregory of Nazianzus completes the list of Greek theologians. Bede transcribed a whole paragraph from the oration on Pentecost without acknowledgement in his commentary on Acts. Years later, in the *Retractation,* he informed his readers of the source from which he had taken over his views on the miracle of tongues, thereby hoping to silence the adverse criticisms called forth by that interpretation.[70]

The *De transitu Beatae Virginis,* wrongly attributed, as Bede himself was aware, to Melito of Sardes, and Latin translations of the *Shepherd* of Hermas, of Athanasius' Life of St. Antony, and of Lucian of Caphar Gamala are also found among Bede's sources, and prove, if proof were necessary, the width or catholicity of his reading.[71] We know from Bede himself that the Acts of the Lateran Council held in 649 under Pope Martin I were brought to England by John the Arch-chanter, and that they

[67] On the Latin versions of Chrysostom cf. P. Bauer in *Revue d'histoire ecclésiastique,* viii (1907), 249–265.
[68] Cf. *T.R.H.S.* 91 [above, p. 113]. To the references there given may be added *PL* xciii. 138 D–139 A on the heretic Nicolaus, a passage based on Rufinus (ed. Mommsen), 261, 6 ff.
[69] *PL* xciii. 58 B–C. Cf. also above, p. 113. I have been unable to trace the passage in Athanasius or in Vigilius of Thapsus.
[70] *PL* xcii. 947 B–D = *CSEL* xlvi. 160, 17–161, 11; *PL* xcii. 999 D.
[71] Cf. for further particulars *T.R.H.S.* 83 and 85 [above, pp. 105–107].

were copied by order of Benedict Biscop. Moreover, reference to that Council was made at the Synod of Hatfield in 680. Definite proof that Bede had familiarized himself with this document is not wanting, but the fact has hitherto been overlooked.[72] In commenting on Mark vi. 49—the miracle of Christ walking on the sea—Bede reproduced the heretical opinions of the Monothelite bishop Theodore of Pharan in Arabia and a sentence from the treatise on the Divine names by the pseudo-Dionysius. The entire passage is copied almost word for word from the Latin version of the Acts of the Lateran Council.[73]

No one will deny that the catalogue of books demonstrably known to Bede is impressive in length and for his age unique. Yet there are some surprising omissions, so that one wonders with what other writings he may have been familiar, although their influence or use cannot be proved from his surviving commentaries. There are, however, certain general considerations that have an important bearing on this question. The bulk of Bede's works were exegetical or homiletic; but very much of the earlier Latin literature of the Church was apologetic or directed against contemporary heresies. Bede, whose strict orthodoxy is obvious wherever he discusses any matter of doctrine or ecclesiastical use, was, it is true, familiar with the general tenets of many heretical sects. But in the main his knowledge of them is derived from the ecclesiastical histories or one of the four doctors.[74] Was he acquainted with the

---

[72] Cf. *H.E.* iv. 17 and 18, with Plummer's notes *ad loc.*

[73] *PL* xcii. 197 B = Mansi, *Concilia,* x. 967 A–B. Plummer, as is evident from his note on *H.E.* iv. 18 (ii. 234), was unaware that Bede had transcribed this passage. Hence he included Theodore and the pseudo-Dionysius in his list of authors (i, pp. li–lii). The other reference to the pseudo-Dionysius is *PL* xcii. 981 A. The biographical part in this passage might be derived from either Jerome or Rufinus. But the statement that Dionysius *ingenii sui volumina reliquit* can hardly mean the pastoral letters of Dionysius of Corinth listed by Rufinus. Thus Bede like every one else in his day seems to have accepted the identity of Dionysius with the author of the so-called pseudo-Dionysian works. But there is nothing to show that he had ever seen any of them; and indeed all the available evidence points to the fact that they did not reach the West till Carolingian times.

[74] E.g. *PL* xcii. 144 C–D, with allusions to Photinus, Arius, and the Manichaeans, is from Ambrose, *in Luc.* (*CSEL* xxxii, iv, 181, 1–10); 275 C–D, on Valentinus, Marcion, and the Manichaeans, from Ambrose, *De fide* (*PL* xvi. 591 A–B). Cf. also the next note.

numerous polemical tracts of Augustine, other than certain anti-Manichaean treatises which, as we saw, were used in the commentary on Genesis? There is no cogent reason for supposing that the anti-Donatist writings of the African Father were known in England in Bede's day; for the Donatist controversy had been localized in a way that Arianism or Pelagianism were not, and it had exerted no obvious influence on western European thought. Bede alludes several times to the sect or to its founder as men who destroyed the unity of the Christian Church; once he makes a passing allusion to their heterodox views on the doctrine of Grace. Again, the teaching of Arius, although it had called forth an immense literature in the fourth century and even later, was hardly a living issue in England in the eighth. And, while Bede makes many allusions to the madness of Arius—*vesania Arrii*—they are, when not repeated verbally from one of his usual sources, not of the kind to make it probable that he had made a real study of the earlier literature on the subject.[75] Pelagianism, on the other hand, was a different matter. Its founder came from the British Isles. It was essentially a Western heresy which had left its mark on both Gaul and Britain, and a century after Bede's death was again to become a vital question on the continent of western Europe. Although it has not been possible to identify any extracts in Bede's works as excerpts from Augustine's anti-Pelagian pamphlets, it is by no means improbable that he had read some of them.

Some authors, noted in their own time, made little or no impression on later generations. The elder Arnobius is a case in point. His book, *Adversus nationes,* was forgotten soon after his death and now survives in only a single manuscript. Tertullian's eclipse, at least after Augustine's time, was to a great extent due to the unorthodoxy of his later teaching. It is evident from the manuscript tradition of his writings that he was little known in the early Middle Ages. A single ninth-century *codex* contains only a portion of his works; for the rest, his modern editors depend on two manuscripts of the eleventh and several

[75] E.g. *PL* xcii. 944 C, a reference to Arius' ghastly end, comes from Rufinus, x. 14. *PL* xcii. 251 A and 950 B, with allusions to the Arian doctrine, are copied respectively from Jerome, *in Matth.* (*PL* xxvi. 157 C) and *Comment. in psalmos* (ed. Morin), 80, 10–16.

of the fifteenth century. Bede nowhere mentions him by name, and evidence is lacking that he had read any Tertullianic treatise.[76] More remarkable is the omission of Lactantius from the authors named by Bede. In Alcuin's day there was a *codex* of this writer at York; which of his works it contained is unfortunately not known. Nor is there anything to show that this or some other manuscript from which Alcuin's was copied, had reached England in Bede's time or before. But amongst the many extant *codices* of the *Divinae Institutiones* are two of very early date (saec. vi–vii) and two of the ninth century. A sentence from the shorter tract, *De opificio,* is quoted by Aldhelm, who names Lactantius as the author. It can hardly be a pure coincidence that nearly all the theological works shown by Ehwald in his monumental edition to have been consulted by Aldhelm were also to be found in Bede's working library. Hence, even without corroborative evidence from his works, one is inclined to assume that Bede was acquainted with the *De opificio,* if not with Lactantius' longest work.

Books by authors of the fifth century which may have been in the library of Wearmouth-Jarrow, or in some other collection accessible to Bede, are the *Instructiones* by Eucherius and the *Commonitorium* of Vincent of Lérins. The latter seems to have left no trace in Bede's works nor is its author ever mentioned by him. Yet, in view of its fame and of Benedict Biscop's sojourn at Lérins, one would expect that keen lover of books to have brought back a copy to his native land. If the evidence for Bede's acquaintance with Eucherius is slight, it is perhaps sufficient to warrant the inclusion of the bishop of Lyons's name here.[77]

It remains to name an author of the sixth century whose

---

[76] Plummer (i. 13) derives the opening sentence in *H.E.* i. 2 from Tertullian, *Adv. Iudaeos.* But are the italicized words, *Brittania Romanis inaccessa,* sufficient to warrant the attribution? In the opinion of the present writer they are emphatically not.

[77] C. W. Jones includes the *Instructiones* among the possible sources of *De temporum ratione.* Bede's language in the commentary on Genesis (*PL* xci. 56 B) is reminiscent of *Instr.* i. 13 (*CSEL* xxxi. 70, 20–22). The explanations of *Hebraica* in *PL* xci. 52 A and 72 B, though they might be from Eucherius, probably come direct from Jerome.

last work is justly ranked amongst the masterpieces of the world's literature. The name of Boethius occurs neither in Aldhelm nor in Bede; nor does the internal evidence of their writings lend any support to the belief that either the *Consolation of Philosophy* or any of Boethius' other works had reached England in their day. The study and elucidation of Boethius became very active in the Carolingian age; and as early as the end of the eighth century some of his treatises were in York. Alcuin's list of books includes the names of Boethius and Aristotle. The former may refer to the *Consolatio* or the theological tractates, or both, while Aristotle is equivalent to Boethius' Latin version of the *De interpretatione* and *Categories*. But even though Bede may never have set eyes on the *Consolatio,* his life and works exemplify to the full the closing words uttered by the 'last of the Romans': [78]

Neither do we in vain put our hope in God or pray to him; for if we do this well and as we ought, we shall not lose our labour or be without effect. Wherefore fly vices, embrace virtues, possess your minds with worthy hopes, offer up humble prayers to your highest Prince. There is, if you will not dissemble, a great necessity of doing well imposed upon you, since you live in the sight of your Judge, who beholdeth all things.

Catalogue of Authors and Works in Bede's Library [79]
(A mark of interrogation against an author or work signifies that the evidence for inclusion in this list is not conclusive.)

Agroecius
Alcimus Avitus?
Ambrosius: De Abraham?
        De fide
        De Noe et arca
        De paradiso
        De poenitentia?
        De Spiritu Sancto
        De virginitate

[78] These concluding words of the *Consolatio* are quoted in the translation of I.T., revised by Stewart and Rand (*Loeb Classical Library*).

[79] The term 'Bede's Library' is used for the sake of convenience. It does not imply that all the works here listed were necessarily in the library of Wearmouth and Jarrow.

     Expositio evang. sec. Lucam
     Hexaemeron
     Hymni
Aponius
Arator
Arnobius junior: Commentarii in psalmos
Athanasius: Vita S. Antonii ab Evagrio traducta
     Opus incertum
Audax
Augustinus: Confessiones
     Contra adversarium legis et prophetarum
     Contra Faustum
     De civitate Dei
     De consensu evangelistarum
     De doctrina Christiana
     De Genesi ad litteram
     De Genesi contra Manichaeos
     De mendacio
     De sancta virginitate
     Enarrationes in psalmos
     Enchiridion
     Epistolae cxlvii, clxvii, ccv
     Quaestiones in evangelia
     Quaestiones in Heptateuchum
     Sermones aliqui
     Tractatus in Ioann. epist. I
     Tractatus in Ioann. evang.
Basilius: Hexaemeron ab Eustathio traductum
Biblia: Versio Graeca actuum apostolorum
     Versio Graeca Novi Testamenti?
     Versio Graeca Veteris Testamenti quae LXX vocatur?
     Versio Hieronymiana
     Versio vetus Latina
Caper
Cassianus: Collationes
Cassiodorus: Commenta psalterii
     Historia tripartita
Charisius
Chrysostomus: Homilia in Nativitatem
     Quod nemo laeditur nisi a se ipso
Constantius: Vita S. Germani

Cyprianus: De habitu virginum
    De lapsis?
    De zelo et livore
    Liber testimoniorum
Cyprianus Gallus
Didymus: De spiritu Sancto liber ab Hieronymo translatus
Diomedes
Dionysius Exiguus
Donatus
Dositheus?
Dracontius?
Eucherius: Instructiones?
Eusebius: *vide* Hieronymum *et* Rufinum
Eutropius: Breviarium
Fortunatus
Fulgentius: Ad Thrasamundum libri III
    Opus incertum
Gennadius: De viris illustribus
Gildas
Gregorius I: Dialogi
    Epistolae nonnullae ad conversionem Anglorum perti-
    nentes.
    Homiliae in Ezech. et in Evang.
    Moralia
    Regula pastoralis . .
Gregorius Nazianzenus: Oratio in Pentecosten a Rufino translata
Gregorius Turonensis: Historia Francorum
Hegesippus: *vide* Iosephum
Hermas: Libri Pastoris versio Latina
Hieronymus: Adversus Helvidium
    Adversus Iovinianum
    Apologia adversus libros Rufini
    Commentarii in Ecclesiasten et in omnes prophetas
    Commentarii in Matth. Evang., in epist. ad Gal. et
    in epist. ad Titum
    Commentarioli in psalmos
    De nominibus Hebraicis
    De situ et nominibus
    De viris illustribus
    Dialogi contra Pelagianos?
    Epistulae liii, lxxi, cvii, cviii, cxii

Eusebii Caesariensis Chronicon
Quaestiones Hebraicae
Hilarius Pictaviensis: Tractatus in psalmum secundum
Iosephus: Antiquitatum versio Latina
      Traductio belli Iudaici ab Hegesippo confecta
      Versio Graeca?
Isidorus: Chronicon
      De natura rerum
      Etymologiae
      Quaestiones in Vetus Testamentum?
Iulianus Eclanensis: Comment. in Canticum Canticorum
           De bono constantiae
Iuvencus
Lactantius: De opificio?
      Divinae Institutiones?
Lateranense Concilium: Acta
Liber Pontificalis
Lucianus e Caphar Gamala
Macrobius: Saturnalia
Mallius Theodorus
Marcellinus Comes
Marius Aventicus
Origenes: Homilia secunda in Genesim a Rufino translata
Orosius
Pascha: Opuscula quattuor quae *Irish Forgeries* vocantur
Paulinus: Vita S. Ambrosii
Paulinus Nolae episcopus
Pelagius: Epistola ad Demetriadem
Petrus Petricoriensis?
Philippus: Commentarius in Iob
Plinius: Historiae naturalis libri ii, iv, v, vi, xii, xiii, xvi, xxxvii
Polemius Silvius
Pompeius
Possidius: Vita S. Augustini
Primasius: Expositio Apocalypseos
Prosper: Chronicon
      Epigrammata
Prudentius
Pseudo-Clemens: Recognitiones
Pseudo-Eucherius: De situ Iudaeae
Pseudo-Melito: De transitu beatae Virginis

Rufinus: Historia ecclesiastica Eusebii a Rufino translata
    Vide etiam Gregorium Nazianzenum *et* Originem
Salonius
Sedulius
Servius
Solinus
Theophilus: Epistolae ad Theodosianum I versio Latina
Tyconius: Expositio Apocalypseos
Vegetius
Victor Capuae episcopus
Victorinus grammaticus
Victorinus Poetovii episcopus
Victorius Aquitanus
Vincentius Lerinensis?
Virgilius

The Latin Versions of Acts
Known to the Venerable Bede*

THAT Bede knew and used several Latin versions of Acts is abundantly clear from his own statements. Moreover, his special interest in this book of the New Testament is suggested by the fact that he composed two separate commentaries on it and may have proceeded, in part at least, from the comparative neglect of Acts by earlier commentators. Neither Bede's Commentary on Acts nor his Retractation can be dated precisely, but this much can be regarded as certain, that the former is an early work, while the latter was composed towards the end of his life. Thus twenty years or more may have elapsed before Bede, following the example of the *eximius doctor Augustinus,* revised errors that he had committed in the Commentary, defended himself against the attack of critics, and added much new material that was the fruit of his ripest scholarship.[1] In

---

* *Harvard Theological Review,* 30 (1937), 37–50. Reprinted by permission of the Harvard University Press.

[1] The Retractation is not included in the list of his own works given by Bede in H.E., 5, 24, and it is therefore a reasonable assumption that it was written after 731. Plummer (ed. of H.E., I, cxlvii) dates the Commentary between 709 and 716, since it was composed before the Commentary on Samuel (c. 716), but after Acca became bishop of Hexham (709). The date of Acca's elevation to the episcopate seems certain, and Bede in his dedicatory epistle addresses him as bishop.

both expositions we find frequent references to several Latin manuscripts of Acts—*quidam codices* or *quidam Latini codices* —as well as to more than one Greek version, *Graeca exemplaria;* [2] in both, but especially in the Retractation, Bede paid great attention to textual criticism and to a comparison of manuscripts accessible to him. Many, but not all, of Bede's readings have been included in the great edition of the Hieronymic version of Acts by Wordsworth and White. Unfortunately these editors were compelled to rely on the printed editions of Bede's works, and these give an entirely false picture of Bede's text and of his Biblical citations. Giles' shocking edition was made from late manuscripts, and the O.L. readings in Bede given by Wordsworth and White from Sabatier are not trustworthy either. Thus not a few corrections need to be made in the Bede citations given by Wordsworth and White in their critical appendix. In the present article, which does not pretend to be either exhaustive or final in its conclusions, the quotations from Bede's Commentary are based on a complete collation of fifteen manuscripts. All of these were copied before 900, four being not later than 820, and six not later than 850. The citations from the Retractation are based on a collation of seven manuscripts. Two of these were copied in the first quarter of the ninth century, one between 850 and 900, two belong to the beginning of the tenth century, and one each to the twelfth and early thirteenth.[3] One other codex is not without importance, a much abbreviated conflation of the Com-

---

Nevertheless Plummer overlooked that Bede in his comment on Acts 13, 21 makes an error in O. T. chronology which he had already corrected in the De temporibus, published in 703. It is surprising that Bede, even though, as he tells us, he composed the Commentary in a hurry, should have left uncorrected a chronological error for which he had been much criticised. Hence one wonders whether, owing to Acca's urgent request, he utilised notes on Acts that he had made much earlier, without stopping to revise them. In this way a mistake committed a good many years before 709 might have been overlooked, whereas, if the comment on Acts 13, 21 had been composed in 709, Bede must have given the chronology found in De Temp., in the De temporum ratione, and finally also in the Retractation.

[2] Cf. the full list of allusions to manuscripts of the Bible or parts of it given by Plummer, H.E., I, liv, note 7.

[3] Mss. of the Retractation are relatively rare. I know of 29 as against 90 of the Commentary.

mentary and Retractation, described more fully in a note at the end. Thus, with the help of a Bede-text based on the testimony of the oldest manuscripts, an attempt may be made to define more closely than could be done in the past the Latin versions of Acts consulted by Bede. It should be emphasised that in all the Acts quotations from Bede which are given hereafter the testimony of the Bede mss. is unanimous, unless the contrary is specifically stated.[4] There are many places where the mss. authority is divided, but I have intentionally omitted these from consideration here. They will be available for study in my forthcoming edition of Co. and Re., but they cannot safely be used to solve the problem with which we are now concerned.

1. Jerome's Vulgate

The text that Bede used most consistently in both his expositions for the quotations from Acts on which he saw fit to write comments is A(miatinus). This ms. left England c. 716, but there were two other copies of this version in Northumbria after that date, which Bede could use in Re. (H.A., 15; Anon., H.A., 20). His dependence on A is proved by a vast number of cases, but it is not necessary to give more than a selection taken from both Co. and Re.

	Vg.	A and Bede
Acts 2, 28	notas fecisti mihi	notas mihi fecisti A, Re.
5, 32	et nos sumus testes	et nos testes sumus A, Re.
7, 31	ego deus patrum	ego dominus patrum A (alone), Re.
7, 43	Rempham	Remfam A, Co.[5]
7, 51	duri cervice . . . resistitis	dura cervice . . . restitistis A, Re.[6]
8, 33	quoniam tollitur de terra	quoniam tolletur a terra A, Co.[7]

[4] The following abbreviations are used hereafter:

Co. and Re. = Bede's Commentary and Retractation respectively.

Vg. = Jerome's Vulgate as given in the text of Wordsworth and White.

W.–W. = Wordsworth and White.

O.L. = Old Latin.

The usual sigla have been used for Bible mss.

[5] Mss. of Co. are not unanimous, but there is a strong preponderance for Remfam. Aug. lxxvii (c. 815) has both in successive lines, the conflated ms. Aug. cxxxv has Rempham in both cases.

[6] One ms. (early 10th c.) has duri.

[7] tollitur is found in one ms. only.

12, 15	illi autem dicebant	illi vero dicebant A (alone), Co.
13, 2	separate	segregate A, Co., Re.
15, 2	alii ex illis	alii ex aliis A, Co.
16, 12	prima partis Macedoniae	prima parte Macedoniae A, Co.
16, 25	laudabant deum	deum hymnum dicebant A (alone), Co.
21, 27	dum autem septem	dum enim septem A, Co.
22, 28	multa summa	multa pecunia A, Co., Re.
28, 2	pyra	pruna A, Re.[8]
28, 3	aliquantam multitudinem	multitudinem (om. aliquantam) A, Co.

However, Bede's general reliance on an A-text did not prevent him from occasionally expressing open dissent from one of its readings, as can be seen in the following instances. In the explanation of Acts 2, 34 in Co. we read, *dicit dominus domino meo,* in fourteen MSS. Only one (late ninth c.) has *dixit,* and in one *dicit* has been changed to *dixit* by a reviser. In Re. all the MSS. read, *dixit dominus domino meo,* and Bede's comment is as follows:

quida⁓ ⸱odices habent, dicit dominus, *sed Graeca exemplaria et in hoc libro et in psalterio (109, 1)* habent, dixit dominus.

There can be no doubt that, when alluding to *quidam codices,* Bede is thinking in the first instance of A. Again in Co., when discussing Acts 18, 18, Bede remarks, *quidam codices plurali numero habent,* totonderunt caput *et* habebant votum. This corresponds to the A-text; indeed, according to W.-W., *totonderunt* is found nowhere else. Years later in Re. Bede reverted to this much disputed passage. In addition to appealing once more to the authority of Augustine and Jerome,[9] which had caused him to reject the readings of A in Co., he turns directly to the Greek text for support. At Acts 2, 1 six MSS. of Co.—all of them belong to the early group—read with A, *dies pentecosten,* the other nine have *pentecostes.* There can, however, be no doubt that the former was in Bede's text when he composed Co.; for towards the end of his life he was at pains to correct his error. In Re. *dies pentecostes* is found in all MSS., and Bede's

[8] One MS. (late 9th c.) reads pyra; in one (10th c.) a corrector has altered pruna to pyra.

[9] Aug. Ep. 82 (CSEL, 34, 358, 5); Jer. Ep. 112 (CSEL, 55, 378, 11–13).

153

exposition there begins, *male quidam codices habent* pente-
eosten, which, as he proceeds to explain, is ungrammatical, because you cannot have a noun in the accusative depending on
a noun in the nominative. As we have already hinted, this
reliance of Bede on an A-text is of no little value to a modern
editor of his two commentaries. Often, where the MSS. are
divided between an A-reading and one surviving in the 'Alcuinian' recension, it is safe to say that the true reading in Bede is
that which agrees with A. This is further demonstrated by the
frequency with which correctors in some of the *codices* have
changed such readings to conform with the text current in
their time, and some of these emenders are contemporary or
nearly contemporary with the manuscripts themselves.

When we pass to other texts of Vg. that Bede consulted, we
find that we are dealing with probability rather than certainty.
We may first consider six passages where he tacitly deviates
from A.

		Vg.	A	Bede
Acts	1, 6	convenerant	convenerunt	convenerant Co.
	4, 12	in alio aliquo	in aliquo alio	in alio aliquo Co.
	4, 22	factum erat	factum fuerat	factum erat Co.
	9, 24	factae sunt Saulo	factae sunt Saulo	factae sunt Paulo Re.
	10, 30	nudiusquartana	nudiusquartana	nudiusquarta Co., Re.
	26, 2	sim defensurus	sim defensurus	sis defensurus Co.

A glance at the critical apparatus of W.–W. will show that there
is only one text of Acts which is, so to say, a common denomi-
nator, namely T(oletanus). T alone agrees with Bede in every
one of these places. From this we may tentatively conclude that
he had access to a Vg. manuscript which, if extant, would
belong to the third, or Spanish, group in W.–W.'s classification.
At the same time we must not lose sight of the possibility that
Bede in some or all of these passages was following a lost O.L.
version, and we must remember that, as Souter has pointed out,
the British text of Acts apparently used by Pelagius two centuries earlier was related to those used in Africa and Spain.[10]

A third type of text, with which Bede seems undoubtedly

[10] A. Souter, Pelagius' Exposition of thirteen Epistles of St. Paul, I, 169.

to have had some acquaintance, was what we may call an ancestor of the Book of Armagh (D); for the correspondences between D and Bede, if not numerous, are too remarkable to be accidental.

At Acts 2, 23 we read in Co. *adfligentes* (*adfigentes* Vg.) in twelve out of fifteen manuscripts. In four of these, moreover, *adfligentes* has been emended by a corrector to the Vg.-reading. In Re. Bede tacitly rejected the reading of D, for all seven codices of Bede give *adfigentes*. At Acts 10, 33 Re., like D, omits *nos* after *omnes,* while at 13, 21 Co. with D and some others omits *deus.*[11] Re. further agrees with D in Acts 19, 9, *cuiusdam Tyranni,* where Vg. omits *cuiusdam* and a few MSS. read *Tyranni cuiusdam.* At Acts 22, 7 Re. comments: *in Graeco et in hoc loco additum est,* durum est tibi contra stimulum calcitrare. D alone has this addition exactly as quoted by Bede, whereas all the O.L. versions, including e, differ slightly. The interpolation (Acts 22, 28) found in D—*quam facile* (+*est* D¹) *te civem romanum dicis*—is quoted in Co. in almost identical words: *alia editio manifestius quid dixerit insinuat. Dixit tribunus: tam facile te dicis civem romanum esse?* The rest of Bede's citation—*ego enim scio quanto pretio civitatem istam possedi*—has as its only parallel the Greek addition in D gr.[12] The Latin is doubtless Bede's own translation; for, when he composed Re., he felt that further elucidation was necessary and suggested *civilitatem* as a better equivalent for πολιτείαν than *civitatem.* Both in Co. and Re. we find, in place of Vg. *nauclerio* (Acts 27, 11), *nauclero.*[13] The latter reading is also found in T and some other MSS. But, since in Co. Bede comments, *nauclerus Graece, Latine navicularius,* and D* here reads *naviculario* (D^mg *naviclero*), we seem to have additional proof that Bede was familiar with a D-text. Finally, in commenting on the words, *reficiebant nos omnes* (Acts 28, 2), Bede remarks,

---

[11] W.–W. are wrong in saying that the Bede-text has *deus.*

[12] All the Bede MSS. read civitatem, not civilitatem as given by W.–W. and, following them, J. H. Ropes, The text of Acts 215, note. Both editors also omit te from Bede's text.

[13] Only one MS. of Co. gives *nauclerio.* All the MSS. of Re. have *nauclero,* save one with the ungrammatical *nauclerus.*

in Graeco scriptum est, recipiebant nos omnes. Now *recipiebant* is found in D alone; at the same time it is possible that our author is here independently translating the Greek προσελάβοντο. We have already, in discussing Bede's occasional criticisms of A, alluded to his correction of *Pentecosten* to *Pentecostes* in Acts 2, 1. When he uses the plural, *male quidam codices habent,* he clearly has more than one codex in mind; and we may hazard the guess that he is thinking also of the D-text, which with A is one of the few that preserve this reading. The presence in Northumbria of an 'Irish' text of Acts in Bede's time is not surprising in view of the close connection between that area and Celtic Christianity. It is interesting to note also that the text of D in the Pauline Epistles has substantial affinities with the Biblical text familiar to Pelagius.[14]

Two other extant Vg.-texts of Acts are connected with Britain in the late seventh or eighth century. The codex F(uldensis), which passed into the possession of Boniface, may have been in Northern England when Bede was at Jarrow, but the evidence is not quite conclusive.[15] The manuscript of Acts, O (Oxford, Bodleian, Selden Supra 30), was written in England, 'probably in a Kentish centre,' in the first half of the eighth century.[16] Either O, or, if it was not written until after Bede's death, the text from which it was copied, might thus have been known to him. It has, however, been impossible to find a clear trace of either F or O in Bede's two commentaries.

[14] Cf. Souter, *op. cit.,* I, 137.

[15] Ropes, *op. cit.,* cxxix, says, without qualification, that F 'lay in Northumbria in the late years of the seventh and early years of the eighth century,' but what is his authority for so positive a statement? Even J. Chapman, whom he seems to be following, is not so categorical. Chapman (Early History of the Vulgate Gospels 157 and 158) argues that Boniface took the codex with him from England and that he obtained it from Jarrow or Wearmouth. But the evidence that he offers, though of some weight, still leaves the matter in doubt, and this Chapman himself seems to have felt. Later in the same book (188) he more cautiously remarks: 'The Codex Fuldensis and the Codex Laudianus of Acts are possibly two of the volumes brought to Northumbria by St. Benet Biscop, and they still survive.' H. Leclercq (Dictionnaire d'archéologie chrétienne et de liturgie, s.v. Fulda) is more non-committal in sketching the wanderings of this famous manuscript, though he admits that the Insular glosses in it may have been written by Boniface himself.

[16] E. A. Lowe, Codices Latini Antiquiores, II, no. 257.

Latin Versions of Acts in Bede

2. Old Latin Versions

We are on safer ground when we turn to the O.L. text most consistently used by Bede. The Latin version (e) in Laudianus gr. 35 (E) was familiar to Bede when he was still a young man, for it is quoted occasionally in Co. Then in Re., in which Bede paid far more attention to textual criticism and to the study of the Greek original, e is the O.L. text that he reproduces in the great majority of instances where he appeals to a second version. Indeed the occasions on which he transcribes e are so numerous that, as in the case of the A readings, we must content ourselves with a few typical examples. We may begin with some from Co.:

Acts 9, 1   spirans minarum Bede, e (aspirans minarum Vg.).

    10, 38   Bede comments: *alia editio dicit:* sicut unxit eum deus (= e alone).

    14, 2   Bede comments: *quod in Graeco sequitur,* deus autem pacem fecit (= e), *quidam Latini codices minus habent.* All the MSS. of Vg. omit this addition, except D, which reproduces it in different words.

    14, 6   Bede comments: *sequitur in Graeco,* et commota est omnis multitudo in doctrina eorum (= e). Paulus autem et Barnabas morabantur in Lystris (= e). *Et hi quoque versiculi in quibusdam nostris codicibus non habentur.* All the Vg. MSS. known to Bede omit these additions.

    18, 23   Bede comments: *alia translatio habet,* profuit multum credentibus per gratiam (= e).

    24, 6–8   Bede comments: *in hoc loco quidam nostri codices aliquot versus habent qui in Graeco ita leguntur,* quem adprehendimus et secundum nostram legem voluimus iudicare. Transiens autem Lysias tribunus cum multa vi de manibus nostris eduxit, iubens accusatores eius venire ante te, quo possis ipse iudicans de omnibus istis cognoscere, *et cetera* (= e).[17] W.–W. omit verse 7, which is found, however, in a good many

[17] Six MSS. read 'versus minus habent,' but this is clearly a later correction, because Bede's words are a little ambiguous. It seems likely that he is thinking in part of A and the corrector of A who adds verse 7. Three MSS. representing one group have *diiudicans.*

Vg. MSS., including A¹ and D; but it is only with e
that Bede's wording corresponds exactly.

Out of a great number of e quotations in Re. it will suffice to
give four:

Acts 5, 38   Bede comments: *in Graeco plus habet,* non coinqui-
nantes manus vestras (= e).

7, 31   Bede comments: *in Graeco ita scriptum est;* facta est
vox de caelo dicens ad eum: ego sum deus patrum
tuorum, solve calciamenta de pedibus tuis. Locus
enim in quo stas, terra sancta est. This corresponds
to e save for the plural, calciamenta (calciamentum
e).[18]

10, 45   Here Bede tacitly abandons Vg. and cites the second
part of the verse on which he is going to comment in
the form in which it appears in e alone: et obsti-
puerunt ex circumcisione fideles qui venerant cum
Petro, quia et in gentibus donum sancti spiritus effu-
sum est (quia et in nationes gratia spiritus sancti ef-
fusa est Vg. W.–W. ignore Bede here).[19]

20, 4   Bede comments: *plus autem habet in Graeco,* comitatus
est autem cum eo usque Asiam (= e).[20]

There can be no doubt that e was not the only O.L. version
known to our author. It is less easy to determine the exact character of the other version or versions that he may have consulted. Nevertheless the available evidence, set out below, is
not without significance.

Acts 1, 12   reversi sunt Hierusalem   Co. with G d gig p Aug.
                (Hierosolymam Vg.)

1, 15   om. simul   Co. with gig p* Aug.

26, 10   Bede comments: *alia editio dicit,* occidendique (*var.
lect.* occidendisque) eis detuli sententiam. This is peculiar to Bede.

---

[18] Three MSS. omit sum; two give dominus for deus. All read *patrum* (*fratrum*
W.–W. wrongly).

[19] One MS. (12th c.) has *spiritus sancti.*

[20] W.–W. attribute to Bede the reading usque ad Asiam, but this is found in
only one MS. (10th c.) of the seven.

27, 15–16   Bede comments: *haec alia translatio manifestius edidit,*
et arrepta navi, cum non possent occurrere vento,
commodata navi flatibus colligere vela coeperunt.
Tunc transcurrimus insulam quae dicitur Caude (*var.
lect.* Caudi); quam occupare non potuerunt, sed
scapha missa adiuvare coeperunt navem praecingen-
tes eam. Trahebant autem et anchoras, timentes ne
occurrerent in Syrtes.[21]

We have quoted the passage in full, as it raises a question of
some difficulty. The words, *et arrepta* to *possent,* are found
also in gig; for the rest the wording is peculiar to Bede, who
after some six lines of explanation goes on to quote part of
Acts 16–17 in the Vg. text and then comments on that. W.–W.,
following Sabatier, treat the whole passage as an exact rendering of the interpolated passage in Acts, but it is perhaps more
likely that Bede, from *quam occupare* to the end, is para-
phrasing the Greek text rather than translating it.[22] He then
goes on to comment on the words, *summisso vase sic ferebantur,*
in the Vg. rendering: *alia translatio sic ponit,* timentesque
ne in Syrtim (var. lect. Syrtem) exciderent laxantes antennam
ita ferebantur. Again the rendering is peculiar to Bede. As he
would hardly, being a modest man, allude to his own translation
as *alia translatio,* we presumably have here a fragment from an
O.L. text.

We may now pass to the more numerous O.L. readings, not
taken from e, that occur in Re.

Acts 1, 15   Bede comments: *unde et in quibusdam codicibus ita
interpretatum invenimus,* quia Iohannes quidem
tinxit aqua, vos autem tinguemini in spiritu sancto.
tinxit Re. only   tinguemini Re. e p*

---

[21] The app. crit. of W.–W. is wrong in several particulars, since Sabatier clearly
relied on late MSS. of Bede or an edition based on such. It is particularly to be
noticed that Bede read Caude, not Claude, and thus supports the better reading.
Souter, Novum Testamentum Graece, ad. loc., should be corrected accordingly.

[22] As for the words, *colligere vela coeperunt,* they correspond to the Greek
συστείλαντες τὰ ἱστία. Of this Ropes (*op. cit.*, 243, 15) says: 'Cassiodorus and Bede,
but no other Latin witnesses, clearly refer to that part of the "Western" text
found in 614, (= Milan, Bibl. Ambros. E 97 sup.).

2, 2   de caelo sonitus
       Vg. and Co. sonus   Sonitus Re. and Vigilius [23]

3, 20 Bede comments: *in quadam translatione hunc versum
       ita propter explanationem sensus positum invenimus,*
       ut, cum venerint tempora refrigerii, veniant et vobis
       a facie domini.
       Re. only. Bede's own explanation of the Greek
       follows.

4, 1   Bede in his exposition remarks: *Latine in quibusdam
       codicibus* praepositum templi, *in aliis rectius* prae-
       torem templi *scriptum invenimus.*
       praepositum e   praetorem h

4, 13 Bede explains: idiotae *autem proprie* inperiti *vocantur.*
       inperiti gig p

5, 39 Bede remarks: *et hic in Graeco plus habet,* neque vos
       neque principes vestri.
       principes D dem gig

8, 1   remanserunt in Hierusalem. This O.L. addition is
       found in Augustine and several O.L. versions (but
       not in e), but only t preserves it in the exact form
       in which it is quoted in Re.

13, 8 Bede comments: *et hic quoque in Graeco habetur plus,*
       quoniam libenter audiebat eos.
       audiebat eos Re. d   eorum audiebat e (Correct
       W.–W. here)

21, 39 Bede explains: *pro* municipe *quidam codices* civem *ha-
       bent.*
       civem d e

22, 17 Bede remarks: *quidam codices habent* mentis excessum,
       alii pavorem, *alii* alienationem. This is a remarkable
       passage, as it implies that our author had consulted
       many MSS.; yet none of these variants is known in this
       verse. In Acts 10, 10, however, where Vg. has mentis
       excessus, p* gives mentis alienatio and e mentis pa-
       bor. This would seem to suggest that Bede in his
       exposition of 22, 17 was thinking of the earlier verse
       and of the variants that he had there observed with-
       out including them in his comment on 10, 10.

[23] I know of no evidence to show that Bede knew Vigilius, De trinitate.

27, 13 existimantes propositum
existimantes Re. s aestimantes Vg.

We may perhaps draw two conclusions legitimately from the above evidence. First, it is certain that, though e was the O.L. text on which he chiefly relied, Bede was acquainted with another that differed substantially from any now extant. Second, it is a notable fact that no less than five instances of correspondence between Bede and p occur; and p in the passages where it agrees with Bede's quotations is an O.L. translation.[24] It thus seems probable that, besides e, Bede had recourse to two other examples of the *Vetus Latina,* one of which has quite disappeared, while the other had strong affinities with certain existing versions; and this plurality of mss. accords with and explains his recurring use of the plural, *codices quidam.* The consonances with p, moreover, and that with t suggest that the third version of the O.L. was a Spanish text or an African text revised in Spain.[25]

In one respect Bede's language is not wholly free from ambiguity; for the frequent use of phrases like, *sequitur in Graeco, in Graeco scriptum est,* might lead one to assume that he is himself translating directly from a Greek text. Actually, in the vast majority of cases, the translation that is supplied corresponds exactly to e. Thus, while Bede, especially when he composed Re., undoubtedly studied the Greek original, he mostly reproduced the Latin version (e) preserved in the same manuscript (E gr.) to which he usually turned for the Greek text of Acts. But the two, as is well known to New Testament scholars, by no means correspond exactly, a fact of which Bede was himself aware, as certain passages quoted below will show. At all events, on the rare occasions when he introduces a translation unknown in any extant ms. of O.L. with a specific reference to the Greek text, a doubt might arise whether the Latin equivalent is his own or taken from a lost O.L. version. The

---

[24] Cf. the excellent description of p in Ropes, *op. cit.,* cviii–cix.

[25] One passage seemed too doubtful to include in the text above. In commenting on Acts 9, 26 in Co., Bede cites 26, 20 in the following form: *in omni regione* (so A: *omnem regionem* Vg.) *et gentibus praedicabam (adnuntiabam* Vg.). W.–W. quote no ms. authority for *praedicabam,* but *praedicavi* is the reading of h. However, it is safest to assume that Bede was here quoting from memory.

few examples that can be quoted leave no doubt that in each case Bede is himself responsible for the variant.

Acts 1, 13 Re.—*nam et in Graeco ita positus est ordo verborum,* et cum introissent in cenaculum ascenderunt ubi erant manentes Petrus et Iohannes, etc. Since Bede goes on to give the order of the disciples' names as found in the Greek, it is probable that manentes (habitantes e) is his own, more accurate, rendering of καταμένοντες·

2, 24 Re.—*verum, si graecam inspexerimus auctoritatem ubi scriptum est,* quem deus suscitavit, solvens per ipsum dolores mortis iuxta quod non erat possibile teneri illum ab eo, etc.

(dolores inferni: propter quod: detineri e)

Bede retains the translation of e in the main, but makes some minor changes, notably mortis to correspond with θανάτου in E gr.

5, 24 Re.—ut audierunt autem verba haec sacerdotes et magistratus templi et principes sacerdotum mirabantur et ambigebant de his quidnam vult esse hoc. In the main this reproduces the text of e, but the first three words are given as in A, while mirabantur et ambigebant de his (mirari coeperunt et confundebantur mente de eis e) is Bede's terser and neater rendering of ἐθαύμαζον καὶ διηπόρουν in E gr.

8, 4 Re.—*pro* dispersis *in Graeco* disseminatos *habet, id est,* διασπαρέντες. This is clearly Bede's own equivalent.

8, 37 Co. Bede quotes the additional verse, omitted from the text of W.–W., thus: dixit autem ei Philippus: si credis ex toto corde tuo, salvus eris. Respondens autem dixit: credo in Christum filium dei. This is the rendering of e save that Bede has added 'tuo' from E gr.[26]

18, 28 Re.—*in Graeco ita scriptum est,* publice et per domos ostendens (in domo e). Bede is dissatisfied with e's rendering of κατ' οἶκον and substitutes his own equivalent for the Greek.

[26] Six MSS. add 'eunuchus' after *respondens autem,* the other nine and Aug. cxxxv rightly omit it. It is clearly a gloss that crept in later to explain the unexpressed subject of *dixit.*

Latin Versions of Acts in Bede

21, 25   Re. Bede reproduces e exactly save that—correct Latinist that he is—he alters 'crediderunt homines' to 'crediderunt hominibus.'

To sum up: our investigation of Bede's quotations from
Acts shows that Bede relied primarily on an A-text of Vg. and
on the O.L. version, e. In addition we have tried to show—with
what success the reader must judge for himself—that he at
various times consulted not less than two other MSS. of Jerome's
translation and two of the *Vetus Latina* which differed substantially from e. His allusions to Greek manuscripts in the
plural prove that E gr. was not the only text of the original
that he knew, and we have recorded above two undoubted
translations of phrases not found in E gr.[27] But the data available are insufficient to define more precisely the character of
this second Greek manuscript of Acts.

Appendix

MS. KARLSRUHE, AUGIENSIS CXXXV

Among the Bede MSS. from Reichenau that now repose in
the Badische Landesbibliothek at Karlsruhe is one (Augiensis
cxxxv) that, according to the printed catalogue, contains Bede's
Commentary on Acts on ff. 1ᵛ to 31ᵛ. The late A. Holder in his
masterly catalogue of the Augienses rarely made mistakes, but
in this instance he failed to note the true character of the manuscript that he was describing. It is in fact a conflation of Co. and
Re. with large sections omitted from both.[28] The MS. was
written in the early part of the tenth century, but I have so far
found no clue to the authorship of this compilation. Where
Bede has commented on the same passage of Acts in both his
treatises the abbreviator usually quotes from Re. first. He
betrays a certain fondness for *Graeca*, while rather ignoring the
more difficult theological passages. Aug. cxxxv is of importance

---

[27] Cf. p. 155 above for a parallel with *Codex Bezae* (D gr.), and for another see
note 22.

[28] I know of three other conflations of Co. with Re., namely, Dijon 153 (s. xii,
from Cîteaux), Oxford, Bodl. Laud. Misc. 268 (s. xiv) and Laud. Misc. 312 (s. x
ex.). In each case the printed catalogue describes the MS. as Bede's Commentary
on Acts. These three conflations are independent of one another, but I have not
enough data at my disposal to say whether any of them is a copy of Aug. cxxxv.

solely for one reason—it provides a link with a lost Insular manuscript of Bede's two commentaries, which may have been written in the eighth century and which in any case cannot be later than c. 800. It is so closely related to Augiensis lxxvii, a codex copied very early in the ninth century and containing both Co. and Re., with which it shares a number of readings found in none of the other MSS., that one's first impulse is to assume that Aug. lxxvii is the manuscript used by the abbreviator of Aug. cxxxv. This, however, is impossible for two reasons. First, the later manuscript contains a number of readings not found in the earlier; and, second, in spite of its relatively late date, Aug. cxxxv preserves some Insular traits that are not found in Aug. lxxvii and which cannot therefore have been copied from it. These traces of an Insular exemplar are: eleven cases of the Insular sign for *autem,* one example of ꝫ for eius, and confusion on several occasions of *post* and *per,* that is to say, the abbreviator misread p with a tail (= Insular *per*) as *post.* We must thus assume that Aug. lxxvii and Aug. cxxxv go back to a common ancestor written in Insular script. The probable relationship may be expressed thus:

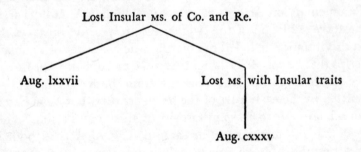

Lost Insular MS. of Co. and Re.

Aug. lxxvii   Lost MS. with Insular traits

Aug. cxxxv

⚓ 9 ⚓

Was Bede the Author
of a Penitential? *

THE recent publication of the more important medieval handbooks of penance in an English version raises afresh the often
disputed question, whether the Venerable Bede was the author
or compiler of a penitential.[1] What may be called the positive
evidence that he did so is slight. In, or soon after, 906 Regino
of Prüm composed his treatise, De synodalibus causis et disci-
plinis ecclesiasticis, in which he refers by name to the penitentials of Bishop Theodore and of the Venerable Bede. In the
second place, there still survive several nearly related penitentials which are ascribed to Bede in the extant manuscripts.[2]
However, this ascription to Bede carries little weight, if un-
supported by other evidence. For several centuries after his
death his authority as a theologian ranked next to that of the
four Latin doctors and the list of works going under his name,

* Harvard Theological Review, 31 (1938), 263–274. Reprinted by permission
of the Harvard University Press.

[1] John T. McNeill and Helena M. Gamer, Medieval Handbooks of Penance
(Records of Civilization, No. xxix; Columbia University Press, 1938). The penitential here discussed will be found on pp. 217–233.

[2] Miss Gamer, who is responsible for an excellent discussion of the MSS in the
Introduction, gives a complete list of them in Appendix V. For the MSS containing various penitentials going under Bede's name see pp. 435–436.

but not by him, is long. Nor is Regino's testimony unimpeachable, for his acquaintance with Bede's writings was not extensive. He does not seem to have used the theological works when composing the De synodalibus causis; and, though he did, when compiling his Chronica, make use of the chronicle inserted by Bede in the De temporum ratione, he did not consult the Ecclesiastical History. Had he been familiar with that basic work on British history, he would assuredly have drawn on it, as so many others did. He would also have found in 5, 24 Bede's own list of his writings. Thus we may suspect that Regino attributed a penitential to Bede merely on the strength of a rubric in a manuscript, and we shall do well to query the accuracy of his statement, unless corroborated by other proofs.

Of the extant penitentials bearing Bede's name the one that has most claim to be considered his was published nearly forty years ago by Dom Bruno Albers.[3] Many of Albers' arguments and assumptions were, however, subjected to severe criticism by W. von Hörmann, and these, as well as the contributions of other scholars to the controversy, have been conveniently summarized by Mr. McNeill.[4] Here it is only necessary to touch on one of the points raised by Albers. The one argument that he could bring forward to sustain his view that the penitential in MS Barberinianus lat. 477 (s. x) was of early date was based on the occurrence at the end of eight canons from the Lateran Council held in 721 and on a reference to a decretal of Gregory II—'item ex decreto pape gregorii iunioris qui nunc romanam catholicam regit matrem ecclesiam.' But since these decretals and the allusion to Gregory II in slightly different wording also occur in the so-called Poenitentiale Martenianum, as von Hörmann first pointed out, it is by no means certain that they belonged originally to the penitential ascribed to Bede, for they might have been added later from another document. Moreover, no one, so far as I am aware, has questioned the latinity of the phrase quoted above; yet it should arouse the suspicions of any one familiar with Bede's language. In the Ec-

---

[3] Archiv für katholisches Kirchenrecht 81 (1901), pp. 393–420.
[4] McNeill, *op. cit.*, pp. 217–221.

clesiastical History Bede refers some eighteen times to the Roman Church but never in these terms. *Romana ecclesia, sancta romana et apostolica ecclesia, sedes romanae et apostolicae ecclesiae, sancta romana ecclesia, romana et apostolica sedes,* these are the turns of phrase that he employs, and once (E. H. 3, 29) we read, *quia romana esset catholica et apostolica ecclesia.* Similarly, when commenting in the Retractatio on Acts 19, 12, he alludes to Gregory II, *qui nunc est apostolicae sedis antistes.* In the De temporum ratione he refers to *sancta romana et apostolica ecclesia* and in the chronicle calls Gregory I *romanae ecclesiae pontifex,*[5] although most of the many mentions in the chronicle of the Roman Church and its bishop are copied by Bede directly from his sources. In the following entry the third sentence is taken verbally from the Liber Pontificalis:[6]

Focas an. VIII.

Huius secundo anno indictione VIII Gregorius papa migravit ad dominum.

Hic, rogante papa Bonifatio, statuit sedem romanae et apostolicae ecclesiae caput esse omnium ecclesiarum, quia ecclesia constantinopolitana primam se omnium ecclesiarum scribebat.

In short, I know of no place in Bede's genuine works where he calls the Roman Church *mater ecclesia,* and one may suspect that, in spite of his unquestioned orthodoxy, his historical sense would have led him to reserve the phrase for the Church of Jerusalem or possibly the Church of Antioch.

Though allowing full emphasis to the criticisms of von Hörmann, Mr. McNeill is still disposed to regard Bede as the author of the Albers penitential, for he remarks:[7]

If we are forced to abandon Albers' argument concerning the date of this work, there still appears no reason to deny the possibility of its early date or even of Bede's authorship of the major part of it. Its close resemblance to the work reputed to be Egbert's and to the Double Penitential, may in fact be probably best accounted for by assuming it to be Bede's. If we consider the close personal relations between Bede and Egbert we need not be averse

[5] PL 90, 494B; MGH: Chron. Min. III, para. 530.
[6] Chron. Min. III, pp. 309–310.   [7] McNeill, *op. cit.,* p. 219.

to the supposition that after Bede's death Egbert utilized penitential materials left by him and gave circulation to them, making such alterations as he chose, in a document which came to be regarded as his own. Bede visited Egbert in 733, about the time of the inception of the latter's work as archbishop. It is not absurd to conjecture that they conferred over the practical aspects of penance with some such roughly-drawn document before them as our present penitential.

Subsequently he observes that the omission of the penitential from the list in E. H. 5, 24 is not conclusive proof that Bede never wrote one, as other genuine works are absent from that list. Moreover, while necessarily admitting the stylistic crudity of the penitential, he does not regard this as decisive against Bede's authorship. 'The most that can be said on this point is that we should hardly have expected the greatest writer of his age to write one of the inferior books of the penitential series.' The unprejudiced reader will feel that Mr. McNeill earnestly desires to uphold the accuracy of Regino and the MSS-headings, but feels extremely uncomfortable in the process!

Let us now turn to the reasons for believing that the Albers document is certainly not by Bede and, indeed, that none of the penitentials bearing his name are from his pen. All of them, whatever the interrelation of their subject matter, have this in common, that they are composed in a Latin that is clumsy, not to say barbarous, and not infrequently ungrammatical. Any one familiar with Bede's style in his theological commentaries will find it impossible to believe that, even in a 'roughly-drawn document' or first draft, he would have committed the solecisms and grammatical monstrosities found in the penitentials; [8] and it is not irrelevant to add that their crudity of expression disappears entirely, when they are translated.[9] Nor is it permissible to blame the medieval scribes. The monks who copied the

[8] I must also confess to feeling great scepticism that Bede would have used *creatura* (McNeill, *op. cit.*, sec. XV, 1), *caritas* (ib. VI, 15), and *causa* (ib. X, 4) in the senses that they bear in the penitential.

[9] Mr. McNeill's translation reads smoothly but it is not entirely free from omissions or errors. On p. 221, line 6, *personam* after 'status,' and on p. 227, last line but one in para. 15, *et sancti Martini* after 'Apostles,' have been left untranslated. On p. 221, line 12, 'many' should be 'most' (*plurimis*) and in line 22, 'even as they judge' must be 'in order that they may judge' (*quomodo iudicent*). On p. 222,

Bede, Author of a Penitential?

Namur manuscript of the Ecclesiastical History or the Orléans manuscript of the Commentary on Acts were very careless. But their carelessness consisted of misspellings, frequently the result of unfamiliarity with the script of their exemplar, or of word-omissions; it did not extend to mangling their author's syntax. Reflection suggests that it was not the scholars of the Church but the practical administrators, whose organizing talents were superior to their literary gifts, who either produced or were the reputed authors of the earlier penitentials. It is surely significant that most of these bear the names of bishops and of abbots —Adamnan, perhaps Cummean, Theodore, Columban, Egbert, Halitgar, even Burchard. However eminent their merits and achievements in other fields, the only one of these men to attain to some note in the world of letters was Adamnan.

Again, it is of course perfectly true that Bede visited Egbert at York in 733 and it may be that amongst other topics the two

---

four lines from the bottom, 'his' should surely be 'His.' In the singularly ill-constructed Latin sentence, *qui volueritis sacerdotalem auctoritatem accipere, inprimitus propter deum cogitet et preparet arma eius,* I take *eius* to refer to God. The arms of God, when dealing with mankind through His ministers, are the psalter, lectionary, and so on. If my interpretation is correct, then Mr. McNeill's suggestion that there might be a reference to works compiled by Bede himself falls to the ground. Nor should any argument be based on the occurrence of the penitential in a tenth century MS which also contains Bede's De natura rerum and De temporibus. For, as Mr. Charles W. Jones kindly informs me, the text of De temporibus in the Barberinianus is very inferior and removed by many stages from the archetype. If, however, Mr. McNeill prefers to adhere to his rendering of *arma eius,* well and good. But in that case I would remark that he cannot 'have it both ways.' The compiler of the penitential was doubtless perfectly capable of confusing the correct uses of *suus* and *eius,* but Bede most certainly was not. On page 227, last line but one of para. 15, 'of a saint' should be 'of the saint' (*illius sancti*); the patron saint of a given geographical area appears to be meant. Even so in the *deprecatio* or *oratio super diptycha* of the Gallican Mass, whose influence extended also to the Irish, after an invocation of the Virgin, apostles, and martyrs, local saints were remembered. See L. Duchesne, Origines du culte chrétien (ed. 5), pp. 220 ff. and Reeves on III, 12 of Adamnan's Life of Columba. On p. 231, fourth line from the bottom, 'powerful men' quite fails to convey to an English reader the meaning in this particular context of *potentes.* It should be rendered 'men of substance.' At the foot of the same page 'he shall set free [some] of his slaves and redeem freemen and captives' is a bad mistranslation for 'he shall let some of his slaves go free and redeem captives.' You cannot (save in a spiritual sense) redeem free men and the Latin is clear enough: *et de mancipiis dimittas (-at) liberos et captivos redimat. Liberos* is used predicatively after *dimittat.* On page 218 of the Introductory remarks De natura temporum should of course read De natura rerum.

169

men conversed about questions of Church discipline. But if so, is it not, to say the least, very surprising that in the letter which Bede shortly before his death addressed to Egbert there is not the slightest reference either to penitentials in general or to any penitential by Bede in particular? Bede in his epistle gives sound advice to his former pupil who had recently been elevated to the archbishopric of York.[10] Besides enlarging on the multiple functions of a bishop, he has much to say about prelates who neglect their responsibilities and who are guilty of avarice, and also about fraudulent monasteries and the vices and abuses current in them. The duties of the clergy towards the laity also receive some mention. Surely in this lengthy communication, if anywhere, we should have expected some allusion to penitential literature, especially if Bede had composed a penitential, or if penance had formed a topic of conversation between Egbert and Bede only a year before.

The truth is that, if Bede really was interested in the 'practical aspects of penance,' he successfully concealed the fact in his genuine works. The word, *paenitentia,* and its cognates are not specially rare in his writings, but the predominant meaning of *paenitentia* is 'repentance' rather than 'penance.' Expressed in another way, it may be said that Bede's interest is in the inner processes of the human heart, in the relation between man and his Creator, and in man's salvation through Christ, rather than in the methods of ecclesiastical discipline. Thus, in commenting on Acts 19, 4, he observes that John's baptism teaches *paenitentiam,* but only Christ's baptism can effect remission of sins. Or again, the widows in Acts 9, 39 are allegorically interpreted thus:

viduae sunt piae cogitationes animae paenitentis, quae sensus pristini vigorem, quasi viri regimen, ad tempus omiserant, quae pro anima delinquente necesse est suppliciter exorent.

Characteristic of the trend of Bede's thought are his remarks on the duties of those vowed to religion, with their emphasis on the fruits of the Spirit: [11]

[10] The best text of the Epistle to Egbert is in Plummer's edition of the Ecclesiastical History, I, pp. 405–423. If the last sentence in the letter is genuine, it is dated Nov. 5, 734.

[11] PL 91, 751 B–C.

abstineant ab otiosis eloquiis, ira, rixa, detractione, habitu impudico, comessationibus, potationibus, contentione, et aemulatione; et e contrario vigiliis sanctis, orationibus, lectionibus divinis, et psalmis, doctrinae et eleemosynis, ceterisque Spiritus fructibus operam impendant, ut qui futurae statum vitae in professione tenent in qua non nubent, neque nubentur, sed sicut angeli dei in coelo.

Even in the following passage the primary emphasis is on the awakening of conscience: [12]

necesse est ut ad conscientiam nostram reversi sollerter opera nostra simul et cogitationes exploremus, et quidquid nos peccasse deprehendimus, digna castigatione purgemus; quidquid de his quae nos recte fecisse credebamus, vitio in nobis elationis perisse comperimus, et hoc humili satisfactione castigemus. Haec enim nobis saepius fit causa flagellorum. Ceterum innocentes et iustos ob augmenta praemiorum flagellari, perfectorum est et donum speciale virorum. Verberibus autem temporalibus ad aeterna tormenta compelli, impaenitentium est poena reproborum.

When we consider how Bede elsewhere employs the word, *flagella*, in a metaphorical sense, it is at least open to question whether the *flagella* and *verbera* in the passage just quoted are to be taken in a literal sense.[13]

Those who have maintained that Bede may have composed a penitential have always argued that Bede's own silence in E. H. 5, 24 is not a definite proof to the contrary, since the genuine works of Bede do not all appear in that list. But what are the facts? Only two works are in question, the De locis sanctis and the Retractatio. The former is not mentioned because Bede had already told the reader about it in an earlier chapter (E. H. 5, 17), after citing considerable extracts from Adamnan's book on which it was based. As for the Retractatio, it has been generally assumed that this work was not composed until after 731, because Bede does not refer to it. In another place I hope to have demonstrated conclusively that the Retractatio is named by Bede, in short, that when he wrote in

[12] *Ibid.*, 92, 148 D–149 A.
[13] The *flagella supernae districtionis* that punished Eadbald (E. H. 2, 5) were madness and an unclean spirit.

E. H. 5, 24, *in actus apostolorum libros II*, he meant the Commentary on Acts and the Retractatio.[14] Thus, if all of Bede's writings, apart from the Epistle to Egbert, were indeed recorded by himself, the above argument regarding the possible composition of an unnamed penitential loses most of its force.

The strongest proof, however, that the Albers document is not by Bede, and that, so far from being compiled in England, it was probably put together on the Continent, is to be found in the penitential itself. No bishop in Western Europe during the earliest period of the Middle Ages devoted himself more wholeheartedly to the duties of his office than Caesarius of Arles. His sermons, of which an authoritative text has recently become available for the first time,[15] abound in references to the vices and superstitions of his age and in suggestions for disciplinary action against them by the Church. It was therefore to be expected that his utterances would continue to be influential after his time, at least on the Continent of Western Europe, and that this was actually the case is proved by reminiscences in seventh and eighth century writers and perhaps in penitentials of continental origin.[16] Now in the Albers document we find one passage which is certainly derived directly from a sermon by Caesarius and another which is probably from the same author. The former occurs in section X of the penitential, dealing with divination and augury, and in Sermo XIII of Caesarius.

[14] The various pieces of evidence showing that the second book of a commentary on Acts and the Retractatio are one and the same work will be set out in full in my forthcoming edition, to be published by the Mediaeval Academy of America.

[15] Dom G. Morin, Sancti Caesarii episcopi Arelatensis opera I: Sermones seu admonitiones (Maredsous, 1937). The reader will find reviews of this work by Alexander Souter in Journ. Theol. Stud. 38 (1937), 432–434 and by the present writer in Speculum 13 (1938), 355–356.

[16] Cf. McNeill, *op. cit.*, p. 277, note 10, referring to a passage in the so-called Burgundian Penitential and quoting from Caesarius, Serm. CXCII (pp. 738–741, ed. Morin). A closer parallel to the passage in the penitential will be found in Serm. CXCIII (p. 743, 11–13) with its mention of *cervulum sive anniculam* and in Serm. XIII (p. 66, 11), *de annicula vel cervulo* (variant readings: *annecula, anicula, agniculis*). One wonders whether *vecola* in the penitential and *veculas* (with variants *vegulas* and *veiculas*) in Pirmin's Scarapsus could possibly be corruptions of Caesarius' *annicula, anniculas*. The supposed reminiscence of Caesarius in the Penitential of Cummean given by McNeill on p. 99, note 5 comes from a homily which Morin rejects as not Caesarian (Morin, *op. cit.*, p. 930).

Albers, *op. cit.*, p. 411

Nolite exercere *quando luna obscuratur,* ut *clamoribus suis ac maleficiis sacrilego usu se defensare posse confidunt, caraios* cocriocos et *divinos praecantatores, filacteria etiam diabolica vel herbas vel sucinos suis vel sibi impendere* vel *V feria in honore Iovis* vel Kal. Ianor. secundum paganam causam honorare, si clerici V annos, laici III vel V annos paeniteat.

Caesarius, ed. Morin, p. 66, 13–22

Et si, *quando luna obscuratur,* adhuc aliquos clamore cognoscitis, et ipsos admonete, denuntiantes eis quod grave sibi peccatum faciunt, quando lunam, quae deo iubente certis temporibus obscuratur, *clamoribus suis ac maleficiis sacrilego ausu se defensare posse confidunt.* Et si adhuc videtis aliquos aut ad fontes aut ad arbores vota reddere, et, sicut iam dictum est, *caraios* etiam *et divinos praecantatores* inquirere, *fylacteria etiam diabolica,* characteres aut *herbas vel sucinos sibi aut suis adpendere* durissime increpantes dicite, etc.

Ibid., 66, 27–8

Isti enim infelices et miseri, qui *in honore Iovis quinta feria opera non faciunt,* etc.

[cf. Sermo XIX (p. 86, 28–9): nullus in ˙honorem Iovis quinta feria observare praesumat, ne aliquid operis faciat.]

As Morin points out, this particular sermon was widely read and quoted after Caesarius' time, and, it may be added, so were several other sermons in which the bishop of Arles castigated the rustic paganism of his age. Thus indebtedness to Caesarius is to be clearly traced in the sermons of Eligius, bishop of Noyon, and in the Scarapsus of Pirmin, founder of Reichenau.[17] But the correspondence between Pirmin's adaptation or Eligius' echoes of Caesarius and the penitential is not exact, whereas, as the passages italicized above show, the penitential copies Caesarius exactly in certain phrases.[18] Thus the possibility that the

[17] The parallel passages between Caesarius, Eligius, and Pirmin have been set out and discussed by G. Jecker in his monograph, Die Heimat des Hl. Pirmin (Beiträge zur Geschichte des alten Mönchtums und des Benediktinerordens, Heft 13 [Münster i. W., 1927]), pp. 131–154.

[18] That Caesarius' *ausu* has been corrupted to the easier, but far less graphic, *usu* is not surprising. For *cocriocos* McNeill adopts Ducange's emendation *cu-*

paragraph in the penitential was only derived mediately from Caesarius, by way of Pirmin or Eligius, is ruled out. The second passage occurs in section V of the penitential, which is concerned with the capital sins, and in Sermo CLXXIX of Caesarius.

Albers, *op. cit.*, pp. 405–406
Nunc igitur capitalia crimina secundum canones explicabo. Prima *superbia, invidia,* fornicatio, inanis gloria, *ira longo tempore,* tristicia[m] seculi, avaricia, ventris ingluvies et Agustinus adiecit *sacrilegium,* id est sacrarum rerum furtum, et hoc maximum est furtum, vel idolathitis servientem, id est auspiciis et reliqua, deinde *adulterium, falsum testimonium, furtum, rapina, ebrietas adsidua,* idolatria, molles, sodomita, maledici, periuri. Ista sunt capitalia crimina, sanctus Paulus et Agustinus et alii sancti *conputaverunt;* pro istis fieri oportet *elimosinas largas* et *longitempore ieiunium* teneatur, etc.

Caesarius, ed. Morin, pp. 684, 27–685, 4
Et quamvis apostolus capitalia plura commemoraverit, nos tamen, ne desperationem facere videamur, breviter dicimus quae illa sint. *Sacrilegium,* homicidium, *adulterium, falsum testimonium, furtum, rapina, superbia, invidia,* et, si *longo tempore* teneatur, *iracundia, ebrietas,* si *assidua* sit, et detractio in eorum numero *computantur.* Quicumque enim aliqua de istis peccatis in se dominari cognoverit, nisi digne et, si habuerit spatium, *longo tempore* paenitentiam egerit, et *largas elimosynas* erogaverit et a peccatis ipsis abstinuerit, illo transitorio igne, de quo dixit apostolus, purgari non poterit, sed aeterna illum flamma sine ullo remedio cruciabit.

Ibid., 686, 1–3
Et ideo continuis orationibus et frequentibus *ieiuniis* et *largioribus elemosinis,* et per indulgentiam eorum qui in nobis peccant, assidue redimantur.

---

riosos, but Ducange had *cararios coriocos* in his MS. One wonders whether the compiler of the penitential also knew the twelfth sermon of Caesarius, where we read (ed. Morin, p. 59, 31–34), *nam et auguria observare, et praecantatoribus adhibere et caragios, sortilegos, divinos inquirere,* and whether *cocriocos* is a corruption, not of a rather pointless *curiosos,* but of *sortilegos* or *sortilogos,* as the word is sometimes spelled (cf. Pirmin's Scarapsus [ed. Jecker], p. 68, 10: *precantatores, sortilogus, karagius*). Palaeographically such a corruption is conceivable and would suggest a misreading, at some stage in the transmission, of an exemplar written in Visigothic minuscule.

It may be admitted that the parallelism of these two quotations is not as close and striking as in the former case. Nevertheless there is a reasonable probability that here too the compiler of the penitential was indebted to Caesarius, especially when we remember the extreme popularity of this sermon in the Middle Ages.[19] In the light of what follows it is not irrelevant to allude to the extant manuscripts in which sermons XIII and CLXXIX are preserved. All the witnesses to the text of Sermo XIII are continental, the earliest being, in Morin's classification, H^5 (s. vii/viii; Luxeuil script), H^{20} (s. viii; French), H^{25} (s. viii/ix; Rhaetic script), H^{53} (s. ix; St. Gall), and H^{71} (s. viii/ix; Reichenau). The only manuscript now in England containing this sermon is one from Silos in Spain (s. xi/xii). For the text of Sermo CLXXIX Morin has utilized four codices and some early printed editions. The manuscripts are L^2 (s. ix), V^1 (s. ix/x), A^1 (s. ix) and W (s. viii); all are of continental origin.[20]

The use of Caesarius in the penitential is a strong, indeed, as I believe, a decisive argument against Bede's connection with it. While it would seem that Caesarius was not wholly unknown in Southern Ireland during the late seventh or early eighth century,[21] all the available evidence suggests that during the same period, and perhaps even in the ninth century, his works, whether under his name or another's, were missing from the English libraries. In his monumental edition of Aldhelm Ehwald has recorded no allusions to, or quotations from, Caesarius. Bede never mentions him by name and, after considerable study, I have been unable to find any passage in

---

[19] Cf. Morin, *op. cit.*, p. 683: 'inter omnes Caesarii homilias nulla fere ita frequens in codd. mss. occurrit, nulla fortasse tanta auctoritate apud medii aevi theologos fuit, sive quod ad dogma purgatorii, sive quod ad distinctionem peccatorum in minuta et capitalia pertinet.'

[20] For Sermo XII he used the ninth century Laudunensis and early printed editions; Sermo XIX survives only in an eighth century homiliary copied in France.

[21] S. Hellmann (Texte und Untersuchungen zur Geschichte der altchristlichen Literatur, ser. III, vol. 4 [Leipzig, 1909], p. 11) has drawn attention to five pseudo-Augustinian sermons which were used by the compiler or compilers of the collectio canonum Hibernensis. Four of these are genuine sermons of Caesarius, viz., Nos. XLIII, XLIV, LIV, and CXCIX in Morin's numeration.

Bede's theological works which would suggest familiarity with the bishop of Arles' works. Boniface once cites from Sermo LIV, but he does so in a letter to Pope Zachary, that is, one written when he had been on the European Continent for more than a quarter of a century.[22] Again, Caesarius' name is missing from the list of writers in the last section of Alcuin's poem on the see and bishops of York; and one may add that no difficulty of scansion, as in the case of Isidorus, would account for the absence of the name in a hexameter poem. Ogilvy in his wide, though incomplete search, finds no trace of Caesarius.[23] It is, of course, true that many of Caesarius' sermons circulated under other names, for example, Augustine's or Faustus' of Riez, but these are included in Dom Morin's monumental edition and are assigned to their true author. The evidence of the extant manuscripts is the most impressive argument of all in favor of our contention; it is immaterial for our purpose under whose name these sermons were transmitted in the Middle Ages.[24] Dom Morin lists nearly two hundred and fifty manuscripts that he has inspected, of which seventy-four are homiliaries or lectionaries containing sermons by various hands. A very substantial proportion of the Caesarius manuscripts proper are of early date, that is, of the seventh, eighth, or ninth centuries.[25] Of the homiliaries more than a third were copied before the end of the ninth century and several are far older, notably H^1 and H^5, written respectively in the Laon *az*-type and the Luxeuil script. There are only three manuscripts prior to c. 900 that at first sight might seem to be connected with England, inasmuch as they are written in Insular script. But Monacensis 6298 (G^1 in Morin), a book of Freising, was evidently a product of a German scriptorium; for Dom Morin calls the collection, of which G^1 is by far the oldest manuscript, specifically Ger-

---

[22] MGH: Epist. III, 301, 21–25. Boniface calls the author of the citation Augustine.

[23] J. D. A. Ogilvy, Books known to Anglo-Latin Writers from Aldhelm to Alcuin (Cambridge, Mass., 1936).

[24] Some of the genuine sermons of Augustine had reached England early and were used, for example, by Bede.

[25] E.g. Morin's L^1, L^2, V^1, M^1, M^2, M^8, M^4, M^{10}, M^{11}, A^1, A^2, W^1, W^2 (fragments only), Q^6 and Q^7.

man.[26] Codex Durlacensis 36 (D), now at Carlsruhe, appears to have originated at St. Gall.[27] There remains only the British Museum manuscript, Arundel 213, in which there are four sermons noted by Morin. Two are genuinely Caesarian, one of them bearing no author's name, the other being attributed to Augustine. The other two, one being assigned to Augustine, the other to Cyprian, are rejected by the editor. Dom Morin would date this codex s. vii/viii, while Zangemeister had thought it of the tenth century; but it would appear that Dom Morin's date is considerably too early. Arundel 213 is not included by E. A. Lowe in the second volume of Codices latini antiquiores and, as he kindly informs me in a letter, was in his opinion copied in the ninth century.

To sum up: if the reader is convinced by the cumulative effect of our argument, he will be led to three conclusions. First, the weight of the evidence is against those who maintain that Bede was the author of a penitential. Secondly, the document published by Albers cannot in any event be attributed to Bede; and, finally, that document, so far from being an English product, was compiled on the Continent of Europe.

[26] Morin, *op. cit.*, p. lx, . . . 'collectio, quam Germanicam ideo appellavi, quod libris in Germania exaratis fere unice servata sit.' There is no MS from an English scriptorium in this family, G⁷, now at Oxford, being 'liber domus clericorum in Doesborch.'

[27] The St. Gall attribution is not certain, though probable (cf. Morin, *op. cit.*, p. lxxii). But even if D were from an English scriptorium, our argument would not, in view of its relatively late date (s. ix/x), be invalidated.

The Carolingian Age

10

Some Early Medieval
Commentaries on the
Old Testament *

IT IS a commonplace that the Biblical commentators of the earlier Middles Ages were traditionalists who copied or adapted the Fathers and rarely added much of their own. At the same time there was much variation in method; for there is a world of difference between the commentaries of Bede or Paschasius, carefully integrated works bearing the impress of the writer's own mind and personality, and compilations that are no more than *collectanea* of Patristic passages strung together but lacking inner cohesion. Between these two extremes are works like those of Hrabanus or even Alcuin. Most of the material in them is borrowed, but its arrangement has been carried out with some skill and the compiler, besides quoting his authorities verbally, gives some variety to his exposition by reproducing part of the traditional teaching in his own words. The commentators also differ greatly in the degree to which they acknowledge their sources. Bede and Hrabanus often indicated their indebtedness to others by specific statements in the text or by a more general reference in the margin to the author

* *Harvard Theological Review*, 46 (1953), 27–46. Reprinted by permission of the Harvard University Press.

cited.[1] Even so the reader needs to be on his guard, because the commentators, by quoting the *ipsissima verba* of their source, may completely mislead him. A palmary example of this occurs in Hrabanus' commentary on Genesis. He introduces (PL 107, 506B) a discussion of Lamech and his seventy-seven descendants who perished in the Flood with the words : "referebat quidam Hebraeus in apocryphis eorum libris." This might easily be interpreted as an allusion to the mysterious Jewish scholar whom Hrabanus is supposed to have consulted and to whom we shall have to return. Actually the whole phrase together with what follows has been copied from a letter (Ep. 36) of Jerome's to Damasus. Similarly, in another passage (PL 107, 166C) Hrabanus remarks, "nomina invenire non potui," again employing the exact words of Jerome in the Quaestiones Hebraicae. Bede, on the other hand, citing the same passage from Jerome, introduces it thus: "Hieronymus se invenire non potuisse testatur." But there is still another reason for exercising caution. Every scholar of experience is aware that, when he meets with a quotation from a classical Latin author in an author of the eighth or ninth century, he must not assume that it has been taken directly from the original source. There are innumerable quotations from Virgil, Cicero, Terence, and others to be found in the works of Jerome or in Isidore's Etymologies, which medieval commentators borrowed at second hand. But the same principle applies also to Patristic citations. Because a ninth century author states that he is quoting Jerome or Augustine, this does not constitute proof without corroboration; he may have filched the whole passage from Isidore, Bede, or Alcuin. In short, the problem of medieval *Quellenforschung* is a great deal more intricate than it seems. If the present inquiry is concerned primarily with one of the less known exegetes of the ninth century, there is ample justification for what might seem, superficially considered, an arid quest. Most of what has been written about Angelomus of Luxeuil and his sources is either demonstrably incorrect or highly misleading. A study of his methods illustrates the problems indi-

[1] Cf. Laistner, Hand-list of Bede MSS, pp. 44 and 50; Journ. Theol. Stud. 34 (1933), pp. 350–354; PL 107, 729B–C and 109, 10A.

cated above. He had access to and used several authors who were, so to say, off the main track of Biblical exegesis in his day. And, finally, an inquiry into his sources may help to throw a little light on what is still an obscure problem—the resources of the library at Luxeuil about the middle of the ninth century.

Angelomus seems to have composed his three commentaries approximately during the decade, 845–855. Genesis engaged his attention first. The exposition of the Song of Songs was finished soon after March, 851, as an allusion to the recent death of Irmingard, wife of Lothar I, shows. The lengthy Enarrationes in libros Regum I–IV must have been completed before the deaths of Lothar and of Drogo, bishop of Metz.[2] In his prefaces Angelomus explains his method of composition and this information, interesting in itself, is borne out by a study of his sources. Several of the authors to whom he is most indebted he does not name at all ; but where he does indicate his authority he can usually be shown to have known him directly and not through an intermediary. On the urging of the priest Leotric, to whom the commentary on Genesis is dedicated, but reluctantly because of his literary inexperience, Angelomus began to compose an exposition of the opening chapters of Genesis. It was based on what he had learnt from his former teacher, Mellinus, and was intended to amplify those parts which Isidore of Seville had left unexplained. Mellinus had then encouraged the young author to read aloud what he had written and had lent him Augustine's De Genesi contra Manichaeos to read for comparison. Subsequently Angelomus set himself to expound the whole of Genesis. In some parts, he says, he has quoted verbally from the Fathers, in

---

[2] That is, in English parlance, I and II Samuel and I and II Kings. References to Angelomus are to PL 115, but the three prefaces have also been published in MGH: Epistolae V. The few facts about Angelomus' life that can be gleaned from his writings have been well discussed by Manitius, Gesch. d. lat. Lit. I, pp. 418–419; but Manitius' treatment of the source-problem is completely unreliable because he has ignored the intermediate sources. Thus, the references to pseudo-Quintilian and Cicero's De senectute come from Jerome. The passages from Josephus and Cassiodorus, the description of Thule, and the philological derivation of *pythonissa* were all taken by Angelomus from Bede. The description of the Dead Sea is also from Bede, not from Isidore. Further details will be found in their context below.

others he has abbreviated their teaching and reproduced it in his own language. There is also some material learnt from others but not to be found in the books in the library, and to this he has added illustrative examples. Though primarily concerned with the historical sense of Scripture, he has not neglected the allegorical and the moral.

The commentary on Samuel and Kings was undertaken at the request of his fellow-monks and was encouraged by his bishop, particularly "quod a nullo doctorum per omnia expositum apud nos haberetur antiquorum," that is, the monastery library possessed no complete exposition by an "ancient" author of these four historical books. Manitius drew attention to the importance of the words *per omnia*, but failed to appreciate the significance of *antiquorum*. Dümmler (MGH: Epist. V, p. 622, note 1) with strange ineptitude observed that evidently Angelomus did not have access to the commentary by Hrabanus, the very book which he used more extensively than any other! The terminology, in fact, is crucial. In the commentary (330D), after a long quotation from Augustine and a briefer one from Bede, Angelomus contrasts *antiqua* and *moderna volumina*. Earlier, in his preface (245A) he had alluded to *multos strenuos doctorum modernos;* and in his commentary on Genesis (117B, 197B) Bede, in contrast to Augustine and Jerome, is described as *doctor modernus*. It is, in short, obvious that by *antiqui* he means the earlier commentators from Origen to Isidore of Seville, while the *moderni* are Bede and those who came after him, especially Alcuin and Hrabanus. Neither of these two is ever mentioned by name as a commentator, although their works were Angelomus' chief standby. Now Hrabanus, in two passages which have been the subject of much discussion (PL 109, 9–10; 281A), alludes to the work of a Jewish scholar which he had consulted. On both occasions he employs the phrase *modernis temporibus,* and it has been generally assumed that the Jew was a near contemporary of Hrabanus'.[3] In view of the evidence from Angelomus this

---

[3] Cf. Wutz, Onomastica Sacra, p. 788: "ein gelehrter Jude der der Zeit des Rabanus Maurus wenig vorangeht." See also S. Katz, The Jews in the Visigothic and Frankish Kingdoms of Spain and Gaul, pp. 69–70, where further references to

assumption is highly questionable. Even if the author of the pseudo-Hieronymic Quaestiones in libros regum composed his book a century or more before Hrabanus' time, he would still be "modern." Indeed, Hrabanus' language elsewhere bears out Angelomus' antithesis. When speaking (PL 109, 671) of Judith, Tobit, Maccabees, and Wisdom, he remarks on the authority of Jerome that these books *apud antiquos* were not regarded as canonical, but that *moderno tempore* the Holy Church had included them among the Scriptures.

To return to Angelomus' preface: he again explains that his commentary is made up of verbal citations, passages abbreviated from earlier writers, what he had learnt from his teacher, and a little additional material of his own. After a long passage in which he maintains that the words of the Bible can be explained in seven senses, he ends by saying that in the commentary he has expounded the literal, the allegorical, and the moral.[4]

The preface to his third work, though long, is less informative. Angelomus compiled his commentary on the Song of Songs from the material that he could garner in the monastic library, and especially from Gregory the Great. In fact much of this preface is either copied directly or adapted from Gregory (PL 79, 473B ff.), including the warning to Lothar, to whom the book is dedicated, that the Song of Songs must be interpreted strictly and solely in an allegorical sense.[5]

---

this controversy will be found. In the ninth century catalogue of Murbach Alcuin is described as *magister modernus,* not Bede. See Hermann Bloch in Strassburger Festschrift zur XLVI Versammlung deutscher Philologen (Strassburg, 1901), p. 269.

[4] This passage has been discussed by H. Caplan in Speculum 4 (1929), pp. 287–288, and by Beryl Smalley, The Study of the Bible in the Middle Ages², pp. 41–42. Angelomus may have borrowed the number seven from Tyconius by way of Augustine, but there is otherwise no similarity between his seven senses and Tyconius'.

[5] The style of the prefaces is verbose and involved. There is a certain fondness for poetic diction and particularly for nautical metaphors (108B, 109D, 331B, 391C–D, 493A–B), which makes one wonder whether Angelomus, before he entered the monastery, grew up on or near the sea-coast. Occasional rare words, like *lampabilis* or *trutinatio* and *exagium* in a figurative sense, may point to his familiarity with the preface to Cassiodorus' Commentary on Psalms (PL 70, 9D) and Cassian's Collations (i, 22, 1; xii, 8, 2).

The Commentary on Genesis

In this work, which survives in five manuscripts,[6] Angelomus has drawn on a variety of earlier authors. The *moderni* are Alcuin, Hrabanus, and, in the opening chapters, Bede; but, as he calls Bede's book Hexameron and some passages from Bede after the third chapter of Genesis are found also in Alcuin and Hrabanus, it is probable that he knew only the shorter version of Bede's commentary.[7] There are also two substantial quotations (174B–C, 197B) from Bede's De locis sanctis, the one reproducing the amusing story of the emperor Vespasian who, to test its buoyancy, ordered some soldiers who could not swim to have their hands tied and be thrown into the Dead Sea. Of the *antiqui* or older authorities Isidore is represented by his Quaestiones in Vetus Testamentum and by a few extracts from the Etymologies.[8] Quotations from Gregory are many and often of considerable length. Angelomus names his author a few times; more often, after expounding the literal meaning of a passage, he continues, as Hrabanus had occasionally done before him, with the word *moraliter*, and what follows is from Gregory. There are enough passages in Angelomus' works to show that he sometimes consulted his author directly; but in the vast majority of instances both he and Hrabanus used Paterius' collection of extracts. This can be proved in two ways: the citations from Gregory correspond exactly with what is quoted by Paterius, and, besides, both Hrabanus and Paterius have incorporated in their works a long passage, running to five and a half columns in the Patrology which they attribute to Gregory. But, as the modern editors have pointed out, it is not to be found in Gregory's extant works.[9] The Gregory extracts in Angelomus are often identical with those in Hrabanus. Nevertheless Angelomus did use Paterius independently; for he reproduces some quotations (141C, 167C–D, 271C, 285B–C) which are neither in Hrabanus nor in Alcuin, or else he cites

---

[6] To the four listed by Manitius must be added MS 744 in the Pierpont Morgan Library; it is a French codex of the twelfth century.

[7] On the two versions cf. Hand-list of Bede MSS, pp. 41–43.

[8] 155A from Et. xi, 3, 13–14; 214C–215C from Et. vii, 7, 5 ff.; 226B from Et. vii, 6, 33–34.

[9] PL 107, 574A–579A and 115, 200A–205B, from 79, 704C–709C.

a passage in full (e.g., 183B–C) which Hrabanus quotes only in part. Both Jerome and Augustine are mentioned by name several times. The real question, however, is how far Angelomus read these authors for himself, since a great many extracts from them appear also in Hrabanus and some also in Alcuin. It is clear that, as he says, he studied the treatise, De genesi contra Manichaeos and introduced quotations from it into his commentary.[10] He also refers his readers to the fifteenth Book of the City of God. He may have found this reference in Alcuin (PL 100, 529B), but, as his quotation is fuller than Alcuin's, he must have looked up the passage for himself. The long extract (219A–220A), however, which is a combination of Jerome's Quaestiones Hebraicae (PL 23, 985A) and some sentences from Augustine's Quaestiones in Heptateuchum (CSEL 28, ii, 47, 19 ff.) cannot be used to prove that Angelomus knew this Augustinian dissertation at first hand, since his text here is identical with that in Hrabanus. Jerome's Quaestiones Hebraicae were a quarry constantly worked by his successors, so that many of Angelomus' excerpts from that book were no doubt taken from one or other of the moderni, usually from Hrabanus.[11] Yet he did go directly to Jerome from time to time.[12] He also quotes from the same writer's commentary on Isaiah, immediately after a citation from the Quaestiones Hebraicae, part of which is also quoted by Bede and Alcuin, and from Jerome's treatises on Hebrew names and on Palestinian geography.[13]

The most interesting of Angelomus' sources, however, is Origen. Baehrens in his exhaustive study of the Latin manuscripts of Origen maintained that Angelomus consulted the homilies on Genesis in Rufinus' version for himself. That is true, but the reasons adduced by Baehrens are quite wrong because he overlooked much of the evidence.[14] Thus, he failed

---

[10] 112D–113A (cf. PL 34, 173); 115C (176–177); 119A (181); 131D (203–204); 132A (*ibid.*); 145A–B (213); 146A (214).

[11] Examples of this are very numerous, so that one instance will suffice: 166A–C, though derived from Jerome, corresponds to Hrabanus in PL 107, 529B–D.

[12] E.g., 119D, just before a quotation from Bede; 141B, 149B, 150A; 169C–D, where Hrabanus follows De civitate dei xvi; 209A–B.

[13] 167B from PL 24, 164A–B; 189C–D from PL 23, 885A–B and 898C.

[14] Texte und Untersuchungen 42 (1920), Heft 1, 76–77.

to see the significance of Angelomus' words (158A): "lege Origenem super hac re contra Apellem disputantem," which conclude a long description of the Ark and its interior arrangement. Origen's explanation became classic and underlies the exposition of many later commentators. Some of them mention Origen by name, others do not, but Angelomus alone refers to Origen's heretical opponent. This is a clear indication that he had gone to the original authority; for Origen begins his next paragraph in the Second Homily with the words: "Sed his omnibus tanta arte compositis obiciunt quidam quaestiones et praecipue Apelles." [15] Hrabanus also (PL 107, 515B) quotes Origen on the construction of the Ark, and his manuscript, like Angelomus', had the reading *congrua*, not *contigua*. Yet Baehrens ignored Hrabanus, and, solely on the basis of readings which are also found in the codex Lugdunensis (A) of Origen, used this passage to prove Angelomus' independent use of the Second Homily. He further asserted that Angelomus derived some of the Origen material from Bede, meaning thereby the commentary on the Pentateuch which is not by Bede at all. The quotation that Baehrens argues from is in 189A, but he has failed to observe that the preceding passage (188B–D) is also a quotation from Origen, and that Angelomus reproduces his source more exactly than the pseudo-Bede does. Again, in commenting on Abimelech (190D–191C) Angelomus is closer to Origen's text. He also cites from the Twelfth Homily; and, finally, there is a lengthy extract from the Fourteenth Homily, where Angelomus (210A–211A) is sometimes nearer to the original than pseudo-Bede, and sometimes not. This evidence, which Baehrens has overlooked, is conclusive: Angelomus cites from four homilies, II, V, XII, and XIV, and he and the pseudo-Bede consulted Origen independently.[16]

[15] GCS: Origenes VI, 27, 17–18.

[16] The commentary on the Pentateuch is not a genuine work by Bede, for its author sometimes copies Hrabanus. Thus the early part of his thirtieth chapter is an abbrebiated version of PL 107, 600A–601B, while the beginning of chapter 26 opens with the middle of a sentence in a passage in Hrabanus (585B–586C). The earliest manuscript of the commentary known to me is Brussels 1354, written in the tenth century. The Lorsch manuscript of the later ninth century (Bodleian, Laud. Misc. 159), which Coxe's catalogue describes as Beda in Octateuchum,

There remain three passages which call for special comment. Although Angelomus never alludes to Alcuin as a commentator, he once refers to him by name in connection with a reading in Genesis 17, 15. He begins by discussing Sarah's change of name and, like the genuine Bede, Alcuin, Hrabanus, and pseudo-Eucherius, he quotes from Jerome's Quaestiones Hebraicae (PL 23, 964A). He then adds some observations of his own, which deserve to be quoted in full, if only because they seem to have been generally ignored by scholars interested in the so-called Alcuinian recension of the Vulgate:

Unde existimant si ita fuerit, antiquam permansisse consuetudinem in ecclesia, ut Sarra vitio scriptorum unum r additum diceretur; quod et in authenticis libris semper ita scriptum reperies. Hinc est etiam quod Sedul <i> us poeta in carmine paschali (I, 107) ait:
 Saucia iam vetulae marcebant viscera Sarae.
At vero nonnulli Sarai, sicut in vetustissimis invenies tomis, non tantum Sari pronuntiare contendunt, et addita littera e, quae per a legitur, postmodum Saraam nominatam autumant; quia inquiunt, sicut Abrahae una littera, ita Sarae est altera addita, prout supra ostenditur. Unde siquidem ferunt quod pater Albinus in bibliotheca quam Carolo principi correxit, quod nos etiam oculis diligenter inibi inspeximus, emendare curavit, videlicet sine uno r Saraam et duo a; et in nostris quibusdam voluminibus ita legitur, quod et nos similiter legendum putamus.[17]

One could wish that our author had been more explicit. From what he says it would seem that he had at some time or other visited Aachen, where he had examined a Bible copied and cor-

---

does not contain it; for this codex is made up of some material apparently derived from Augustine, Book 1 only of Bede's commentary on Genesis, and then Wigbod's Collectaneum; on this last cf. Harv. Theol. Rev. 40 (1947), p. 30 with note 27.

[17] 160C–D. For *bibliotheca* in the sense of Bible or one or other of the two Testaments see Thesaurus, s.v. The usage is first found in Jerome; to the examples in the Thesaurus should be added the Latin Acts of Pilate (Tischendorf, Evang. Apocr., p. 409), where the *magna bibliotheca* must mean the Law and the Prophets. We have it on the authority of Alcuin (MGH: Poetae I, p. 283, no. lxv) that by his time the word had come into general use, though he himself favored the older *Pandecte*, which had already been employed by Cassiodorus (Inst., ed. Mynors, 37, 20 et al.). It is also found in library catalogues of the ninth century; cf. Becker, Cat. bibl. ant. 11, 1 (St. Riquier) and Lehmann, Mittelalt. Bibliothekskat. I, p. 71, 35 (St. Gall).

rected for Charlemagne under Alcuin's direction. Furthermore, we learn that Luxeuil possessed one or more Bibles of the Alcuinian recension. The accepted reading in the new edition of the Vulgate sponsored by the Vatican authorities is "Sarai uxorem tuam non vocabis Sarai sed Sarram"; but there still exist many manuscripts, some of early date, which give Saraam not Sarram.[18]

The mysterious figure of Melchisedech (Genesis 14, 18) stimulated Angelomus to comment at some length. At the end he refers his readers to Jerome and Isidore, though much of what he had put down himself corresponds closely to Alcuin's observations on the same subject. The priest-king had long since attracted the attention of the Fathers in connection with Psalms 110, 4 and Hebrews 7, 3. He had, on the one hand, inspired a heresy, and, on the other, had been interpreted as a prototype of Christ and been used by Christian expositors in their anti-Jewish polemic.[19] But the main interest of Angelomus centred in the name. After quoting Hebrews 7, 3, he introduces a Jewish tradition which he had found "in cuiusdam (v. l. "quodam") vetusto volumine," to the effect that Melchisedech's father was named Melchi and his mother Sedech; and that, as he was a posthumous child and his mother died in childbirth, he was called Melchisedech after his two dead parents. The Latin commentators, following Jerome, knew the correct meaning of Melchisedech as *rex iustus* perfectly well; and the variant explanation discovered by Angelomus in an old book finds no place in their exegesis. But in the Syriac version of the Book of Adam and Eve Melchisedech's father is named Melchi and his mother Yo-Sedek; while in the short historia de Melchisedech, wrongly ascribed to Athanasius, the parents are called respectively Melchi and Salem.[20] Thus there is "authority" for this etymo-

---

[18] E.g. the Theodulfus Bible (Paris, B.N. 9380; saec. viii–ix) and a Tours Bible (Paris, B.N. 11514) which Rand has placed in his class IVB (A.D. 800–820). The corrector of the Maurdramnus Bible (Amiens 6–11; saec. viii²) also favored Saraam.

[19] See the admirable article, 'Melchisédech dans la polémique entre juifs et chrétiens et dans la légende" by Marcel Simon in Rev. d'hist. et de philos. religieuses 17 (1937), pp. 58–93.

[20] I owe this information and the following references to the kindness of Profes-

logical oddity which must have found its way into some Western, that is, Latin, source now lost, and one wonders whether
it could have been the first of the *homiliae mixtae* by Origen
to which Jerome refers (Ep. 33). The manner in which Angelomus specifies his source is almost identical, as we shall see, with
that in which he quotes from the Quaestiones in libros regum
by an unindentified Jewish writer; and it is very likely that no
author's name was attached to the treatise in the "old book."

The extended commentary on Genesis 49 (232D–242C) reproduces the De benedictionibus patriarcharum, a tract which
was probably compiled by Isidore (cf. PL 83, 276C–288A), who
seems to have used Rufinus' longer treatise with the same name.
Isidore's version reappears with occasional modifications in
Alcuin, Hrabanus, pseudo-Bede, pseudo-Eucherius, and our author, whose text is sometimes nearest to Alcuin's, sometimes to
Hrabanus'.[21]

The Commentary on Samuel and Kings

In this commentary which, to judge by the number of extant
manuscripts,[22] became the most popular of Angelomus' books,
he is more reticent about his authorities. There are, it is true,
four references to Gregory, two to Augustine, and two to
Jerome; but, beyond the general statement that he had consulted "modern" writers (330D), there is no hint of the true
state of affairs.[23] This is, that between two-thirds and three-
quarters of this long commentary is copied almost word for
word from Bede and from Hrabanus! Just as in the commentary
on Genesis Angelomus at first worked with a good deal of inde-

sor Harry Wolfson of Harvard University. Cf. Carl Bezold (ed.), Me 'arat Gazo, p.
116, 11, 4–5, and id., Die Schatzhöhle, pp. 27–28; pseudo-Athanasius in PG 28,
525A.

[21] E.g., in 233C Angelomus includes a sentence from Hrabanus that is missing
in Alcuin, but in 235A the Hebrew etymology is from Alcuin. Hrabanus omits it.

[22] Manitius lists eight. To these should be added MS 92 in Trinity College,
Cambridge (Christ Church, Canterbury; saec. xii), Angers 41 (St. Aubin, saec. xii)
and Angers 42 (St. Serge, saec. xii). See M. R. James, The Ancient Libraries of
Canterbury and Dover, pp. 21 and 506; L. W. Jones, Studies in Honor of E. K.
Rand, p. 144, note 11, and p. 151.

[23] Gregory: 273C, 305A, 334B, 351C; Augustine: 306D, copied from Hrabanus,
328D; Jerome: 348A ("noster interpres in tribus linguis peritus") and 393C.
Jerome's treatise on Hebrew names was used in 347B and 383C.

pendence and introduced what appear to be his own observations, while the later chapters are little more than a cento of excerpts from Alcuin and Hrabanus, so, in expounding Samuel and Kings, he began by combining various sources with some skill, but from the beginning of chapter 5 of his third Book to the end of Book 4 he copies Bede-Hrabanus with scarcely any change.[24] The works of Bede more or less incorporated in the commentary are Quaestiones XXX, De templo Salomonis, and Quaestio 8 in the Aliquot quaestionum liber, but Hrabanus had already followed the same procedure.[25] The question thus arises whether Angelomus knew any of these works by Bede at first hand. Quaestio 8 of the Aliquot quaestionum liber he seems to have copied from Hrabanus; for where there are slight divergencies from the printed text of Bede it is with Hrabanus' text that he agrees. He also made small alterations, presumably for greater simplicity, as when he changes *enucleatius* in Bede and Hrabanus to *manifestius*. In De templo the occasional cuts made by Hrabanus reappear in the text of Angelomus, and the only passage which might suggest that Angelomus had inspected Bede's treatise for himself is a Virgil citation followed by ten words of explanation (411C). Both the couplet and what follows are missing in the printed text of Hrabanus; but in view of the shockingly faulty texts of all three authors in Migne's Patrology, it would be unsafe to draw any conclusions from this discrepancy.[26] Quaestiones XXX, however, Angelomus consulted in-

---

[24] 404D–550C. The only exceptions are two short pieces of allegorical interpretation (453A–B and 469C–D) which I have failed to trace elsewhere, and a brief addition in 473A–B. These may well be Angelomus' own contribution!

[25] It has not been generally recognized that Hrabanus "lifted" the whole of De templo Salomonis for his own commentary. In their catalogue for 1947 the Rosenbach Company of Philadelphia and New York (Item 492) announced a manuscript written in France in the later twelfth century, which they described as follows: "De templo has been incorporated chronologically into Rhabanus Maurus' Commentary on Kings and as here written forms an integral part of the third book of the latter work." Clearly this codex, so far from being unusual, is a normal manuscript of Hrabanus' commentary. For the Aliquot quaestionum liber cf. Paul Lehmann, Munich SB. 1919, Heft 4, and Heinrich Weissweiler, Beiträge z. Gesch. d. Philosophie und Theologie des Mittelalters XXXIII, Fasc. 1–2 (1936), 54 ff.

[26] At 430D Angelomus agrees with Hrabanus against Bede's slightly different wording. The occasional cuts made by Hrabanus in Bede's text are uniformly

dependently, for example, in 277B and 278A, where he copies twenty-five lines from Bede, which Hrabanus has left out. Both commentators relied heavily on Isidore's Quaestiones and on Paterius; but again Angelomus' independent use is demonstrated by quotations which are missing in Hrabanus.[27] The classic authority on the Witch of Endor was Augustine who composed a short dissertation on this subject for Simplicianus. It is therefore not surprising to find it quoted in full by Isidore, Hrabanus, Claudius of Turin, pseudo-Eucherius, and our author; but Angelomus alone adds to it a few lines taken from Bede's commentary on Acts.[28] Book III opens with a long quotation (393C–394B) from Jerome's letter to Nepotian (Ep. 52). Hrabanus copied much from the same source, but the section describing the old age of Cato, Plato, and Isocrates is reproduced only by Angelomus, a clear proof that he had read Jerome's letter for himself. The most unusual source, however, is the short commentary by the unknown Jewish scholar to whom we have already referred. Here too Angelomus worked independently of Hrabanus; for, though many quotations from the Quaestiones in libros regum are common to both, Angelomus added many others which his predecessor disregarded.[29] But, like Hrabanus, he introduces these extracts with phrases that are tantalisingly vague: "ut legi in cuiusdam disputatione," "prout in quodam volumine legi," "unde in Hebraeo ita habetur." As he does not quote from his source in the opening chapters of Book III, it is possible that his manuscript of the Quaestiones belonged to the class which lacks this book.

From what has been said it will be apparent that the material which Angelomus owed to the oral teaching of Mellinus—save insofar as Mellinus reproduced what he had gleaned from books in the library—and what he added himself amounts to very little.

---

passages of allegorical interpretation. Pseudo-Eucherius also incorporated De templo in his commentary and he retained the parts which Hrabanus, and following him Angelomus, excised. But see Note at the end of this article.

[27] E.g., 271C (PL 79, 789D–791A) and 285B–C (ib. 791B); 290A–B (PL 83, 396D–397A), 363B–C (ib. 412A–B), 396A (ib. 413D–414D).

[28] 328D–330C; cf. PL 40, 101 ff.; Bede on Acts (ed. Laistner), p. 63, 24–28.

[29] E.g., 287A, where Angelomus inserts six lines from the Jew between two passages taken from Bede, 301B–C, 310D–311A, 332B, 339B.

There are a few passages which it has been impossible to identify, but the only one of any length and interest is an excursus on various heresies of the Later Roman Empire. It forms part of Angelomus' comment on I Samuel, 13, 19–20 (297C–299D), because the Philistines prefigure the heretics: "Philistim, quorum ingens numerus esse perhibetur, omnium haereticorum magistros figurasse non dubium est." As a general guide for this disquisition he may well have turned to the chapter on heresies in the Etymologies (viii, 5) of Isidore.

The Commentary on the Song of Songs

This book is virtually compiled from four authors, Gregory, Aponius, Alcuin, and Justus of Urgel; and, apart from the verbose remarks addressed to Lothar I,[30] there is little or nothing of Angelomus' own. He quotes a couplet from Sedulius and adds two excerpts from Isidore, as well as a little material from Jerome.[31] His main sources call for brief comment, since all four have been the subject of controversy in modern times. The authorship of the commentary on the Song of Songs printed among Gregory's works was long a matter of dispute; but it has now been established that this book is made up of two genuine homilies on Cant. Cant. 1, 1–8 followed by the compilation of Robert of St. Vigor (late 11th century).[32] Again, the authenticity of Alcuin's Compendium in Cantica Canticorum (PL 100, 642–664), on which earlier editors had thrown doubt, was rightly defended by Froben on general grounds of style. His arguments are corroborated by the fact that the compendium appears among the works of Alcuin in the catalogue of Reichenau within less than a generation of his death, and later in the ninth century it is

[30] 577A–C and 627D–628D. The second passage contains the story that Theodosius II copied out Priscian with his own hand and is found also in Aldhelm's De metris. The tale arose out of a confusion between Theodorus of the imperial chancellery and the emperor. Cf. Schanz, Gesch. d. lat. Lit. IV, ii, 230, Keil, Gramm. lat. II, viii, and Aldhelm in MGH: Auct. ant. XV, 203, 22 ff. Ehwald assumes that Angelomus copied from Aldhelm, but both may have copied from a common source now lost.

[31] 562B from Carmen paschale I, 335–336; 538A–B from Isidore, Et. xvii, 8, 4; 623C from Et. xvii, 9, 30; for Jerome see below.

[32] See B. Capelle in Revue bénédictine 41 (1929), pp. 204–217. Among the MSS of the two Gregorian homilies listed by Capelle are several that were copied in the ninth century.

attributed to Alcuin in the catalogue of Lorsch. A shorter version of the compendium, in which the commentary on chapters 1–4 is much abbreviated, has been printed among the works of Isidore and it was apparently a manuscript of this version which Angelomus used.[33]

The brief exposition by Justus of Urgel, which appears to have passed into oblivion during the later Middle Ages, enjoyed a certain popularity in the ninth century when there were copies of it at St. Riquier, Reichenau, St. Gall (now Sangall. 110), and Murbach; and there is no valid reason for doubting Justus' authorship.[34] It has long been known that Angelomus consulted the elaborate commentary composed by Aponius probably near the beginning of the fifth century; but only the first editor, Johannes Faber, seems to have realized fully the extent of Angelomus' debt to his predecessor. Faber saw that the text of Angelomus might be used as a check on his faulty manuscript of Aponius, but neither the more recent editors nor Witte in his monograph have appreciated the importance of Angelomus.[35]

[33] The manuscript of the shorter version collated by Froben is now Cod. Reg. Christ. 69 (saec. ix–x) in the Vatican Library. See A. Wilmart, Codd. lat. regin. I, p. 153: "Alcuini in Cant. Cant. compendium immo de cap. I–IV magis contractum; quae sub forma Isidori iam impressa est" (PL 83, 1119–1132). Although it is not assigned to Alcuin in this manuscript, it is included in a collection of Alcuin's letters.

[34] Several early manuscripts survive. One, an uncial codex (saec. viii med.) in the Vallicelliana at Rome, was probably copied in France. E. A. Lowe in C(odices) L(atini) A(ntiquiores) IV, No. 433 says of it: "Written north of the Alps in a fine centre of calligraphy," but the manuscripts with which he compares it are from N. or N.E. France. Schanz, *op. cit.* IV, ii, 95, and Manitius, *op. cit.* I, p. 50, disputed the attribution and proposed to assign the pseudo-Cassiodorus commentary to Justus. Neither offered any proof. Moreover, on p. 359, note 3 Manitius referred to the commentary by Justus, meaning the work printed under Justus' name, and Krüger on pp. 629–630 of Schanz's book did the same! *Delirant reges, plectuntur Achivi!* The pseudo-Cassiodorus commentary has recently been attributed to Isidore by Vega in La ciudad de Dios 154 (1942), 143 ff., but I have not seen this article.

[35] I have used the reprint of Faber's edition in M. de la Bigne, Sacra Bibliotheca SS. Patrum (ed. 2: Paris, 1589) I, pp. 763 ff. The only complete text of Aponius in print is that by H. Bottino and J. Martini (Rome, 1843), and the references to Aponius given below are to the pages of that edition. It is, however, very faulty. J. Witte, Der Kommentar des Aponius zum Hohenliede (Diss. Erlangen, 1903), pp. 5–6, is critical, but is himself far from impeccable. He finds some parallels (p. 85) between Aponius and Ambrose, meaning by Ambrose the

We are now in the position to analyze the sources used by Angelomus. The prefatory letter contains a long quotation from Gregory (PL 79, 473B–C). For his Introduction Angelomus has drawn on two works by Jerome, the preface to the commentary on Ecclesiastes and the preface to his translation of Kings. He may well have been familiar also with Alcuin's commentary on Ecclesiastes, which in fact is little more than a repetition of Jerome. But, although Angelomus does not copy Jerome as sedulously as Alcuin does, his text here and there reproduces the text of Jerome more closely; and an extant manuscript of Jerome's exposition was copied in the eighth century in the type of minuscule commonly called the Luxeuil script.[36] There are also two long quotations from Aponius in the Introduction and one from Gregory.[37] The commentary itself, as far as the sources are concerned, falls into three parts. From 562C to 577A Angelomus copies Gregory's two homilies almost word for word, adding a sentence from Alcuin at the end of 562C and two substantial excerpts from Aponius.[38] The second section begins where the genuine Gregory ends and extends to 607A. Most of this is from Aponius, but Angelomus has shortened his authority a good deal. He also has changed the order here and there and occasionally paraphrases Aponius instead of giving his exact words. In addition, there is in this section a good sprinkling of

pseudo-Ambrosian compilation (PL 15, 1851 ff.) which in fact was put together by William of St. Thierry in the twelfth century. His comparison between a passage in Aponius and one in Gregory on Cant. Cant. 8, 2, is no less unfortunate, since that part of "Gregory" is by Robert of St. Vigor. As we shall see, Witte also underrated the extent to which Angelomus copied from Aponius.

[36] This manuscript is now in the Stiftsbibliothek of St. Paul in Carinthia (25.2.36). Angelomus retains Jerome's subjunctives and the verb *nuncupare*, whereas Alcuin changes the subjunctives to the indicative and *nuncupare* to *appellare*. Jerome and Angelomus also read *per sententias* for which the printed text of Alcuin has *praesentibus*, but this may be a corrupt reading. So, too, Angelomus took the Hebrew titles of Proverbs, Ecclesiastes and the Song of Songs from Jerome's preface to Kings (cf. Biblia Sacra iuxta latinam vulgatam versionem 5 [Rome, 1944], p. 7), not from Isidore, Et. vi, 1, 7, as he retains Jerome's *praenotant*. Hrabanus, De inst. cler. 3, 7 (ed. Knöpfler, p. 200), copies Isidore.

[37] 558A–560A from Aponius 5–7 and 561C–562A from Aponius 3–4; 561B–C from PL 79, 561B–C.

[38] 562D–563B from Aponius 10, and 566C–568B greatly abbreviated from Aponius 10–15.

extracts from Alcuin and from Gregory-Paterius.[39] For the third section, from Cant. Cant. 4, 3 to the end, Aponius' help evidently was no longer available; that is, as Witte had already observed, since Angelomus did not copy from Books VII to XII of Aponius' commentary, his manuscript of that author belonged to that class of manuscripts which contains only the first six Books. At any rate, the third section is much briefer. It is little more than a conflation of Alcuin and Justus, whose exposition is at first paraphrased and later is quoted without acknowledgment *verbatim*. Usually Angelomus gives two interpretations of a verse, Alcuin's and then another, often introduced by *aliter* or *item*, taken from Justus. Here and there, as in the previous sections, he has also woven some quotations from Gregory-Paterius into the texture of his discourse. It thus becomes apparent that, when Witte quoted four passages from Aponius in Angelomus' commentary and further observed that there were in it a good number of other citations from the fifth-century author, he was guilty of serious understatement. A rough calculation shows that out of a total of seventy-seven columns in the Patrologia Latina no less than twenty-six are derived from Aponius and from Gregory about eighteen. Angelomus once (559A) alludes to Aponius by name, a fact which Witte seems to have overlooked. Later, at the beginning of Cant. Cant., chapter 2 (586D), Angelomus introduces what follows with the words: "dicamus uberius beati Ambrosii dicta ponentes"; but the quotation is not from Ambrose, but from Aponius, 57 ff. Is Ambrosius an error in the printed text or in the manuscript from which it was taken, as the citation does not appear to be in the works of Ambrose? It may be objected that Angelomus would be unlikely to refer to Aponius as *beatus*. The riddle must remain unsolved, but at least it is certain that Angelomus copied the whole paragraph from Aponius. A final point is worth noting. Angelomus did not have access to Bede's long commentary on the Song of Songs, but Alcuin did. The verbal parallels between Bede and Angelomus are found in the quotations which Angelomus copied from Alcuin's com-

---

[39] From Alcuin: 580D, 581A, 585D, 589C, 591C, 599C; from Gregory-Paterius: 594C, 603A, 604D–606A.

pendium. One must also bear in mind that all three commentators were heavily indebted to Gregory the Great.[40]

The Library at Luxeuil in the-Ninth Century

Angelomus, as we have seen, on several occasions alludes to his monastic library. No medieval catalogue is known to survive, but during the French Revolution an inventory of it was compiled. By that time the collection had shrunk to "thirty-three manuscripts and a few others," and a good many of these can still be identified.[41] Even if the number of earlier authors consulted by Angelomus was modest compared with the numerous predecessors quoted or paraphrased by Bede or Hrabanus, it was still respectable; and this evidence may be of some value to any palaeographer who may hereafter attempt a study of the scriptorium and library at Luxeuil. Unhappily the existing palaeographical evidence is not conclusive. A dozen or more codices of the late seventh or early eighth century survive, written either in late uncials or in a variety of Merovingian minuscule to which the name, Luxeuil script, has long been assigned. Yet it is not certain that Luxeuil itself was the centre in which any or all of these manuscripts originated, though the *Schriftheimat* of all appears to have been in E. or N.E. France.[42] By the ninth century some of these manuscripts had travelled far, but the exemplars were still presumably in the scriptoria

[40] Cf. Bernhard Bischoff in his valuable article on John of Mantua (Festschrift für Walter Goetz zum 80. Geburtstag [Marburg, 1948], p. 27): "Da die homiletische Auslegung Gregors des Grossen nur für Kap. 1, 1–8 erhalten geblieben war, wurde für die lateinischen Erklärer des Frühmittelalters Beda die beherrschende Autorität."

[41] See Leclercq in Dictionnaire d'archéologie chrétienne et de liturgie IX, ii, 2780–2781. Mr. Leslie Webber Jones in his article on three Luxeuil manuscripts and another now at Oxford (Bulletin of the J. Rylands Library 23 [1939], 3–18) overlooked this inventory, since he remarks (p. 4): "We may be sure, then, that all four manuscripts were present at Luxeuil at the beginning of the eighteenth century." The manuscripts that he analyzes are Nos. 4, 11, 14, and 7 in Leclercq's description of surviving manuscripts.

[42] See E. A. Lowe, CLA I, nos. 92–94 and 106; II, 163 and 173; III, 300; IV, 497; V, 548, 579, 614, and note particularly Dr. Lowe's remarks on V, 579 (Paris, B.N. 9427). The homiliary collated by Morin and described by him as *litteris typi luxoviensis exaratus* (S. Caesarii opera I, lxxxix), which was formerly Ashburnham Barrois 57, is now MS 17 in the Pierpont Morgan Library. See De Ricci and Wilson, Census II, p. 1368.

where the extant copies had been made. Several contain works of Gregory the Great and one was made up of extracts from the Fathers.[43] Many of the treatises and commentaries which Angelomus had at his elbow were, as the surviving catalogues show, commonly to be found in the larger libraries of E. or N.E. France and of Alemannia. That inter-library loans, even if sometimes attended by difficulties, were not unusual, is known from the correspondence of Servatus Lupus. Since Corbie was founded from Luxeuil, one might expect continued contact between the two houses and their libraries; and, although no catalogue of Corbie earlier than the eleventh century has been preserved, the number of extant manuscripts copied in the eighth and ninth centuries in its scriptorium is large. Nevertheless, some of the rarer works consulted by Angelomus suggest that the librarians of one or two collections geographically nearer to Luxeuil, particularly the chapter library in Rheims and the library in Murbach abbey, may have borrowed manuscripts from Luxeuil in order to have copies made for their own use. Thus, among extant manuscripts from Rheims is one donated by Hincmar, and its contents arouse curiosity; for there, together in one codex are pseudo-Jerome on Kings, Bede's *Quaestiones* XXX, and Gregory's two homilies on the Song of Songs, together with several other works by different authors. As the three works named were all at Luxeuil in Angelomus' time, one is tempted to assume that the librarian in Rheims had borrowed his exemplars from Luxeuil.[44] A codex from Murbach, now MS 78 in the municipal library at Épinal and copied about the middle of the ninth century, contains Jerome on Ecclesiastes, his translation of two of Origen's homilies on the Song of Songs, and the first six books of Aponius.[45] Bottino and Martini did not

---

[43] Cf. CLA V, 548. The illustration shows the beginning of a series of excerpts from Gregory: "Excarpsum ex libro beati Gregorii papae in Hiezechel propheta." This is the kind of selection, other than that of Paterius, to which Angelomus might well have had recourse.

[44] For Rheims 118 see *Catalogue général* 38, 109 ff. and especially F. M. Carey in *Studies in Honor of E. K. Rand*, pp. 52–53. Mr. Carey assigns it with a number of other manuscripts to the period 845–882.

[45] Cf. Baehrens, *op. cit.*, pp. 160–161; *Cat. gén.* (in quarto) 3, p. 431. The writer of the catalogue says "Apponius super totum librum eiusdem" but the explicit is not that of Book XII, but of Book VI.

use this manuscript for their edition, in spite of its early date. The rarity of the commentary in the ninth century—there was also at the same date a codex at Lorsch which seems to have disappeared—makes the conclusion almost irresistible that the exemplar of the Murbach Aponius was the manuscript used by Angelomus at Luxeuil. So too with Jerome's Commentary on Ecclesiastes. The extant codex of it which is now in St. Paul in Carinthia is written in the so-called Luxeuil script. A comparison of its text with the text in Épinal 78 would probably settle the question whether the one is the exemplar of the other. Finally, a perusal of the Murbach catalogue leads one to wonder whether it is pure accident that that library owned copies of nearly all the works consulted or copied by Angelomus.[46] At least it may be suggested that further study of the scriptoria and libraries at Rheims and Murbach may at the same time throw some much needed light on the books at Luxeuil during the Carolingian Age.

Note on the pseudo-Eucherius

This essay was already in proof when there came to my attention the important article, "Claudio de Turín, autor de los comentarios 'In genesim et regum' del Pseudo Euquerio" by Dom Bellet in Estudios Bíblicos 9 (Madrid, 1950), pp. 209–223. The authorship of the two commentaries wrongly ascribed to Eucherius of Lyons (PL 50, 893–1208) has long been a problem. The opening chapters of the Genesis commentary in a variant version were published by Carl Wotke in 1897 from Augiensis CXCI, and this publication was used by Baehrens (*op. cit.* 77 and 205). Dom Bellet has now shown that this version, which explains only Genesis i–iv, 1, survives also in MS Autun 27 (saec. viii) and MS Hague 130 E 15 (saec. ix–x). It was in fact Claudius of Turin's first attempt to compile a *collectaneum* on Genesis. Somewhat later Claudius put together a fuller commentary on the whole of Genesis. This survives in MS Paris 9575 copied in 811, as well as in MS Vienna 69 (saec. xii, Heiligenkreuz), the codex from which Brassicanus published his *editio princeps* at Basel in 1531. Clearly Dom Bellet has not himself seen the manuscript at Karlsruhe, since, like Wotke and Baehrens, he assigns it to the tenth century. I am deeply indebted to the di-

[46] Cf. Bloch, *op. cit.*, pp. 262–273.

rector of the manuscript section in the Landesbibliothek at Karlsruhe, Dr. K. Hannemann, who, in answer to my inquiries, kindly
sent me a detailed description of Aug. CXCI which amplifies the
information in the printed catalogue. The present codex is made
up of two distinct manuscripts which were only bound together
in the fifteenth century. The former (Aug. CXCI, foll. 2r–116r)
was correctly dated by Holder saec. viii/ix and contains Quaestiun-
culae on the Gospels collected from various fathers. The second
manuscript (foll. 117r–150v) begins with the text printed by Wotke
(foll. 117r–131v), which is introduced, as in the Autun manuscript,
by the phrase, "Isidori Iunioris expositionum sententias intexui-
mus." This second part of the present codex on palaeographical
grounds may be assigned provisionally to the period 825–840 and
may be a product of the Reichenau scriptorium. But, as Dr. Hannemann has rightly pointed out, certainty regarding both date and
Schriftheimat will only be attainable after a comprehensive study
of the writing-school in Reichenau has been made by a competent
scholar. Dom Bellet further points out that the commentary on
Samuel and Kings by Claudius of Turin is to be found in MS
Pistoia 51 and MS Mantua C.V.2, both of the eleventh century. The
commentary going under the name of Eucherius is in fact the commentary by Claudius with the addition of Bede's De templo Salomonis. This conflation survives in the same manuscript at Vienna
which contains Claudius' second and enlarged commentary on Genesis.

I can find no evidence that Angelomus used Claudius' exposition
of Samuel and Kings. But in the opening chapters of his commentary on Genesis (cf. PL 115, 127B, 129B, 135A–C) there are occasional comments where, in spite of verbal differences, the correspondence between Angelomus and pseudo-Eucherius is rather close.
It is therefore possible that Angelomus had access to the earlier
version by Claudius of Turin.

11

Fulgentius in the
Carolingian Age[*]

THE remarkable revival of letters in western Europe under
Charlemagne and his successors in the ninth century is a subject fascinating alike to the student of history, of theology, and
of literature. Intellectual activity in that age manifested itself
in the main under two forms. On the one hand, various theological questions gave material for vigorous, if not always charitable, disquisitions. Since a clear understanding of the Scriptures
was a needful prerequisite for discussing those problems, and
since the authority of the Fathers was regarded as second only
to that of Holy Writ, it was natural that this period should
witness the production of many biblical commentaries and
that these should for the most part reproduce, sometimes in
amplified, more often in abbreviated, form the expositions of
the great theologians of the fourth and fifth centuries. On the
other hand, the study of the classical and later literature of
pagan Rome was revived, and this renewed interest might mani-
fest itself in various ways, in the unique scholarship of a Servatus Lupus, which did so much to preserve classical writers for
a later age, in commentaries on grammatical and other works

[*] *Mélanges Hrouchevsky* (Kiev: Ukrainian Academy of Sciences, 1928), 445–
456.

suitable for use in monastic schools, and in original compositions, mostly in verse, which are rarely quite devoid of indi-
viduality, even when they are most closely modelled on earlier
poets, from Vergil to Sedulius and Fortunatus. The four massive
volumes of the *Monumenta Germaniae Historica* doubtless
represent only a fraction of the poetic output of that epoch. If
the ninth century produced no poet of the first rank, one can
nevertheless divide the verse written then, as one can that of
any other age, into good, bad, and indifferent. It would be idle
to deny that the writers of earlier ages, who enjoyed popularity
in the Carolingian period, are also of very unequal merit. Sometimes authors who appear to have been widely read then, may
seem to us quite unworthy of such posthumous fame. No better
instance of undeserved popularity could be found than that
of the subject of this paper, Fulgentius. Much has been written
on the identification of Fulgentius, the mythographer; but,
whereas it is perhaps hardly permissible categorically to deny
that he is identical with Fulgentius, bishop of Ruspe, it must
be emphasised that the arguments which have been educed
in favour of the identification are not convincing.[1] That the
writings both of the mythographer and of the bishop were well
known in the ninth century, it is the purpose of these pages
to demonstrate. But the two men will be separately considered,
not only because it is in itself highly improbable that the profane and the theological works, which bear the name Fulgentius,
are by the same hand, but because the scholars and writers of
the ninth century themselves appear never to have identified
or confused the bishop with the mythographer.[2]

---

[1] See on this whole question M. Schanz, *Römische Litteraturgeschichte*, IV,
2, pp. 196 ff. where ample references are given to the earlier literature on the
subject. Among recent protagonists for the theory of identifying the two Fulgentii,
the late F. Skutsch (Pauly-Wissowa, *Realencyclopädie;* art. Fulgentius) and his
pupil, O. Friebel (*Fulgentius, der Mythograph und Bischof,* 1911) are the most
prominent.

[2] The attribution of the fragment *Super Thebaiden* to the bishop in the
single ms., where this work is preserved, does not disprove the contention made
above; for the ms. belongs to the thirteenth century. Similarly, it is no more than
a scribe's error, if in some mss. the *Sermones antiqui* are attributed to Fulgentius,
the bishop. (For these mss. cf. Wessner, *Commentationes Philologae Ienenses,*
VI, 2, p. 128).

The Mythographer

Among the remnants of an effete and expiring classicism none are more pretentious, yet essentially trivial, than the three treatises which bear the name of Fabius Planciades Fulgentius, namely, the *Mitologiae* in three books, the *Expositio Virgilianae Continentiae* and the *Expositio Sermonum Antiquorum*. A fourth work, *De Aetatibus Mundi et Hominis*, though its author's name appears in the manuscripts as Fabius Claudius Gordianus Fulgentius, is without doubt by the same writer as the other three.[3] The general similarity of style, and particularly the fantastic etymologies, proclaim the common authorship. However unworthy of survival these compilations may seem, there is abundant evidence that the *Mitologiae* at all events were extensively read in the Carolingian age. It is true that reminiscences of, or citations from, Fulgentius are often very brief; they are also widely scattered. But the cumulative evidence derived from writers of the ninth century, together with that provided by extant manuscripts and the catalogues of monastic libraries, justify the contention that the *Mitologiae* and, to a less degree, the other works of Fulgentius, were among the more popular (school?) books used in that period.

As has already been said, by far the largest number of reminiscences come from the *Mitologiae*. The brief, though often inaccurate, descriptions of various episodes in Greek and Roman mythology, followed by more or less fanciful allegorical interpretations, appealed alike to the commentators and versifiers of that age. Sometimes, too, it is not the subject matter but the exotic language of Fulgentius which appealed to those writers. To them echoes of the tortured and artificial periods of Fulgentius introduced into their own works were marks of a high style. A strange contrast indeed to the pure latinity of Lupus, which is the product of an intimate study of classical prose writers like Cicero, and a no less thorough familiarity with the Vulgate! No actual commentaries on Fulgentius appear to have survived, though it is not improbable that such existed. At all events a commentator on some other work might use Ful-

---

[3] For a detailed analysis of these works see Schanz, *op. cit.*

gentius for purposes of illustration, as was done, for example, by John Scotus. In his commentary on Martianus Capella, there are a number of allusions to the *Mitologiae,* and in one place John refers to the author by name, calling him briefly Fabius.[4] Moreover it is in this very passage that he disagrees with Fulgentius about the interpretation of the name Atropos. This is not an isolated case, for his derivation of the name Heracles, his account of Dionysus, and his interpretation of Saturn with his sickle, all differ from those of the older writer.[5] Elsewhere John's elucidations agree with those found in the *Mitologiae;*[6] hence we see that he was thoroughly familiar with that work, but did not hesitate to correct, and we may add, improve interpretations given in it. Whether the Irish Dunchad, who was slightly older than John Scotus and also wrote a commentary on Martianus, was familiar with Fulgentius, must remain doubtful. There are, at all events, three passages in his fragmentary work which resemble information found in the *Mitologiae.*[7] The Martianus commentary by Remigius of Auxerre contains a reference to Fulgentius by name,[8] but, as Remigius used older commentaries on Martianus freely, we cannot be certain that the few reminiscences of Fulgentius are the result of first-hand acquaintance with him. They may have been borrowed from John Scotus or perhaps from Martin of Laon. The last named writer's *Scholica* also show some acquaintance, either direct or derivative, with the *Mitologiae.*[9] Moreover in the same *Scholica* there is a passage which throws some light on a much disputed question. At the end of his edition of Fulgentius, Rudolf Helm published a fragment entitled *Super Thebaiden,*

---

[4] John's commentary on Martianus was partly published by Manitius in *Didaskaleion,* I, pp. 157 ff. and II, pp. 43 ff. Cf. I, p. 169—"ut Fabio placet."

[5] I, p. 172; II, pp. 46 and 58.

[6] I, p. 167 (Polymnia); pp. 171–172 (Hecate), p. 172 (Proserpina); II, p. 44 (Forcus and the Medusae).

[7] Dunchad's commentary was also published in *Didaskaleion,* I, pp. 138 ff. The three passages in question are: p. 143 (Mercurius; cf. *Mit.* p. 29, 8 in Helm's edition); p. 147 (Sol—Apollo: cf. *Mit.* 23, 4–5); p. 155 (Gorgones; cf. *Mit.* 32, 3 and 33, 8).

[8] *Didask.* II, p. 67.

[9] See my articles in *Bulletin of the J. Rylands Library,* Manchester, VII, 1923, pp. 421–456 and IX, 1925, pp. 130–138.

in which the same kind of allegorical interpretation is applied to Statius' *Thebaid* as is applied to the *Aeneid* in Fulgentius' *Expositio Virgilianae Continentiae*. This fragment has only survived in a single manuscript of the thirteenth century (Paris. Lat. 3012). While some scholars have accepted it as a work of Fulgentius, others have argued that it is the compilation of a medieval writer.[10] For this assertion only one definite proof has been produced; it is maintained that Surculus as a nickname for Statius is not found before the tenth century. Helm tries to strengthen his case by arguing that even Fulgentius would not have perpetrated such a Greek etymology as is found in the fragment (p. 183, 10–1): *Polis Grece multum dicitur Latine, nichos victor; unde dicitur chere Cesar anichos*. The *argumentum ex silentio*, which in this case has been used about the name Surculus, is always dangerous; but the whole argument for authorship in the tenth century or later falls to the ground because a part of the very sentence just quoted is found in the ninth-century *Scholica* (K 5; cf. Misc. 2). The fragment was therefore not written in the tenth century; nor can it be reasonably maintained that the specimen of Greek lore is any worse than some which occur in the *Mitologiae* or in the other works of Fulgentius.[11] There seems then to be no reason for doubting the Fulgentian authorship of the *Super Thebaiden;* that it was less popular than the allegorical interpretation of the *Aeneid* will occasion no surprise, but is perhaps rather some indication of the relative popularity of Vergil and Statius in the Middle Ages. Incidentally, it may be added that there appear to have been other works bearing Fulgentius' name, which survived in the Middle Ages, but which are now lost.[12]

Sedulius Scotus, the contemporary and fellow countryman of

[10] See Schanz, *op. cit.* pp. 199–200; Helm, *praef.* p. xv, in which works further references are given.

[11] e.g. *Mit.* 19, 10 (Posidonian—quasi pion idonan etc.); 48, 4–5 (Fedra quasi odoratus, velut si dicat feronedon quasi adferens suavitatem). *Virg. Cont.* 102, 10 (Anchises enim Grece quasi anon scenon id est patrium habitans).

[12] cf. for instance the *Liber Differentiarum Fulgentii* recorded in a ninth-century catalogue of St. Gall (P. Lehmann, *Mittelalterliche Bibliothekskataloge,* I, p. 89, 22). [But see now Bernhard Bischoff in *Byzantinische Zeitschrift* 44 (1951), 51, note 3.]

Erigena, was another prominent teacher and writer of the period, who shows familiarity with the *Mitologiae* and the *Sermones Antiqui*. A number of reminiscences in his *Liber de Rectoribus* make this clear, but it is noteworthy that Fulgentius' name does not appear in the *collectaneum*, which the same writer compiled from classical and patristic literature.[13] It is rather more surprising that Paschasius Radbertus, whose interests were wholly theological, should nevertheless betray a little knowledge of the *Mitologiae*. The opening sentence of that work is transcribed in a passage of the *Epitaphium Arsenii*,[14] while traces of Fulgentius occur also in Radbertus' letters.[15] Ermenrich of Ellwangen in his long and rambling epistle to Grimold, which is mainly a compilation from Boethius, Bede, Priscian, Alcuin, and others, took his explanations and etymologies of the Fates and the Furies verbally from Fulgentius.[16] Again, a writer of somewhat later date, Gunzo of Novara (floruit circa 960), refers to the same work in a way which suggests that he knew not only its name, but its general content.[17] Finally, there is a remarkable letter, written in the second half of the ninth century by A to his former master E. It has not been possible to identify either the writer or the recipient of this letter, which contains many points of interest and some obscurities.[18] The letter opens with the following flamboyant dedication:

Ulixeo intuitu se regenti, Syrenarum tractus facili impulsu transeunti, adnullanti Charybdin et Scylleos latratus modesta severitate calcanti ac per hoc ideali theoremate cathedralem eptadin iure

---

[13] See S. Hellmann, *Sedulius Scotus* (= Texte und Untersuchungen zur Lateinischen Philologie des Mittelalters, I, 1906) and the list of references given by him on pp. xiv–v.

[14] *PL*, 120, 1562D (Nonne legisti . . . effectu = *Mit.* p. 3, 2). In *PL*, 1576D and 1607C he uses the word *glaber* in a context, which suggests that he remembers *serm. ant.* p. 117, 3–4 (glabrum vero lenem et imberbem).

[15] *MGH: Epist.* VI, p. 134 (salsura); also 142, 41 and 143, 7 with Dümmler's notes *ad loc.*

[16] *MGH: Epist.* V, p. 563, 33–36 (= *Mit.* 21, 8–10; 20, 21).

[17] *PL*, 136, 1289B–C; there do not appear to be any citations from Fulgentius in the letter.

[18] This is the second of three letters first published by Dümmler in *Neues Archiv*, XIII, pp. 345 ff. from a Leyden ms. (Voss Lat. 88). It was reprinted in MGH: *Epist.* VI, pp. 182–186.

tenenti regentique in apotelesmaticen, perfectam scilicet consum-
mationem plectra Phoebea, domino vere sancto et desiderabili de-
siderandoque magistro E. A. voto perpete suus, quadriformem
agonem in cyclo Phenonis, Pegaseam sessionem in circulo solis
Gorgoneamque parthenen in intentione virtutis usque ad bravium
salutis perpetuae et gloriam felicitatis aeternae.

When editing this curious example of high style, Dümmler, no
doubt rightly, saw an allusion to Martianus Capella in the use
of Heptas and of the name Phenon for Saturn, but beyond this
he offered no comment. It seems clear, however, that the writer
was even more familiar with Fulgentius, who provided him
with these mythological allusions and adjectives derived from
proper names.[19] The word *Apelleas* in the body of the letter
may come from the same source,[20] but any doubt that might
still exist that A is indebted to the *Mitologiae* is dispelled by
his use of the rare *apotelesmatice,* which in Fulgentius occurs in
the following context:

sed . . . . . vox canora descendit et quia apotelesmatica fonascica
omnia praebet . . . . . voluptatum reddit effectus (*Mit.* p. 79, 1).

At the end of the third letter in Voss Lat. 88, which follows immediately on the letter under consideration, there are, written
in the same hand as the third letter, four glosses. The second
of these reads:

fonascus: medicina vocis.

Is this a mere coincidence, or did the scribe recognise the source
of the allusion to *apotelesmatice* in the previous letter, which is
copied in a different hand? If so, he added the gloss to show his
own learning. At the end of the same manuscript a number of
verses or short poems have been written by various hands of
the twelfth and thirteenth centuries. Their content is for the

[19] cf. *Mit.* p. 48, 8–9 (Fabula Ulixis et Sirenarum. Sirenae enim Grece tractoriae
dicuntur); p. 49, 3 (Fabula Scyllae). The adjective *Gorgoneus* is used twice by
Fulgentius (pp. 8, 6 and 12, 19).

[20] *MGH: Epist.* VI, p. 185, 36. In *Mit.* 9, 7 Helm prints *Pelleae,* following one
ms. against the consensus of the others, which have *Apelleae.* For the third letter
see *MGH: Epist.* VI, pp. 186–187. The gloss *Politeia multorum vel plurimorum
deorum* is perhaps another Fulgentius gloss (on *Mit.* p. 19, 2).

most part obscene, since they allude to vices practiced at Sens, Paris, and Orléans. It is not at all clear whether these Fescennine compositions were actually composed in the twelfth and thirteenth centuries or belong to an earlier date. Dümmler seems to imply that they were written in the later period of the Middle Ages, but at all events, one couplet is unintelligible save to one familiar with the legend of the birth of Erichthonius. This the medieval reader would find most readily in the *Mitologiae*.[21]

The poets or versifiers of the Carolingian age supply further proof of Fulgentius' popularity. Sometimes they cull rare words from that source, sometimes they borrow mythological allusions or even brief etymologies. For the former practice we may instance Engilmodus, Sedulius Scotus, and Milo;[22] for the latter, Milo, Hucbald, the author of a poem on St. Landbertus, and the writers of the *Carmen de Sancto Cassiano* and of the *Carmen de Sancta Benedicta*.[23]

Occasionally poems written at this period are elucidated by contemporary *scholia*, whether written by the poet himself, or by some friend or pupil. Such annotations often provide more than a brief explanation of a single word; they give citations from, or allusions to, older sources. Thus, in one of the *scholia* accompanying Heiric's poem on St. Germanus of Auxerre there is a reference to Fulgentius by name.[24] An even more instructive example of this practice may be found in the *Gesta Berengarii*. This remarkable poem was composed between 915 and 924; the elaborate *scholia*, which are appended to it, are contemporary

[21] Dümmler edited these verses in *Neues Archiv*, XIII, pp. 358–360. The couplet in question is as follows: Hostis nature, cui non est gignere cure, in vetitum gremium fundis Eritonium (cf. *Mit*. p. 57, 5–7).

[22] Engilmodus: see *MGH: Poet.* III, pp. 62, 13–15; 63, 35–36; 66, 156, with L. Traube's notes *ad loc*. Sedulius: *ibid*. pp. 166, 5; 180, 10. The latter passage, strangely enough, was missed by Traube, who commented on *vernulitas* in the poem thus: "vernulitas a ver vernum novam vocem deduxit Sedulius." Yet the word occurs three times in Fulgentius (pp. 3, 13; 7, 1; 14, 5), and previously (*Poet*. III, p. 62) Traube had himself cited one of these very passages. Milo: *ibid. de sobrietate*, I, 1. 837.

[23] Milo: *ibid*. II: 830–834. Hucbald: Poet. IV, 1, ll. 1–4 of the prologue to the *ecloga de clavis*. Carmen de S. Cass.: *ibid*. p. 182, 25. Carmen de S. Landberto. *ibid*. p. 143. Carmen de S. Bened.: *ibid*. p. 211, 17.

[24] *MGH: Poet.* III, p. 436.

with the poem, and some part of them was written by the poet himself.[25] Fulgentius' *Mitologiae* are used a number of times, but the scholiast was also familiar with the *Sermones antiqui*, as the use of *sandapilis* and *tucceta*, together with their glosses, seems to show. Fulgentius is once mentioned by name.[26]

It is very regrettable that our information regarding the distribution of Fulgentius manuscripts in the ninth century is so incomplete. It is also a remarkable fact that, whereas the literary sources discussed above for the most part show indebtedness to the *Mitologiae*, it is the *Sermones* which are found most frequently in extant manuscripts.[27] Of the oldest surviving codices which contain three works of Fulgentius (*Mitol., Virg. Cont.* and *Serm.*) one was written towards the end of the eighth, the other early in the ninth century. The two manuscripts were copied from the same archetype, but while the former (Vat. Reg. 1462) cannot be assigned to a particular scriptorium, the latter (Vat. Pal. 1578) is a book of Lorsch.[28] There was a ninth-century manuscript of the three works at St. Amand, of which only two leaves have survived because they were used to bind up another codex in the St. Amand library at a much later date.[29] Two important tenth-century codices contain only the *Mitologiae;* one is now at Trèves, the other at Cassel. The latter was

[25] For the *Gesta Berengarii* and *scholia* see *MGH: Poet.* IV, 1, pp. 355–401. The note on Book 2, line 207 is clearly by the poet himself. See generally the valuable introduction and notes to the poem by Winterfeld.

[26] cf. the *scholia* on 1, 4, 1, 123; 2, 80, and Winterfeld's note on 1, 67. To the passages which he illustrates from Fulgentius I should add the gloss on 1, 244 (Thetis secundum fabulam mater fuit Achillis; sed ponitur pro mari. cf. *Mit.* p. 70, 4; 71, 10). *Sandapilis* is used in 1, 271, *tucceta* in 4, 160; Fulgentius is named in the note on 1, 123.

[27] See the list of over fifty codices, containing the *Sermones*, which Wessner has drawn up in his introduction to the edition of that work (Commentationes Philologae Ienenses, VI, 2).

[28] The discussion of these two manuscripts by W. M. Lindsay (*Palaeographia Latina*, III, 1924, pp. 23–24) supersedes the information to be found in Helm and elsewhere. Lindsay calls the script of Vat. Reg. 1462 "pre-Carolingian north Italian minuscule."

[29] See L. Delisle in *Journal des Savants*, 1899, pp. 126–129, who explains "Les deux feuillets dont il s'agit servent de gardes à un manuscrit de l'abbaye de Saint Amand, aujourdhui conservé à Valenciennes, no. 278 du catalogue de Mangeart, et no. 288 du catalogue de M. Molinier."

originally at Fulda.[30] To the same century belong several lesser manuscripts of the *Mitologiae* and *Virgiliana Continentia,* while a tenth-century catalogue of Bobbio records no less than three copies of the former work.[31] The best surviving manuscript of the *De aetatibus mundi* (Vat. Pal. 886) is a Lorsch book of the ninth century.[32] The same work was to be found early in that century at St. Riquier.[33] To sum up: while it must be admitted that our knowledge regarding the distribution of Fulgentius manuscripts in the Carolingian period is very fragmentary, such evidence as we have, coupled with the numerous traces of that author in the writers and poets of that era, as well as the more abundant evidence for manuscripts of the tenth century, justify the contention that Fulgentius was a favourite author in that period of the Middle Ages.[34]

The Bishop

Since the theological writers of the Carolingian age were admittedly so prolific, and since it is equally clear that they were earnest students of earlier patristic literature, it might seem superfluous to single out for consideration a sixth-century author, who is after all only in the second rank, and to estimate his influence in the ninth century. It so happens, however, that in a recent and authoritative work an effort is made to minimise the extent of Fulgentius, the bishop's, influence in later times; hence it has seemed worth while to marshall the evidence for

[30] For these two mss. see P. Lehmann in *Rheinische Museum,* 61 (1906), pp. 107 ff.

[31] See G. Becker, *Catalogi bibliothecarum antiqui,* 32, nos. 445, 610 and 665.

[32] See Lindsay, *loc. cit.* Helm had dated this codex in the thirteenth century.

[33] See Becker, *op. cit.* 11, no. 86.

[34] Was Fulgentius known in England before the end of the ninth or beginning of the tenth century? Harleian 2685 (saec. IX–X) and 2682 (saec. XI) were both once at Cologne (cf. A. C. Clark in *Class. Rev.* 1891, p. 372). For an early tenth century ms. in the Bodleian cf. Madan, *Cat. of western mss.,* no. 20627; it, too, is presumably a Continental codex. Neither Aldhelm nor Bede show any acquaintance with Fulgentius. On the other hand, Lindsay (*Palaeographia Latina,* III, p. 24) gives palaeographical reasons for supposing that Vat. Pal. 1578 was copied from "an exemplar in Insular script." This need mean no more than that the writer of the exemplar was an Anglo-Saxon resident in a German monastery. The archetype in question need not have been written in England.

the use of Fulgentius in the period that we are considering.[35] The truth seems to be that most of the more important writers on theological subjects in western Europe during the ninth century show acquaintance with the works of Fulgentius; if the geographical boundary be extended, we may add Claudius of Turin to the list. He includes Fulgentius among the important ecclesiastical authors, whom he enumerates in the preface to his commentary on Matthew.[36] This alone shows that Fulgentius' writings must have been available in many monastic libraries; the evidence of early catalogues points in the same direction. At least one venerable codex of Fulgentius has survived, the original home of which was in France.[37] It was written in uncial and half-uncial script in the sixth or seventh century. The libraries of Friaul, St. Vandrille, Compiègne, Lorsch, and Würzburg contained at least some of Fulgentius' works in the ninth century.[38] Early in the previous century the compiler of the *Liber Glossarum* had included some extracts in his huge dictionary from the *contra Fabianum libri decem* of Fulgentius and possibly from some other works as well.[39]

[35] Gustav Krüger, in Schanz, *Röm. Litt.* IV, 2, p. 581, asserts: "Die Nachwirkung des Fulgentius war nicht so gross, wie man es nach den ihm oft gespendeten Lobeserhebungen annehmen sollte. Während Isidor ihn feiert, erwähnt ihn Beda überhaupt nicht (vgl. Hinkmar v. Rheims, praed. diss. post. 3. M. 125 Sp. 88A). Alcuin nennt ihn adv. Elipandum 4, 4 (M. 101, Sp. 288D) einen *luculentus ecclesiae catholicae scriptor.*" The solitary reference to Alcuin is most misleading. As a matter of fact, Fulgentius is mentioned by name in Alcuin's letters (*MGH: Epist.* IV, pp. 337, 3; 468, 35) and he appears also in the list of ecclesiastical writers to be found at York (*MGH: Poet.* I, p. 204, line 1544).

[36] *MGH: Epist.* IV, p. 594, 13.

[37] Vat. Reg. 267, foll. 99–228. See E. A. Lowe (*A Handlist of halfuncial mss.* in *Miscellanea Francesco Ehrle*, IV, no. 110), who adds "From the abbey of St. Benedict at Fleury the ms. migrated to St. Martial at Limoges."

[38] Friaul: Becker, *Cat. bibl. ant.* 12, nos. 19 and 35 (837). St. Vandrille (823–833): Becker, 7. no. 25. Compiègne: Lindsay, *Notae Latinae*, p. 477 (= Bibl. Nat. lat. 17416; "from Compiègne written before 837"). Würzburg: Becker, 18, no. 35. See also the letter of bishop Humbert of Würzburg to Hrabanus Maurus in *MGH: Epist.* V, p. 440, 21–22. Lorsch: Lindsay, *Palaeogr. Lat.*, III, p. 10 and line 8 of the left-hand column on Plate II.

[39] See, for example, the following entries in the *Liber Glossarum* (*Glossaria Latina*, I, 1926): AE 313, AR 341, DI 3, DI 24, DU 107, ID 67, MI 98, PA 370, PA 373, SI 259. All these bear the label "Fulgenti"; AE 313, MI 98, and SI 259 could be definitely assigned by the editors to the treatise *contra Fabianum*.

It is, indeed, not surprising that the theologians of the ninth century should have consulted the works of the African bishop. Several doctrinal questions, which in the eyes of the orthodox affected the very foundations of Christian belief and ecclesiastical authority, produced long and often exceedingly bitter controversies in that age. Thus, the attacks of Photius on the western Church, and the letter in support of him addressed by the emperors Michael and Basil to the Bulgarian king, led Pope Nicholas I to communicate with the Frankish bishops towards the end of 867, and to invite them to rebut the charges. It was especially the question concerning the Procession of the Holy Spirit which led to embittered discussion. Of the three lengthy replies written to the eastern Church by Frankish prelates, that by Odo of Beauvais has not survived, but the disquisitions of Aeneas, archbishop of Paris, and of Ratramnus of Corbie can still be studied by historians of dogma. To maintain their argument these writers of course make extensive use of patristic literature, and Fulgentius is among the authorities cited. In his *contra Graecorum opposita* Ratramnus quotes a lengthy passage from a lost work of Fulgentius on the Procession of the Holy Spirit.[40] Aeneas, whose treatise is little more than a *collectaneum* of passages from earlier writers on theology, also includes excerpts from the bishop of Ruspe.[41]

For his acrimonious controversy with Claudius of Turin, Jonas of Orléans would find little material in Fulgentius, but in his treatise on monarchic government he cites the bishop at least once.[42] Ratramnus, to whom reference has already been made, was also a protagonist in the Eucharistic controversy of the ninth century. In his *de Corpore et sanguine Domini* he invokes Fulgentius' authority.[43] Allusions to Fulgentius and considerable quotations from his *Letter to Ferrandus* are found also in Florus of Lyons' dissertation on the Mass.[44]

Again, we find in the reports of several Councils of the late

---

Only fragments of this work are however preserved, and the other extracts, which it was not possible to identify, may be from lost portions of that work. (See however the editors' apology, *ib. praef.* p. 13).

[40] See *PL*, 121, coll. 295–297A.   [41] *ibid.*, 121, coll. 712–715.
[42] *ibid.*, 106, coll. 289C–D.   [43] *ibid.*, 121, coll. 165B–166B.
[44] *ibid.*, 119, coll. 15c; 23C; 30C; 70B.

eighth and early ninth centuries appeals to the authority of the African bishop.[45] One sentence in particular, from the treatise *De Veritate Praedestinationis* (II, 38), is cited more than once:

Quantum pertinet ad huius temporis vitam constat quia in ecclesia nemo pontifice potior, et in saeculo Christiano nemo imperatore celsior invenitur.

It was in debating the doctrines of single and double predestination that the works of Fulgentius were most extensively used by both sides in the controversy. Discussions arising out of that doctrine were of course no new thing,[46] but the teaching and writing of Gottschalk raised the whole topic in a particularly acute form and produced what may be called without either exaggeration or impiety an ecclesiastical *cause célèbre*. The works of Fulgentius from which authority was chiefly sought and from which most citations were adduced, were the *Liber de veritate praedestinationis,* the *Liber de fide,* and the first of the three books addressed to Monimus, which bears the sub-title, *De duplici praedestinatione Dei.*[47] To the most orthodox opponents of Gottschalk, Fulgentius himself was not free from the suspicion of heresy on this particular question. Hence Hincmar of Rheims pens a general warning, though otherwise he speaks of him with becoming respect.[48] Many of the writings which were called forth by this controversy are little more than collectanea from the Fathers; others show more originality in form, if not in content. But in all alike we meet with the name of Fulgentius and, what is more important evidence, with quotations from him. The weight of his authority is of course not comparable with that of Augustine, Ambrose, Jerome,

[45] See *MGH: Concilia Aev. Carol.,* I. p. 111, 33; II, 492, 25; 610, 39; 627, 33; 650, 41; 705, 22; 715, 12; *MGH: Capit. Reg. Franc.,* II. 29, 28; 47, 1.

[46] Cf. the two letters written by Pope Hadrian I shortly before the period which we are considering (between 785 and 791), which contain *inter alia* long citations from Fulgentius (*MGH: Epist.* III, pp. 642, 6 ff.; 646, 10 ff.).

[47] For the works of Bishop Fulgentius see *PL,* 65. It is high time that a new and critical edition of this author were produced. Particularly there is need of full information about the extant manuscripts. The present writer regrets that, through inability to get access to all the needful library catalogues, his remarks on this topic may not be exhaustive.

[48] See *PL,* 125, coll. 86–88. There are further references to and citations from Fulgentius in later parts of Hincmar's book (cf. coll. 96–105; 122–125).

Fulgentius in the Carolingian Age

Gregory the Great, and some others, but it is not negligible. Thus besides Hincmar himself, we find our author used by Hrabanus, Prudentius of Troyes, Lupus of Ferrières, Remigius of Lyons, Ratramnus, and Gottschalk himself.[49] In conclusion, even if we allow for the borrowing of citations from one another by participants in this acrimonious controversy, there still remains sufficient evidence to prove that some at least of Fulgentius' works were to be found in many monastic libraries and that they were considerably studied by the Carolingian theologians. Assuredly the *Fortleben* of Fulgentius was not unimportant.

Addendum

Another ninth-century author, who names Bishop Fulgentius among the Latin Fathers with whom he is familiar, is Smaragdus of St. Mihiel (PL, 102, col. 13 C.).

To the mss. of Bishop Fulgentius named above should be added: Paris, Bibl. Nat. Lat. 1796, written in the ninth century, partly in Visigothic script, partly in Carolingian minuscule. See C. U. Clark, *Collectanea Hispanica*, p. 50, no. 645.

Further, the first in a collection of homilies from Luxeuil, now in the Rylands Library at Manchester (no. 12 in M. R. James' catalogue; saec. VIII–IX), is a homily by Fulgentius.

No. 4 in the Beatty collection appears also to contain works by the bishop, but the catalogue was inaccessible to me. See however E. A. Lowe in *Journal of Theol. Stud.* 29 (Oct. 1927), p. 33.

---

[49] Hrabanus: *MGH: Epist.* V, pp. 389, 25 (general reference only); 418, 8 (ref. to a work now lost); 492, 38 ff. Prudentius: *PL*, 115, coll. 1055A, 1075A, 1156A, 1246B, 1304B, 1309C, also 989D–993C, containing a whole chapter from *ad Monimum*, I, and 1001A–B. Lupus: *PL*, 119, col. 642C; 656D. Remigius: *PL*, 121, coll. 1000C, 1003A, 1105–1106. Ratramnus: *ibid.*, coll. 49–54. Gottschalk: *ibid.* coll. 350A and 357A. The nickname, Fulgentius, which Walahfrid Strabo applied to Gottschalk (see, *MGH: Poet.* II, p. 362), has sometimes been regarded as an allusion to Gottschalk's part in the predestination controversy, i.e. Gottschalk was a second bishop of Ruspe. But L. Traube (*MGH: Poet* III, p. 708, note 2) is probably right in seeing in the nickname an allusion to the mythographer. As he says, not without a touch of humour, Gottschalk and Walahfrid were friends in their boyhood (W.'s poem alludes to this), and the two were more likely to have read the *Mitologiae* together, than to have jointly ruminated over the doctrine of predestination at that tender age.

12

A Ninth-Century Commentator

on the Gospel according to

Matthew*

THE subject of this paper, Christian of Stavelot, though he is one of the less familiar figures of the Carolingian revival of learning, whose only substantial work is a commentary on the First Gospel, should be of interest to any student of monastic education. Yet, apart from an admirable essay by Ernst Dümmler and a shorter, but very useful, article by Manitius, recent research has not paid much attention to this writer.[1] A study of his commentary throws a good deal of light on the methods followed by commentators of that age in compiling their expositions of the Scripture, as well as on the system of teaching adopted in the monastic schools. Not the least remarkable characteristic of Christian is his independent spirit, which contrasts markedly with the slavish adherence to earlier authorities noticeable in some of his contemporaries. Indeed the sentiments expressed by Christian at the beginning of his epistle dedicatory

* Harvard Theological Review, 20 (1927), 129–149. Reprinted by permission of the Harvard University Press.

[1] E. Dümmler in Sitzungsberichte, Berlin Academy, 1890, pp. 935 ff.; M. Manitius, Geschichte der Lateinischen Literatur im Mittelalter, I, p. 431. For the MSS. of Christian's work, see J. Lebon, Revue d'histoire ecclésiastique, IX, 1908, pp. 491 ff.

are such as to arouse the interest of the reader at once in the man and his work. He says:

I have aimed to follow the historic rather than the allegoric (*spiritalem*) meaning, because it seems to me illogical to look for an allegorical understanding in any book and to ignore the historical utterly; for history is the foundation of all intelligence and we must seek her from the first and embrace her, and without her we cannot successfully pass on to other knowledge.[2]

The known facts of Christian's life are few. Sigebert of Gembloux (end of the eleventh century) calls him a native of Aquitania, and this statement has been generally accepted,[3] but it is probable that Sigebert merely deduced this from a single passage in Christian's commentary.[4] More is to be said for the view that he came from Burgundy, for several passages in his work support it.[5] When he wrote his commentary he was a monk in the abbey of Stavelot, and with the help of internal evidence the date of that sojourn can be fixed in the second half of the ninth century. The abbey of Stavelot was situated in what at that time was wild and dangerous country—*in locis vastae solitudinis in quibus caterva bestiarum germinat* [6]—in the heart of the Ardennes. Originally in the diocese of Maastricht, it was later in that of Liége. It had been founded between 648 and 651 at the same time as the neighboring religious house of Malmédy, both being for long under the rule of a single abbot. The founder of Stavelot, St. Remaclus, was a native of Aquitania, and in due course became abbot of Cougnon in the diocese of Trèves. Later he was appointed head of the newly founded religious settlement in the Ardennes. The rule of St. Columban was at first followed in Stavelot, but later—there would appear to be no evidence for determining the precise

---

[2] The epistle dedicatory is included among the letters published in MGH: Epistolae, VI, pp. 177 f.

[3] So by Dümmler and Manitius. The identification of Christian with Druthmar of Corbie has long been exploded; for this topic see Dümmler, p. 936.

[4] Col. 1379D, where Christian contrasts the attitude of the Vascones and Spaniards with that of the Franks on the subject of dancing.

[5] So Hauck, Kirchengeschichte Deutschlands, II, p. 565, note 2.

[6] MGH: Diplomata, I, 22 (diploma of King Sigebert II of the year 648).

date of the change—the rule of St. Benedict was introduced, and Christian himself was a staunch admirer of that saint.[7]

In Migne's Patrologia Latina, volume 106, we find under Christian's name a lengthy commentary on Matthew and two very brief "Expositiones" on Luke and on John. The genuineness of these two short tracts is open to grave doubt. Dümmler inclined to accept them as genuine, but thought them to be first drafts for a longer work. It has, however, since been pointed out that the two so-called expositions are made up of extracts from the commentaries of Bede and Augustine.[8] That most of the extracts deal with allegorical interpretation, if it shows anything, suggests that Christian was not the man who made these excerpts. In his genuine work allegorical interpretation, though by no means lacking, is assigned a subordinate place, for he is true to his own declaration in the preface quoted above. Nor does the fact that Christian, in the same preface or dedicatory epistle, indicates that he may, if the commentary on Matthew be a success, follow it up by composing treatises on the Third and Fourth Gospels, prove that the two short tracts that have come down to us are his work. The matter is really immaterial, because the degree of Christian's excellence as an expositor and teacher can be appraised solely from his large commentary.

A passage from the epistle dedicatory has already been quoted; Christian there further tells us that he has undertaken to expound the First Gospel, because the younger members of the abbey, after two readings of the Gospel according to Matthew, are still ignorant of it. Jerome's commentary is too advanced for these beginners in theology, and Christian has tried to be as simple in his exposition as possible, since, he says, it is folly, when expounding any book, to speak in such a way that the commentary requires another commentator to explain it. Al-

---

[7] Cf. Gallia Christiana, III, 939; Hauck, I, p. 270.

[8] J. Lebon, Revue d'histoire ecclésiastique, IX, 1908, p. 453. Lebon leaves the authorship of the two expositions undecided. It is significant, too, that of the four extant MSS. which contain the commentary on Matthew, two omit both the tracts, and one omits the commentary on John. Besides Dümmler, Hauck also accepts the tracts as genuine (Realencyclopädie für protestantische Theologie, art. 'Druthmar').

legorical interpretation, he continues, must therefore be a secondary consideration. If his work be a success, he will write commentaries on Luke and John, but Bede's on Mark has made another on that gospel superfluous. Augustine on the Fourth Gospel is again too difficult for beginners, and of Bede's treatise on Luke, Christian had only seen, he says, *quasdam homilias.*[9] The modesty and good sense of this introduction at once predispose the reader in the author's favor. In Dümmler's excellent essay several aspects of Christian's work have hardly received sufficient attention, and some further inquiry into these may be of value. The points in question are the sources used by Christian, his method of compilation and composition, and in connection with this topic the nature of the Bible text used by him and the extent of his knowledge of the Greek language.

A number of commentaries on the First Gospel had been composed before Christian's time, for example Jerome's, that attributed to Bede, and the lengthy expositions of Hrabanus Maurus and Paschasius Radbertus. Of these four works Jerome's is basic, a composition in fact on which all subsequent commentators relied. Christian studied it carefully and used it extensively, as is proved by what he himself says in his introduction, by occasional references to Jerome by name, and by a general comparison of the two commentaries. The commentary on Matthew now included among the works of the Venerable Bede need not detain us, since it has been conclusively shown that, so far from being a genuine work of the great English scholar, it is a very abbreviated and not too successful adaptation of the commentary of Hrabanus Maurus.[10] That Christian used Radbertus there seems to be no proof whatever, but it does seem probable that he was not unfamiliar with the work of Hrabanus. It might be thought a simple task to demonstrate such indebtedness, but in reality it is far from easy for two reasons. First, Christian, unlike Hrabanus himself,

[9] It must remain an open question whether Christian's comment on *parasceve* (col. 1496B) is indebted to Bede on Luke 23, 54 or to Hrabanus, who copies Bede exactly.

[10] A. E. Schönbach, 'Ueber einige Evangelienkommentare des Mittelalters,' Sitzungsberichte, Vienna Academy, philosophisch-historische Klasse, CXLVI, no. 4, 1903.

adapts rather than copies his authorities and in adapting allows himself considerable freedom and adds what is clearly expository matter of his own. Again, in most of the passages where there is some degree of correspondence between the two, we find that Jerome's exposition formed the basis of both, Hrabanus generally copying word for word. As Christian used Jerome's commentary at first hand—this is indisputable—such passages prove nothing for the question whether he used Hrabanus. Again, when Christian comments on Matthew 21, 21 (*si monti huic dixeritis tolle et iacta te in mare, fiet*), he relates a story about Gregory of Nazianzus, who, wishing to build a church in a certain place situated between a rock and a mountain, prayed to God that the mountain might recede. In the morning his prayer had been fulfilled (1435 A). Now this miracle is told by Bede in commenting on Mark 11, 23, a passage that contains the same teaching of Christ, and Hrabanus copies this verbally from Bede, when explaining Matthew 21, 21. Nevertheless, in view of Christian's glowing eulogy on Bede's commentary on Mark in his epistle dedicatory, it seems safe to assume that Christian used Bede directly. When all such passages where an earlier writer has been used are eliminated, the remainder in which it is possible to trace a correspondence between Christian and Hrabanus is small. Yet it is sufficient to show that Christian did occasionally consult the work of the older author, without however being greatly indebted to it.[11] The question of dependence by one author on another is really a very difficult one, as can be illustrated by an error made even by so careful a scholar as Hauck. He asserted that Christian had used the "Collectiones" of Smaragdus (early ninth century) on the New Testament, on the evidence of a single sentence that occurs in both writers.[12] What Hauck failed to observe was that precisely the same sentence is to be found also in Hrabanus, and that all three presumably took it from Jerome, where it first occurs.

[11] Some examples of correspondence between the two commentators may here be given: Christ. 1335A, Hrab. 873D; Christ. 1340A, Hrab. 882D; Christ. 1380D, Hrab. 961B–C (cf. however Rufinus xi. 28); Christ. 1490B, Hrab. 1137A–B.

[12] Realencyclopädie f. protest. Theol., art. 'Druthmar.'

Christian is much indebted to Isidore's Etymologies, though Dümmler's remarks on this indebtedness go too far.[13] The interpretation of Hebrew names, especially in the first chapter of Matthew, can in part be found in Isidore; but a considerable number of them, given by Christian with their interpretations, is not in Isidore. They stand, however, in Jerome's treatise, "De nominibus Hebraicis," and it seems a reasonable hypothesis that this book was accessible to Christian.[14]

The number of passages on other topics where Christian is indebted to Isidore is very considerable, but only in a relatively small number of cases does he copy him verbally. Three such passages arouse our special curiosity, because they seem to give a hint of the type of Isidore manuscript available in the Stavelot library. They are the comments on *theriaca,* on *lepra,* and on *furtum.*[15] In each of these passages in Christian we meet with readings in the Isidore quotations that are found only in a Leyden manuscript of that author (Voss. lat. F 74, called *C* by W. M. Lindsay in his edition of the Etymologies) from the hand of the first corrector. Nothing appears to be known about the history of this manuscript before the beginning of the seventeenth century, when it was in the possession of Gruter; [16] but, as there had apparently once been a fair library at Stavelot,[17] it is conceivable that this manuscript was formerly there.

---

[13] Dümmler, p. 942.

[14] See also the exhaustive work, with full indexes, by F. Wutz, Onomastica Sacra (Harnack and Schmidt, Texte und Untersuchungen, ser. 3, vol. XI), 1915. An alternative hypothesis would be that Christian used some list of Onomastica Sacra, similar to that contained in Cod. Vat. Reg. 215; for this see my article in Bulletin of the John Rylands Library, Manchester, VII, 1923, pp. 446 ff.

[15] Theriaca in 1292B; Isid. Etym. xii. 4, 11 ('pastilli,' codd. Isid.: 'partelli,' C¹: 'pastelli,' Christ.). Lepra in 1325B; Isid. iv. 8, 11 ('lepidae herbae similis,' codd. Isid.: 'lapide,' C¹: 'lapidi similis,' Christ.). Furtum in 1389B; Isid. v. 26, 18 ('a furvo, id est fusco, vocatum,' codd. Isid.: 'furco,' C¹: 'dictum est a furto, id est nigro,' Christ.).

[16] P. C. Molhuijsen (De Navorscher, XLIX, 1899, p. 591) leaves it uncertain whether this manuscript was one of those that Suffridus Sixtinus got from Gruter's library and that passed later into Voss's hands, or whether it reached Voss through some other channel.

[17] The Royal Library at Brussels contains manuscripts that were once at Stavelot (see for possible early examples W. M. Lindsay, Notae Latinae, p. 448). A seventh-century MS. of Orosius, of which only a few leaves have survived, was once at Stavelot. Since the note in the MS. which gives this information is written

Its date, according to the latest editor of Isidore, is the ninth or tenth century (the first corrector seems to be contemporary or nearly so); it would, however, be interesting, if the manuscript could be reëxamined, first, to ascertain whether a slightly earlier date could be assigned to it on palaeographical grounds, and, secondly, to see whether the codex furnishes any clue to its original provenance.

References in Christian to other patristic writings are few. Augustine, Gregory the Great, and Origen (doubtless in a Latin version) are appealed to on certain points.[18] Among historical writers, Josephus (again, no doubt, in a Latin translation) is mentioned by name in several instances, and this work was used in other passages without acknowledgment; but in some cases Christian quoted him at second hand, merely reproducing the reference that he found in Jerome. Solinus and Orosius are specifically named only once each, but the use of them can be traced in other passages.[19]

The commentary repeats a number of anecdotes from Roman history, the source of which Dümmler briefly indicated as Aurelius Victor and Eutropius. But the matter is not quite so simple and deserves a little further elucidation. In the first place, Aurelius Victor's "Liber de Caesaribus" was not used by Christian, but only the epitome of that work. The epitome was compiled at the end of the fourth, or beginning of the fifth, century by an unknown author, and contains sundry anecdotes not to be found in Victor. It is one or two of these that reappear in Christian. For example, there is a story of what Diocletian said when he decided to abdicate from the imperial throne. Orosius too mentions the abdication, but without allusion to the fine vegetable-garden which Diocletian said was awaiting his attention when he retired into private life.[20] Another anecdote in

---

in a fifteenth-century hand, we cannot tell whether this is the ms. actually used by Christian in the ninth century. See the preface of Zangemeister's edition of Orosius, p. xi.

[18] Cf. generally Dümmler, pp. 941 ff.

[19] For instance, the remark on the hyena's habit of frequenting tombs (1453B) is probably based on Solinus, ed. Mommsen, p. 135, 16. The solitary reference to Orosius by name (1454D) is to his history generally, not to a particular incident in it.

[20] 1323D; Epitome 39, 6; Orosius, vii. 25, 14.

Christian relates a story of the emperor Valerian and his captor, the Persian king Sapor.[21] This is told both by the epitomist of Victor and by Orosius. Internal evidence makes it probable here that Christian followed Orosius. Again, there are two stories of the emperor Titus; one of these is certainly from Eutropius, the other either from that author or from the epitomist of Victor.[22] We see then that Christian had access to Orosius, Eutropius, and the epitomist of Victor, but that it is not always possible to tell with certainty which source he used in a given passage. Finally, there is a somewhat unpleasant story of Flamininus, who gratified the sadistic proclivities of his mistress by executing a prisoner before her eyes at a banquet, and was subsequently expelled for this act from the senate. Not so terrible a sin, says our commentator, as the offence of Herodias and her daughter. Dümmler overlooked the fact that this story is cited by Jerome, whence Christian took it over. It appears also in the tract of uncertain authorship, "De viris illustribus." [23] Christian had access too to a Latin version of Eusebius's history,[24] and he refers from time to time to the lives of saints and to the passions of certain apostles; for example, St. Peter, Saints Celsus and Martinus, St. Lambert, and St. Leger. We are not surprised to find St. Lambert (Lampertus) among the saints named, for during his earthly life he had been bishop of Maastricht, and had also spent seven years in retreat at Stavelot, where his memory was no doubt cherished with the utmost piety. St. Leger (Leodegarius), again, had played a prominent part in Burgundian politics; if the assumption that Christian came originally from Burgundy be correct, his interest in this saint becomes more in-

[21] 1448C; Epitome, 32, 6; Orosius, vii. 22, 4. The occurrence of the word 'adclivis' in Christian and 'adclinis' in Orosius makes it probable that Orosius was the source.

[22] 1379C, cf. Eutropius, vii. 21, 4 (verbal quotation); 1323D, cf. Eutropius vii. 21, 3 and Epitome 10, 9.

[23] 1380B–C; Jerome on Matt. 14, 11; cf. De vir. illust. 47, 4. This story seems to have originated with the notorious Valerius Antias, and then to have been frequently repeated by Roman historical writers, including Livy. See fragment 48 of Valerius and H. Peter's note in Historicorum Romanorum Reliquiae, I (2nd ed.).

[24] We may compare, for instance, 1378C with Rufinus i. 11, and 1380D with Rufinus xi. 28 (but, as pointed out above, Christian may here be following Hrabanus).

telligible.[25] There is also a reference to a certain martyr who, when he was being tortured, exclaimed "I am the wheat of God, I am being ground by the teeth of wild beasts." [26] C. Weyman, in a review of Dümmler's essay, identified this martyr as St. Ignatius, pointing out that the citation is to be found in the letter to the Romans attributed to that saint (chap. 4).[27] But the story found its way also into Jerome's "De viris illustribus"; [28] and yet it seems unlikely that Christian took the story from either of these sources, unless he was quoting from memory something that he had read long before. Otherwise we should have expected him to refer to St. Ignatius by name, and not to have told the story vaguely about *quidam martyr*. A few lines of poetry are to be found scattered here and there through Christian's commentary, drawn from Sedulius, Juvencus, and the Disticha Catonis.[29] There are, besides, three citations from Vergil, one from Juvenal, one from Martial, and one from the Latin Anthology, but with regard to these a word of caution is necessary.[30] Two of the Vergilian quotations, and those from Martial and Juvenal, are cited by Isidore in the Etymologies, and the context in which they are found in Christian leaves no room for doubt that he took them from Isidore. The remaining Vergilian quotation is Eclogue 4, 7; one cannot of course deny that Christian had access to Vergil and read him; but it cannot be proved, for he may well have got this line also from an intermediate source. Similarly, the line from the Latin Anthology is quoted, not in the form in which it appears in the best manuscripts, but as cited by a sixth-century grammarian.[31] This seems to be significant.

It is when we analyse Christian's commentary, apart from the

---

[25] St. Lampertus and St. Leodegarius are named together in 1305A.

[26] 1294A–B.   [27] Historisches Jahrbuch, XI, 1890, p. 805.

[28] Jerome, De vir. illust. 16.

[29] Sedulius, Carm. pasch. v. 188–195 in 1490A; v. 322–325 in 1500A. Juvencus i. 241 in 1281B; Dist. Cat. i. 17, 2 in 1438D.

[30] Vergil: 1267C, Ecl. 10, 67 (Isid. vi. 13, 3); 1302B, Aen. iv. 174 (Isid. v. 27, 26); 1427B, Ecl. 4, 7; Martial, xiv. 73 (Isid. xii. 7, 24) in 1347D. The line from Juvenal (14,139, Isid. i. 36, 11) is cited three times, 1373C, 1404B, and 1418C.

[31] Anthol. Lat. 256, 2, in 1330A; it is cited in the same form as in Cassiodorus, De orthographia (Keil, Gramm. Lat. VII, 156). The remaining verse citations in Christian are two from Bede and one from the Sibyl. The Bede quotations are:

question of sources, that we find something unique in it for the time at which it was written. It is couched in simple language and contains much elementary teaching on grammar, because the author never forgot that he was instructing beginners and that some words in the Bible were no longer clearly understood by the illiterate in the ninth century. Thus Christian explains that *proficiscens* is the present participle of a deponent verb (1465C), and to the phrase *mi pater,* he adds *mi vocativus possessivi est, a meo veniens* (1478D). *Sata dicuntur seminata* he writes in another place (1361D), for, as glossaries show us, in ordinary speech *serere* had gradually been displaced by *seminare* (Fr. *'semer'*).[32] There are scarcely any rare words in the commentary and, to us a matter for regret, only one trace of the vernacular. This single passage in which a Germanic word occurs is of some interest; Dümmler, though he cites the passage in a footnote, does not appear fully to have understood it.[33] Commenting on the sentence, "a reed shaken by the wind" (Matt. 11, 7), Christian equates *arundo* with *canna,* following Isidore (Etym. xvii. 7, 57); then he adds one of those touches of local color that are a token of his excellence as a teacher:

Such reeds abounded in Judaea just as they do in Italy, so that they make fences out of them and other necessary objects, and they

Nulla erit suspicio	O quam infelix anima
Salutis vel remedii,	Privata hoc convivio,
Janua clausa thalami	Quae ultra in memoriam
Completis sponsi nuptiis (1464D);	Non revertetur domini (1465A).

These verses do not appear to be found in any of the extant poems attributed to Bede. The line from the Sibyl, which is quoted immediately after the verse from the fourth Eclogue, reads:

E coelo rex adveniet Christus per saecla futurus (1427B).

It looks as if Christian, or rather his source, had in mind Oracula Sibyllina, iii. 286,

καὶ τότε δὴ θεὸς οὐρανόθεν πέμψει βασιλῆα

(cf. also iii. 652,

καὶ τότ' ἀπ' ἠελίοιο θεὸς πέμψει βασιλῆα

which is quoted by Lactantius, vii. 18). I am indebted for these three references to Professor Nathaniel Schmidt.

[32] Similarly in 1317D, to the quotation (Matt. 6, 26), "Respicite volatilia caeli, quomodo non serunt" he adds "id est seminant." The Migne editor printed these three words in italics, as though they were part of the citation.

[33] Dümmler, p. 938, note 6.

grow in marshy places *in modum herbae quae apud nos ros vocatur* (1355B).

So the text in Migne and no doubt in the manuscript followed by the editor: but does it mean anything? Surely what Christian wrote was *ror* (O. H. G.*'rôr'*; Mod. Germ. *'Rohr'*); this makes good sense, and anyone who is even slightly familiar with final R and final S in certain types of eighth-century and ninth-century minuscule, will recognise how easy it was for a scribe to make the mistake in copying (especially after the preceding *nos*). It is a pity that there are not more references to the vernacular, such as occur, for example, in his contemporary, Martin of Laon. Christian's method of exposition is, as already indicated, unusual for the time at which he wrote. Though he makes extensive use of Jerome's commentary and of Isidore's Etymologies, it is generally his practice not to copy his source verbally, as was done by Hrabanus, but to give in his own words the gist of what his sources contain, and usually that is the same as to say, in simpler language. Again the method of the good teacher is apparent. He adds touches of his own too; for instance, in an excursus on visions and prophecies (1277B–D), which seems to be based on Isidore (Etym. vii. 8, 33), some of the examples he gives, as well as the order in which he classifies different kinds of such manifestations, appear to be wholly his own. Similarly, in the classification of the *tria genera philosophiae* (1266B–D) based on Isidore (Etym. ii. 24), some of the illustrative matter is not to be found in the earlier writer.[34] In commenting on the two robbers on Calvary (1491C), Christian has clearly consulted Jerome on the passage;[35] but it is his own comment that the repentant robber had the three virtues of faith, hope, and charity, doubtless a conscious reminiscence of 1 Corinthians, chapter xiii, on the part of the commentator. The robber had faith because he believed that the Lord would reign; hope, because he adjured Jesus in the words, "Lord, remember me when thou comest into thy kingdom";

[34] 'Logica,' which is first spelled correctly, then appears twice as 'loyca.' Is this merely a scribe's carelessness or an indication of the way in which the word was then pronounced?

[35] Jerome on Matt. 27, 44.

charity, because he reproved his fellow robber for reviling Christ.

Christian knew his Bible well, and reminiscences, tacit or expressed, for the purpose of illustrative comparison, are many. Thus the suicide of Judas Iscariot reminds him of Achitophel's self-murder by hanging (2 Sam. 17, 23); [36] while we are provoked to a smile when Christian, speaking of the destruction of Jerusalem in the forty-second year after the Lord's ascension, goes on to say that this time was given to the Jews, and "because they refused to repent, two bears, Vespasian and Titus, came forth from the forest of the Gentiles (*de saltu gentilium*) and slew 1,100,000 of them and took 100,000 prisoners." [37] Clearly Christian had the story of Elisha and the children of Bethel in mind, and it was fortunate that even the number forty-two fitted in, though rather awkwardly; there are two bears and forty-two children in the tale (2 Kings 2, 23 f.).

Reference has already been made to what may be called touches of local color in the commentary. Thus, in annotating the words *et iussit eos discumbere supra fenum*,[38] Christian remarks:

> During the summer in these lofty mountains grass customarily grows in abundance, a similar sight to that which is familiar to those who have sojourned in our Alps. And, as the distance from cities and villages was great, for that reason no man cut it.

Again he contrasts the season at which thunder occurs in the eastern countries with the time of the year at which it may be expected in that part of the world where he lives.[39] More than once he refers to the poverty and woodland-character of the neighboring regions, comparing them to the wealth and resources of Palestine. The social conditions of the time cause Christian to strike more than once the note of pessimism and reprobation: [40] he compares many clerics and laymen of his

---

[36] 1485C.   [37] 1493D.

[38] Matt. 14, 19 (where the reading is 'et cum iussisset'); Christian's comment is in 1382D.

[39] 1369A.

[40] For these passages and others it is sufficient to refer to Dümmler's very full analysis (pp. 943 ff.).

day to wolves, because of their injustice and rapacity, and there are many other like criticisms scattered through the commentary.

A matter of some interest, which has not received the attention that it deserves, is the nature of the Biblical text used by Christian. The citations from the gospels and elsewhere are of course printed in italics in Migne's edition; but the editing has been carelessly done, so that in a number of instances words that are part of Christian's annotation have been printed as though they were Biblical quotations. This adds to the difficulty of determining the nature of Christian's Biblical text, and a critical edition of the commentary is needed before anything like a final estimate can be formed. Nevertheless some conclusions can safely be drawn. If the citations from Matthew in Christian's work are carefully collated with a critical text of the Hieronymic version, two things will be noticed: [41] first, Christian occasionally conflates his text by adding or substituting words from one of the other gospels, where these narrate the same event or parable as Matthew. Secondly, there are a good many divergences from what is probably the true text of Jerome's translation. With regard to the first matter, an illustration or two will help to make the point clear. In the story of the healing of the paralytic, the Latin text of Matthew is *surrexit et abiit in domum suam*.[42] In Christian the quotation appears thus: *surrexit et tulit in quo iacuerat et abiit in domum suam*, a version which adds a detail from Luke. Again, in Jerome's translation of Matt. 12, 25, we read *omne regnum divisum contra se;* in Christian [43] the citation appears as *omne regnum in se ipsum divisum*, which is actually Luke's version of the same phrase. The words *arundinem quassatam non confringet* in Matt. 12, 20, are part of a quotation or transcription of Isaiah 42, 3. Christian however cites the words, not as they appear in the gospel, but as they stand in the original context in Isaiah, *calamum quassatum non conteret*.[44]

---

[41] Wordsworth and White's text of the gospels has been used throughout, and for the Greek text of the New Testament the edition of von Soden.
[42] Matt. 9, 7; Christian 1334A; Lk. 5, 25 (tulit lectum in quo iacebat).
[43] 1366B, Lk. 11, 17.   [44] 1365B.

The cases where Christian's text diverges from the standard are numerous. In forming the following conclusions the present writer has ignored trifling differences. But even if only the more noteworthy divergences are observed, we get an unmistakable indication of what Christian's New Testament looked like. In nearly a score of cases Christian's readings correspond to those found in the manuscript now called R; in nearly as many instances we find parallels to E. In a smaller number of cases the readings are those also found in D, L, and Q. Now, what are these manuscripts? R is Codex Rushworthianus, now in the Bodleian Library, E is Codex Egertonensis in the British Museum, D is the famous Book of Armagh, Q the equally well-known Book of Kells, and L is Codex Lichfeldensis, the so-called Book of St. Chad. All these manuscripts contain what Biblical scholars call an Irish text. Wordsworth and White, while they are cautious about the origin of this recension, agree that DELQR form a clearly defined group of manuscripts and add: "In these we frequently recognize corrections made from Greek codices and readings of great value. It would not be difficult therefore to construct the Irish recension of Jerome's Vulgate from these and similar manuscripts." [45] There can be no doubt, then, that the manuscript of Matthew used by Christian belonged to this Irish family of manuscripts,[46] but to assume from this that at some time there was considerable Irish influence at Stavelot, or even the presence of Irish monks there, is hazardous in the absence of more definite evidence. Still, it should be remembered that in the early days of the abbey the monks followed the Rule of St. Columban and that later Stavelot was in the diocese of Liége. And in the early part of the ninth century there was an Irish colony at Liége, the most illustrious member of which was Sedulius Scotus. Finally there is one characteristic of Christian which at once suggests that he, at all events, came under Irish influence at some stage of his career—he knew some Greek.

Dümmler and others would seem to have underestimated

[45] Novum Testamentum Latine ed. Wordsworth and White, praef. p. x.
[46] The more important variants have been set out in a short appendix at the end of this paper.

Christian's knowledge of that language.[47] What is the evidence provided by the commentary? Near the beginning of it (1265D–1266A) Christian, after some remarks on the composition of the four gospels, in which he is probably adapting Isidore (Etym. vi. 2, 35–39), tells us that he had seen gospels which were supposed to have belonged to St. Hilary and in which the order of the four gospels was unusual, namely, Matthew, John, Luke, Mark.[48] He goes on:

> *Interrogavi enim Euphenium (Euphemum?) Graecum cur hoc ita esset: dixit mihi: in similitudinem boni agricolae, qui quos fortiores habet boves primo iungit.*

This Euphemus may of course have been a Greek, as his name, if genuine, suggests; but the fact that he is called 'Graecus' need not by itself mean more than that he knew some Greek. For 'Graecus' is a sobriquet applied to Irishmen who had some acquaintance with that language.[49] The 'Graeca' in Christian's commentary are in the main single words, for which the Latin equivalent is given, with or without a further explanation. A goodly number of such words with their Latin equivalents are derived from the two sources to which Christian owed most, Jerome and Isidore.[50] But even when all these words are elim-

---

[47] Traube's opinion of Christian's Greek was somewhat more favorable, because of Christian's remarks on the abbreviation of the name Jesus (1278C–D). See L. Traube, Nomina Sacra, p. 6.

[48] This is of course the regular "Western" order of the gospels, as found in Codex Bezae, Codices Vercellensis (*a*), Veronensis (*b*), Brixianus (*f*), Palatinus (*e*), and many other Old Latin MSS., as well as in some Greek codices; see Zahn, Geschichte des Neutestamentlichen Kanons, II, pp. 370 f.; Gregory, Textkritik des Neuen Testamentes, II, pp. 854 f. On Hilary's use of a text not unlike the sixth-century Irish Codex Usserianus (r), see A. Souter, Text and Canon of the New Testament, pp. 87 f.

[49] We may instance the Irish bishop who came to Bavaria and who is called 'Tuti Grecus' (Meichelbeck, Historia Frisingensis, II, 91) and also 'Dobda Grecus' (MGH: Script. XI, p. 6). Wattenbach, in his note on the latter passage, cites a charter of Charlemagne in which the name appears as 'Dodo Grecus peregrinus.' At all events there is no doubt that the bishop was an Irishman. A further instance we find in the 'Ellenici fratres' at St. Gall; cf. J. M. Clark, The Abbey of St. Gall, 1926, pp. 109–111.

[50] One or two instances will suffice: the explanations of εὔνουν (1309B), ἐπιούσιον (1314D), κυλλούς (1391D), are all from Jerome, those of λατρεία (1299D) and 'paropsis' (1443D) are derived from Isidore.

inated from the list, a fair residue of knowledge remains for which Christian himself deserves the credit. He distinguishes between ὅσιος and ἅγιος,[51] explains carefully the principle on which the name Jesus is abbreviated,[52] gives the derivations of ἐπιφάνια and θεοφάνια.[53] In another place a distinction is drawn between προσκυνῆσαι and κλίνειν;[54] this appears to be Christian's own, although in the passage which immediately follows he is indebted to Isidore. The quotation λατρεύειν αὐτῷ is also given correctly from Luke 1, 74. Occasionally Christian makes blunders, but the derivation of Haceldema from ἀγρός and αἷμα is no worse than many etymological experiments in Isidore and elsewhere.[55] He cites the words ἀπὸ τοῦ Καιάφα (the name is given in Roman characters) correctly from John 18, 28, but with more logic than grammatical accuracy calls this an ablative.[56] The equation of 'dormitorium' with κοιμητήριον he may have found in a glossary,[57] but we are impressed by a philological note in which he explains how an initial aspirate in Greek appears as initial s in the corresponding Latin word.[58] Finally, there are three passages which strongly confirm the general impression formed from the evidence already given, that Christian knew a good deal of Greek and used a Greek New Testament.

1. Commenting on Matt. 16, 22, where Peter rebukes Christ, Christian quotes the Greek version in this form: "ἱλεώθητί σοι, quod est, propitius esto tibi" (1398C). We should say that he was copying Jerome, but Jerome cites the words as they are now found in the passage "ἵλεώς σοι, κύριε." No authority for Christian's reading is known, and it is probable that Christian was quoting from memory. But if he was, the use of the imperative of the aorist passive of a verb argues some familiarity with the grammar of the Greek language.

2. Neither Jerome, Bede, Hrabanus, nor Radbertus gives the Greek version of the Aramaic Eli, Eli, lama sabachthani (Matt. 27, 46) spoken from the cross. Christian quotes the Greek in the following form: [59] ὁ θεός, ὁ θεός μου ἵνα τί ἐγκατέλιπές με·

[51] 1276D. [52] See note 47, above. [53] 1286A–C. [54] 1299C.
[55] 1486B. [56] 1481D.
[57] 1493C; cf. Corp. Gloss. Lat. V, 430, 22 (a Eusebian gloss). [58] 1498A.
[59] 1492B.

This rendering does not correspond exactly to what we find in either the first or the second gospel, but is a combination of the two.[60] In fact, the form he cites of this Greek sentence shows the same conflation that has already been noted in the case of some of his quotations from the Latin.

3. Christian also quotes another saying from the cross,[61] the sentence, *Pater, in manus tuas commendo spiritum meum,* which does not occur in Matthew, but only in Luke 23, 46. The Greek words in Christian's version read thus: εἰς χεῖράς σου παραθήσομαι τὸ πνεῦμά μου. Here παραθήσομαι (a correction after the Greek text of Psalm 30, 6, as against the better reading παρατίθεμαι of codices ℵAC KMPQUXII and others) shows that Christian is using the text of codices EGHLSVΔΛ and others, that is, the text of the group held by von Soden to represent the oldest form of the Antiochian, or Lucianic, text (K).[62]

When we bear in mind that, in the passages just indicated, Christian is, so far as can be ascertained, quite independent of earlier commentators, who either do not quote the Greek version at all or quote it in a different form, and when we add this strong evidence to the by no means negligible indications of Greek scholarship in the rest of the commentary, we are led to the conclusion that he belonged to that very small band of ninth-century scholars who really had a practical knowledge of Greek and not merely a small vocabulary of Greek words derived from Isidore or from some glossary.

It is always a fascinating, if dangerous, pastime to form a picture of a man for ourselves from his writings, dangerous, especially, if he lived in an age remote from our own. Christian we should judge to have been an earnest yet kindly disciple of St. Benedict; not untypical of his age in his judgments on women [63] and on wine; [64] charitable to the poor and to humbler

---

[60] Matt. 27, 46 θεέ μου, θεέ μου, ἵνα τί με ἐγκατέλιπες. Mk. 15, 34, ὁ θεός ὁ θεός μου, εἰς τί ἐγκατέλιπές με (so codd. AEFGKPΓΔII and many others; ἐγκατέλιπές με is the order of ℵBL and a few others).

[61] 1492D.

[62] Presumably C. Weyman had this passage in mind when he referred to Christian's exposition as "anknüpfend an die Traditionen der antiochenischen Exegetenschule" (Histor. Jahrb. XI, 1890, p. 805).

[63] "Curiosum animal est femina et ardens novitate" (1483C).

[64] "Quod non est vitium, si moderate potetur (sc. vinum)" (1358B).

232

folk in general; intolerant of the oppressor, and withal a teacher of exceptional ability and, for that age, of unusual originality. Among the lesser scholastic figures of the Carolingian Age he deserves to be assigned a foremost place.

Appendix of Readings from the Latin Text of Matthew

In the first table (A) is given a selection of readings as they appear in the Vulgate (Wordsworth and White's edition) and in Christian respectively. Correspondences of Christian's readings with one or more of the Irish group of MSS. are indicated by the usual symbols for the Vulgate codices. Other codices such as Epternacensis, cited by Wordsworth and White, which occasionally agree with the Irish group, have been ignored.

In the second table (B) some of the more important divergences of Christian's text which seem not to be attested in existing MSS. of the Vulgate, are set out. In many cases these variants seem to be due to conflation with the version in another gospel, and in these cases a reference to this other source has been added. A study of the Old Latin codices might show the source of some, perhaps many, of these harmonizations.

A

Vulgate	Christian
Matt.	
3, 10 radicem	1293A radices (DLR)
3, 12 permundabit	1294A mundabit (L)
5, 18 amen quippe dico	1306D *om* quippe (*om* R)
5, 38 quia dictum est	1311C quia dictum est antiquis (Q)
6, 29 quoniam nec Salomon	1318C quia nec Salomon (DEL)
8, 12 regni	1327D regni huius (DELQR)
9, 17 rumpuntur; effunditur	1337D rumpentur; effundetur (rumpentur LR: effundetur DELQ; cf. Lk. 5, 37)
9, 35 omnem infirmitatem	1342D omnem infirmitatem in populo (R)
10, 13 revertatur	1348A revertetur (DLQR)
10, 18 et ad praesides et ad reges	1348C et ad reges et praesides (ER; cf. Lk. 21, 12)
12, 9 transisset	1364A transiret (DE)
12, 29 domum illius	1367A domum eius (DE)
13, 11 mysteria	1372B mysterium (misterium DEQ)

233

13, 16 quia; quia	1372D qui (LQR); quae (LR)
13, 24 simile factum est	1374A simile est (ER)
13, 33 farinae	1375B farina (DQR)
13, 47 congreganti	1376D congregati (Q)
14, 21 mulieribus et parvulis	1383D parvulis et mulieribus (E)
16, 27 secundum opus eius	1400D secundum opera sua (opera DLQR; sua R)
17, 5 bene	1402D *om* bene (*om* L)
17, 12 quia Helias	1403D quod Elias (E)
18, 18 ligata et in coelo	1410C ligata et in coelis (EQ)
21, 23 docentem	1435C *om* docentem (*om* R)
21, 25 e coelo *bis*	1435C–D de caelo *bis* (E)
22, 26 similiter secundus et tertius usque ad septimum	1443C similiter duo et tres usque ad septem (II et III usque ad VII D)
22, 40 universa lex	1445B tota lex (R; Radbertus 757D)
24, 20 ut non	1457A ne (R)
24, 27 paret	1458A apparet (DQR)
24, 29 commovebuntur	1458D movebuntur (E; cf. Mk. 13, 25)
24, 30 parebit	1458D apparebit (DEQR)
24, 33 haec omnia scitote	1459D haec fieri scitote (E)
24, 44 fur venturus esset	1461D fur veniret (E; cf. Lk. 12, 39)
24, 50 manducet; bibat	1462D manducat; bibit (R)
25, 14 sicut enim	1465B *om* enim (*om* LR)
25, 30 illic	1469B ibi (E)

B

Vulgate	*Christian*
Matt.	
2, 4 congregans	1282C convocans
5, 12 quoniam merces	1305B ecce enim merces (Lk. 6, 23)
5, 33 iterum audistis quia dictum est	1310C *om* audistis quia
5, 34 ego autem dico vobis non iurare omnino	1311A nolite iurare
5, 35 est pedum eius	1311B pedum eius vocatur
5, 41 f. (*These verses are transposed*)	
6, 11 supersubstantialem	1314C quotidianum (Lk. 11, 3; *below in the exposition Christian uses* supersubstantialis)
6, 27 vestrum	1318B nostrum
6, 30 deus sic vestit	1318D Deus tali decore vestit (*Is* tali decore *merely the interpretation of Christian?*)

7, 8	invenit	1320B inveniet
7, 9	lapidem porriget ei	1320B lapidem dabit illi (Lk. 11, 11)
8, 29	et ecce clamaverunt	1331C et clamabant
9, 7	et surrexit et abiit in domum suam	1334A et surrexit et tulit in quo iacuerat et abiit in domum suam (cf. Lk. 5, 25, tulit lectum in quo iacebat)
9, 10	venientes discumbebant	1335C *om* venientes (cf. Mk. 2, 14)
9, 16 f.	inmittit commissuram panni rudis in vestimentum	1337B commissuram panni rudis mittit in vestimentum
9, 18	adorabat	1338A adoravit (*also in some codices, cf. Wordsworth and White, ad. loc.*)
10, 11	donec exeatis	1347C *om* donec exeatis (cf. Lk. 10, 7)
10, 14	receperit; audierit; exeuntes foras de domo vel de civitate excutite pulverem de pedibus vestris	1348A receperint; audierint; exeuntes excutite pulverem de pedibus vestris in testimonium illis (Mk. 6, 11)
11, 1	et praedicaret	1353C *om* et praedicaret
11, 21	factae essent	1358D factae fuissent (Lk. 10, 13)
12, 25	omne regnum divisum contra se	1366B omne regnum in se ipsum divisum (Lk. 11, 17)
12, 33	fructum..bonum; fructum.. malum	1368A fructus..bonos; fructus..malos (cf. Lk. 6, 43)
13, 4 f.	quaedam ceciderunt secus viam; alia autem ceciderunt in petrosa	1371C–D aliud cecidit secus viam; aliud cecidit super petram (Lk. 8, 5 f.)
13, 7	alia autem ceciderunt	1372A aliud cecidit (Lk. 8, 8)
13, 19	venit malus et rapit	1373A venit diabolus et tollit (Lk. 8, 11)
13, 20 f.	super petrosa; accipit; in se	1373B super petram; suscipit (cf. Lk. 8, 13, *om* in se)
13, 54	in patriam suam	1377B in terram suam
13, 54	synagogis	1377B synagoga (cf. Mk. 6, 1)
14, 3	posuit in carcerem	1379B religavit in carcere
14, 7	postulasset	1379D postularet
14, 19	et cum iussisset turbam discumbere	1382D et iussit eos discumbere
14, 20	tulerunt	1383C sustulerunt (Mk. 6, 43)
14, 23	et dimissa turba ascendit in montem solus orare. vespere autem facto solus erat ibi	1384A vespere solus erat ibi. ipse ascendit solus verticem montis orare et discipuli laboraverunt in mari in remigando tota nocte (cf. Mk. 6, 48)
14, 26	et videntes eum supra mare	1385B–C et videntes eum supra mare

ambulantem turbati sunt dicentes quia phantasma est

ambulantem putaverunt phantasma esse (cf. Mk. 6, 49)

14, 35 et cum cognovissent eum viri loci illius

1386C cognoscebant autem dominum de frequenti visione (*this seems to be a paraphrase by Christian*)

14, 36 et quicumque tetigerunt

1386C et quotquot tangebant

15, 9 mandata

1387D *om* mandata

15, 29 sedebat ibi

1391C erat ibi

15, 35 praecepit turbae ut discumberet

1392C praecepit turbae discumbere

15, 37 omnes; plenas

1392D *om* omnes; *om* plenas

16, 26 detrimentum patiatur

1400A detrimentum faciat (cf. Lk. 9, 25, detrimentum sui faciat)

17, 14 filio meo

1404A mei filii (*also in some codices, cf. Wordsworth and White*)

17, 25 vel censum

1406C *om* vel censum

21, 28 habebat

1436A habuit

22, 7 civitatem illorum

1440A civitatem illam

23, 23 graviora sunt

1450A maiora sunt

24, 6 haec fieri

1454D haec primum fieri

24, 7 consurget

1455A surget

24, 14 veniet consummatio

1456A erit consummatio

24, 22 breviati fuissent

1457C abbreviati essent (adbrebiati T; *cf. Wordsworth and White*)

24, 34 dico vobis quia non praeteribit

1460A *om* quia non

25, 32 segregat

1469D separat

26, 3 et seniores populi

1472A *om* et seniores populi

26, 17 accesserunt discipuli ad Iesum dicentes

1475A accesserunt discipuli eius Petrus et Andreas (cf. Lk. 22, 8, et misit Petrum et Ioannem)

26, 68 prophetiza nobis, Christe, quis est qui te percussit

1483B si propheta es, dic per prophetiam quis est qui te percussit

Miscellanea

Richard Bentley: 1742-1942[*]

IN THE summer of 1742 even the notoriety of a long and embittered feud between the lately deceased Master and the Fellows of a Cambridge College was completely eclipsed by more stirring or distracting events at home and abroad. So we may suspect that the reading public felt only a languid interest in an inconspicuous entry that appeared among the obituary notices of the *Gentleman's Magazine* for July, 1742:

> July 11. The Rev. Dr *Richard Bentley*, Master of *Trinity College, Cambridge*. A critic, by the Testimony of Dr. *Clark, omnes omnium temporum criticus longe longeque antecellens.*

Clarke, who had been dead a dozen years at this date, had inserted his eulogy of Bentley, which the editor of the *Gentleman's Magazine* did not quote quite accurately, in an edition of Caesar's *Commentaries* published in 1712. Of Bentley's two most famous detractors, Swift in the very year of Bentley's death entered the ultimate stage of the disease which was not to carry him off till 1745; while Pope, whose last and most virulent attack on the Master of Trinity is contained in the fourth Book

[*] *Studies in Philology*, 39 (1942), 510–523. Reprinted by permission of the editor of *Studies in Philology*.

of the *Dunciad* issued early in 1742, survived his enemy by only two years.

Comparatively little is known about Bentley's boyhood and student days at Cambridge, but there is no doubt that from an early age intellectual precocity was combined in him with an enormous capacity for hard work.[1] His appointment to be tutor to Dean, afterwards Bishop, Stillingfleet's second son, a post that he held for six years, was momentous for two reasons: it brought him the interest and friendship of Stillingfleet himself and it gave him access to the exceptionally rich library which that eminent divine had built up. Bentley was not quite twenty-nine years of age when his first published work appeared in the form of a long letter included as an appendix in Mill's edition of the Byzantine chronicler, John Malelas or Malalas. *Ex pede Herculem!* Even among classical scholars there are probably few today who have ever perused the *Epistola ad Millium.* Yet the brilliance with which Bentley corrected and explained the many garbled quotations in Malelas from classical authors and especially from the Greek dramatists, brought him the enthusiastic praise of great scholars like Graevius, who saw in him a new and bright luminary on the horizon of scholarship.[2] The *Epistola* is notable also because various topics are there treated which Bentley was to discuss more fully and with even greater brilliance in the *Dissertation on the Epistles of Phalaris,* which first appeared in 1697 and then in a revised and greatly augmented form in 1699.

Only a year after Mill's edition of Malelas was published Bentley had an opportunity of proving his mettle in another way. He was the first preacher chosen under the terms of the will left by the famous physicist, Robert Boyle, which provided

---

[1] For the facts of Bentley's life, J. H. Monk's biography, *The Life of Richard Bentley, D.D.* (2 vols.; 2nd. ed. revised and corrected, London, 1833) is still indispensable. Of shorter studies the best is *Bentley* by R. C. Jebb (English Men of Letters; London and N.Y., 1882). There is an admirable bibliography by A. T. Bartholomew and J. W. Clark entitled, *Richard Bentley, D.D.: A bibliography of his works and of all the literature called forth by his acts or his writings* (Cambridge, Eng., 1908).

[2] Cf., for instance, Graevius' letter in *The Correspondence of Richard Bentley* (London, 1842), pp. 43 ff.

an annual stipend of fifty pounds to be paid to a 'divine or preaching minister' who should 'preach eight sermons in the year, for proving the Christian religion against notorious infidels, viz., Atheists, Deists, Pagans, Jews, and Mahometans; not descending to any controversies that are among Christians themselves.' Bentley's eight sermons were printed under the title, *The Folly of Atheism and (what is now called) Deism even with respect to the present life.* Their theological doctrine is of slight interest to-day, save perhaps to the historian of dogma; but they are invaluable for a study of their author's intellectual grasp and growth. They show him as an able controversialist and the master of a vigorous and highly individual English style; they also throw not a little light on his scientific reading. He had of course studied mathematics at school and in the university, but in these sermons he displays great familiarity with the latest developments in physics. The four famous letters which Isaac Newton wrote to him in answer to certain queries, letters in which the fifty-year old Newton treats the thirty-year old divine as an intellectual equal, are an accolade of which any man might be proud. But Bentley's interest in contemporary scientific progress went further than this. In his second sermon he shows acquaintance with the use of the microscope and with the discoveries of Harvey and Boyle; in the fourth he quotes Descartes' *De formatione foetus* and, in the course of a long argument to disprove the old belief that insects and flies can be generated from putrefying matter, he appeals to the authority of Francisco Redi, Malpighi, and Lewenhoeck. Years later Bentley, as Master of Trinity, gave practical proof of his continued interest in scientific research. He brought about the appointment of the first professor of astronomy in the university and the building of an observatory for his use over the entrance gateway to Trinity College; further, for the professor of chemistry, J. S. Vigani, 'he repaired and fitted up an old lumber house as an elegant chemical laboratory.' [3]

Phalaris in its final form is probably Bentley's greatest book. At all events, although the literary coterie whose scholarly pretensions had led to its composition continued to vent their

[3] Monk, *op. cit.*, I, 204.

spite against its author, it established his reputation as the first critic of the age among discerning readers at home and among leading scholars abroad. Even now, after more than two centuries, when our knowledge of many phases of classical antiquity is vastly greater than in Bentley's day, the consummate mastery of his exposition, like the astonishing range of his knowledge, embracing with equal ease Greek and Latin authors, religion, social customs, numismatics, metrology and other branches of archaeology, fills one with awe; while the vigorous style, slightly colloquial, now witty, now shot through with biting sarcasm, carries the reader along breathlessly even through the discussion of scholarly *minutiae* which in other hands would, however learned, have become insufferably arid and dull. A decade passed before any other considerable work from Bentley's pen saw the light; but his surviving letters of the period provide a remarkable picture of his zest for the classics in the midst of the varied business caused by official duties and of the multiple quarrels to which they led. Not less striking and instructive are the many letters addressed to him, often as the ultimate authority on a disputed question, by Dutch and German scholars. At last, between 1709 and 1713, three important works appeared. Two of these—a treatise on fragments of Menander and Philemon provoked by Le Clerc's most faulty edition and by an attack on Bentley himself, and the two parts of the *Remarks* on Collins' *Discourse of Free-thinking*—were published under the pseudonym of Phileleutherus Lipsiensis, but Bentley's authorship was recognized from the first by the *cognoscenti*. The assumed character of a German Lutheran divine adopted by Bentley in the *Remarks* adds a certain piquant humor to some of the strictures on Collins, which would have been impossible, if he had composed the book in his own character. The third work to appear at this time was the long awaited edition of Horace (1711). Bentley's edition of Terence, Phaedrus, and Publilius Syrus followed *longo intervallo* in 1726, and the *Manilius*, though he had begun to work on this author as a young man, not until three years before his death. He had other projects which were never carried out, but emendations on more than twenty other Greek and Latin authors were entered by him in the margins of manuscripts and editions in his possession or communicated to other scholars engaged on editorial work.[4] There is, however, one of his proposed undertakings which demands somewhat fuller comment. As early as 1691, as is clear from an addendum in the *Epistola ad Millium,* Bentley had become interested in the text of the New Testament, but we do not know how far he may have pursued his inquiries during the next few years. At least we may be sure that he quickly discovered the poor quality of the printed texts which were then in universal use, but which had been constructed from few and very late manuscripts. In 1707 Dr. John Mill, after many years of labor, brought out a text with notes in which he recorded approximately 30,000 variants derived from manuscripts that he had collated. To emend a pagan author was a harmless occupation, to print, even though only in foot-notes, a vast mass of collations which might lead to tampering with the received text of Holy Scripture, was quite another. As one recent writer remarks: 'Holy Scripture was considered in the period *circa* 1600 to 1760 as identical, even to its *minutiae,* with the Word of the Lord. Any one who suggested changes in the so-called *Textus Receptus* was accused of tampering with the pure Word of God.' And again: 'The suspicion aroused in England [by Mill's edition] was very similar to that which disturbed the orthodox Christians at Basel in 1730, greatly to Wettstein's discomfiture. In England, as later in Switzerland, many Fundamentalists feared that the vast number of variants found in different MSS., and the use which scholars would make of them, would endanger the authority of the pure Word of God.' [5] If the orthodox were alarmed, free-thinkers like Collins were delighted to use this information for their own ends. In his reply to Collins Bentley defended Mill's book and maintained that text-critical work on the New Testament was desirable and would not endanger the essential truth of Christianity. But let us hear the Doctor himself on the subject: [6]

But I have too much value for the ancients to play booty about their works and monuments, for the sake of a short answer *to a fool*

[4] These all appeared posthumously; cf. Bartholomew and Clark, *op. cit.,* Nos. 138–143; 186–204.

[5] C. L. Hulbert-Powell, *John James Wettstein* (London, 1938), pp. 1 and 302.

[6] Bentley's *Works,* edited by Alexander Dyce (London, 1838), III, 359–360.

according to his folly. All those passages, and all the rest of their remains, are sufficiently pure and genuine to make us sure of the writer's design. If a corrupt line or dubious reading chances to intervene, it does not darken the whole context, nor make an author's opinion or his purpose *precarious.* Terence, for instance, has as many variations as any book whatever, in proportion to its bulk; and yet, with all its interpolations, omissions, additions, or glosses (choose the worst of them on purpose), you cannot deface the contrivance and plot of one play; no, not of one single scene; but its sense, design, and subserviency to the last issue and conclusion, shall be visible and plain thorow all the mist of *various lections.* And so it is with the sacred text; make your 30,000 as many more, if numbers of copies can ever reach that sum: all the better to a knowing and serious reader, who is thereby more richly furnished to select what he sees genuine. But even put them into the hands of a knave or a fool, and yet, with the most sinistrous and absurd choice, he shall not extinguish the light of any one chapter, nor so disguise Christianity but that every feature of it will still be the same.

It was, however, only after his meeting with J. J. Wettstein, who had already begun collecting material for the monumental edition of the New Testament that finally appeared at Amsterdam in 1751–52, that Bentley decided to bring out an edition himself. In 1716 he addressed a letter to the Archbishop of Canterbury; he followed this up by printing his Proposals for a new edition in which he outlined the plan to be followed and as a specimen appended the twenty-second chapter of *Revelation* in Greek and Latin with an *apparatus criticus* containing variants from manuscripts, from the Coptic, Syriac, and Ethiopic versions, and from the citations in the works of the Fathers. For years thereafter Bentley himself collected material, while first Wettstein and then Walker made numerous collations for him on the continent. He also procured a collation of the fourth-century *codex Vaticanus* made by two Italian scholars. But there the matter rested. No edition ever appeared; the material that he and others for him had collected was left to his nephew who in due course bequeathed it to the library of Trinity College. In spite of this, Bentley's labors in this field are of the utmost importance, although it was long before the fact was adequately recognized.[7] Undoubtedly his defense of Mill in the *Remarks* and his decisive arguments, justifying the text-critique of the Bible as something necessary and not incompatible with belief in Christianity, encouraged later scholars to persevere along the path that he had blazed. To the student of Bentley himself this material is also of primary interest.[8] It reveals the same brilliance in emendation, with occasional lapses into arbitrary wilfulness, that we find in his work on pagan authors, a brilliance which enabled him in a number of instances to forestall readings whose soundness has since been confirmed by the oldest manuscripts. It demonstrates his extensive knowledge not only of manuscripts but of the Greek and Latin Fathers, the importance of whose Biblical citations to students of the Bible-text is now universally recognized, but which were little considered before Bentley's time. And, finally, it proves that, although Bentley was wrong in some of his assumptions, in certain essential features he was a pioneer, a forerunner of Lachmann, Tischendorff, Westcott, Hort, and other leading scholars of the nineteenth century.

Bentley's edition of *Paradise Lost* appeared in 1732. It is marked by the same brilliance as his other works, but it fails to convince primarily because it is based on a hypothesis—the blind Milton at the mercy of a careless copyist and an unscrupulous editor—for which no adequate evidence exists. But even if we pass it by as a strange aberration of a great intellect, it should not influence our final judgment of him, any more than Newton's occupation with an outmoded theology or Oliver Lodge's devotion in his later years to spiritualism should seriously affect our estimate of their place in the history of science. Of Bentley the man it is difficult to form a fair judgment. Like many another man of genius, he was full of apparent contradic-

---

[7] See, for instance, the review of editions by Alford, Tischendorff, and Lachmann in the *Edinburgh Review* 191 (1851), pp. 1–46, in which the writer does justice to Bentley's work done more than a century before.

[8] Until 1862 little more than Bentley's *Proposals* for a new edition and certain portions of his treatise against Collins were available to students of Bentley's studies in the text of the New Testament. But in that year A. A. Ellis in his *Bentleii Critica Sacra* (Cambridge, Eng.) collected the more important materials from Bentley's notes and marginalia.

tions in his character. In his relations to the Fellows of Trinity and to some of his ecclesiastical superiors his imperious arrogance is as undeniable as it is distasteful, even after every allowance is made for the provocations that he received and for his earnest efforts to remedy existing abuses, whereby many genuine reforms both in his college and in the university were set in train. On the other hand, we have ample proof of his cordial relations with distinguished contemporaries like Newton and John Evelyn and with many continental scholars. He seems also to have been uniformly kind and helpful to younger men from abroad who came to him with introductions, and in some instances he was instrumental in securing them good academic posts. He appears to have taken a compassionate interest in the unfortunate Germans who were forced to emigrate from the Palatinate in 1709.[9] In his family circle he was by no means the tyrant that might have been expected; on the contrary, his grandson has left a singularly lovable picture of the old gentleman as he was in his declining years.[10] Lastly, the accusation sometimes levelled against him, that he was subservient to the great, is based on no satisfactory evidence; for the fulsome dedication of his *Horace* to Harley followed a polite and generally recognised convention in an age when the patronage of the great was still all but universally sought by authors and artists.

The universal character of Bentley's genius as a scholar is nowadays too often forgotten. The average student of Classics learns to think of him as the rash editor of Horace; the student of English literature may be familiar with the allusions to Bentley in Pope and with the satirical diatribes of Swift, especially the *Battle of the Books,* and will hold up his hands in horror at the man who would improve on Milton. Certainly the methods and broad principles which Bentley advocated all his life are instructive not merely to students of Greek and Latin literature but to all philologists alike. Already in his life-time methods analogous to his were used with conspicuous success by Theobald on the text of Shakespeare. One of the most wide-spread errors about Bentley's critical work is the

[9] Cf. *Correspondence,* pp. 383–385.
[10] Monk, *op. cit.,* II, 401–404; Jebb, *op. cit.,* p. 188.

belief that he belonged to that class of emendator whom one of
the outstanding Latin scholars of our own day has described in
apt, if scathing terms: [11]

Those classical scholars who occupy themselves with what is called
'feet-on-the-hob' emendation have a poor opinion of the extant
MSS. They sit by the fire with Virgil in one hand and a pencil in
the other and jot down in the margin any alteration of a word or
a line which caprice suggests. When the marginal litter has accumu-
lated they send it, under the misleading title, 'Emendations,' to an
indulgent magazine editor.

Bentley's procedure was nothing like that, as any reader of his
letters or books can quickly determine for himself. He constantly refers his correspondents to manuscripts and, when these
are not available, to the earliest printed texts. He himself says
more than once of his own conjectures that he is guessing
(*hariolari*) and even that, in the absence of manuscript evidence,
a lacuna or corrupt passage had best remain untouched.[12] A
most illuminating passage occurs in a letter that he wrote to
Gottfried Richter in 1708. After speaking of the manuscripts of
Manilius which, he remarks, are 'portentously and almost un-
believably faulty,' he thus advises Richter: [13]

In those old manuscripts many interpolations were made at the time
of the renascence of letters about three hundred years ago and new
readings used to be inserted after the old had been erased. If there
are such new readings in your manuscript, as doubtless there are,
you will easily distinguish them by the color of the ink or by the
form of the letters or by traces of erasure, which never disappear.
Consequently you will take care to indicate each place which has
been changed by a second, interpolating hand; and, if possible, you
must ascertain what was previously written by the first hand, i.e.,
the reading now lurking under that erasure. Furthermore, that
you may not fill up the entire margin of your copy, if you write
down the complete words, it will be enough to mark the letters
[which have been emended] only by a small line drawn underneath
and to put the variants in the margin approximately thus: . . .

[11] W. M. Lindsay, *Palaeographia latina* II (St. Andrews University Publications,
XVI, 1923), p. 53.
[12] *Correspondence*, p. 281: neque vero sine codice suppleri debet ex coniectura.
[13] *Ibid.*, p. 387. The original of the letter is in Latin.

He then sets out a few examples of what should be done. Again, his intimate knowledge of the authors whose texts he was trying to emend enabled him to correct a corruption in one passage on the basis of another similar passage in the same writer. We see this particularly clearly in his emendations of Aristophanes, in which he not infrequently succeeds in righting an error in one play on the authority of a like phrase in another. Similarly he proposed an emendation in I Timothy 6, 3 on the basis of other passages in the Old and New Testament, and Bentley's reading has since been proved to have very early manuscript support; for it is found in the fourth century *codex Sinaiticus*.[14] This is by no means the only instance in which he anticipated the readings of the oldest manuscripts, which in his day were often unknown or unused. We know that already in his student days he had spent many hours in poring over the grammarians and lexicographers of the Byzantine period; for these were crammed with citations from classical authors, citations that as a rule were derived from earlier and often better manuscripts than those to which Bentley and his contemporaries had access.

Another curious notion about Bentley, which is widely prevalent and has marred his reputation, is that he was so intent upon the letter that he forgot the spirit. Even an admirer, when writing about Bentley's reply to Collins' *Discourse of Free-thinking*, can pass the following grotesque judgment: [15]

To the scholar the chief interest of the book is to watch Bentley *for once* interpreting the thought, rather than the language of the ancients. The mastery with which he extracts the whole meaning and nothing but the meaning from a difficult passage of Lucan (IX, 546–568) *shows what he could have done, had he chosen,* in this part of a scholar's business.

That the chief interest of the book to the scholar is the discussion of the lines from Lucan is a matter of opinion; for the

[14] *Works*, III, 357.

[15] J. D. Duff in *Cambridge History of English Literature*, II (Cambridge, Eng., 1913), 378. The italics are mine. Lucan with the notes of Hugo Grotius and Bentley was published at Strawberry Hill Press in 1760, edited by Richard Cumberland (Bartholomew-Clark 193).

book, like most of its author's larger works, shows an astounding range of interest and knowledge. The *Reply* is one of the most valuable sources for what we know about Bentley's earlier work on the text of the New Testament; it contains an illuminating passage, especially for the time at which it was written, on the Samaritan Pentateuch; it defends the authenticity of Plato's *Thirteenth Epistle,* as indeed of them all; it discusses Egyptian and Greek religious beliefs, and reviews the opinions about religion held by Aristotle, Epicurus, Plutarch, Varro, Cato, and Cicero. Of all this there is no hint in Mr. Duff's paragraph on the *Reply.* More serious, however, is the suggestion that Bentley usually concerned himself only with words and language. It is, of course, true that, as the text of Lucan in the passage discussed was free from corruption, Bentley was able to give all his attention to explaining the poet's meaning. But you cannot interpret an author's thought until you are sure of what he has said; and the essential point is that in Bentley's time few printed texts of classical writers were free from textual blemishes of all kinds. Much of our knowledge of Bentley as a textual critic comes not from his published works but from marginal annotations made in manuscripts and books that he used. In such cases the insight of the critic into his author's thought is not expressed; but one need only peruse his emendations of Aristophanes to see that his proposed corrections proceeded from a profound knowledge of the thought and the language of the dramatist. In the case of two plays, the *Plutus* and the *Clouds,* we have two long letters from Bentley to Ludolf Küster, in which the treatment is fuller; the critic constantly explains Aristophanes' meaning as well as improving his text.[16] So, too, in the famous letter to Hemsterhuys, in which he tells the young Dutch editor of Pollux that he must be thoroughly familiar with Greek metrics before venturing to edit fragments from the poets, he often translates an emended passage into Latin in order to make the sense clearer.[17] And has Mr. Duff forgotten the brilliant interpretation of an epigram by Callimachus which Bentley introduced in the preface to the second edition of *Phalaris?* As Bentley himself says, a fact which Jebb appears

[16] *Correspondence,* pp. 305–323; 326–364.   [17] *Ibid.,* pp. 270–293.

to have overlooked, he derived a hint from Suidas and on the basis of this he emended and interpreted the epigram correctly for the first time. And what, to cite but one other example, of the fifteenth chapter of *Phalaris* which is concerned with the content of the letters? To quote Bentley once again: 'But, to let pass all further arguments from words and language, to me the very matter and business of the Letters sufficiently discover them to be an imposture.' Thereupon he deals with 'the matter and business' at length.

The judgment of modern critics on the relative merits of Bentley's Greek and Latin scholarship inevitably tends to be influenced by the primary interest of the critic himself. Thus, Bentley's biographer, Jebb, whose chapter on Bentley's *Horace* is the least satisfactory part of his book, clearly thinks him greater as a Grecian than as a Latinist. Yet A. E. Housman, no mean judge, can remark of Bentley's *Manilius* that it was a greater work than either his *Phalaris* or his *Horace*.[18] This surely implies that the Latinist Housman had a very much higher opinion of the *Horace* than did Jebb, whose own interests and contributions to learning were in the field of Greek literature. In fairness to Jebb one must add that elsewhere he remarks: 'the notes on Horace and Manilius, for example, constantly fail to persuade, but seldom fail to teach,' and again, 'the fact which has told most against the popular diffusion of Bentley's fame is that he is much greater than any of his books.'[19] Tyrrell, speaking of Bentley's *Terence*, ranks him first among editors of that author and adds that some of the greatest nineteenth-century editors of Terence, like Ritschl and Fleckeisen, trod in Bentley's footsteps and to a great extent employed his methods.[20] Tyrrell himself in his edition adopted approximately 160 of Bentley's corrections and readings. Kauer-Lindsay in theirs, while rejecting most, nevertheless cite many of Bentley's variants in the apparatus criticus and adopt some manuscript readings which Bentley had anticipated by conjecture. Furthermore, Kauer-Lindsay, but not Tyrrell, were able to use the shorter

[18] A. E. Housman, *Manilius* I (London, 1903), xvi.
[19] R. C. Jebb, *Bentley*, pp. 211 and 213.
[20] R. Y. Tyrrell, *P. Terenti Afri Comoediae* (Oxford, 1903), preface.

commentary of Donatus, first published by Wessner in 1902, and in addition Kauer collated seven manuscripts which no previous editor had used. There is progress even in the editing of ancient authors, and even where a Bentleian correction has not stood the test of time, it has frequently formed the starting point for improvements by later scholars. Most of Bentley's emendations of Aristophanes' *Plutus* no longer find a place in a modern text of the play, but they have notwithstanding been an inspiration to editors after his time; and his correction of lines 1012–1013, which every one accepts, is a fine example of Bentley at his brilliant best. What Tyrrell has indicated in the case of one author, is indeed generally true. Bentley's influence, which was great on men like Porson and Elmsley, was perhaps even more profound on German classical scholarship of the late eighteenth and of the nineteenth centuries. It was by German enterprise, not in the country of Bentley's birth, that his *Horace* was reprinted in 1869.

It is easy to cavil at Bentley's work when superficially considered, but the greatest classical scholars after his time will usually be found to honor him most, even though they may differ from him on many points. He sometimes, as Housman wittily put it, treated the manuscripts as if they were fellows of Trinity College. Sometimes he was arbitrary in his judgments; so on occasion were Lessing and Hazlitt. He might carry a sound principle too far. What pioneer of genius has not done the same? The effect of the digamma on the scansion of Homeric verse was a fundamental discovery compared to which the fact that Bentley sometimes applied his rule incorrectly is of secondary importance. The metres of Plautus and Terence are a problem about which even now there is no complete agreement among scholars. Bentley in his edition of Terence laid a foundation on which all later investigators have built, even as he was the first clearly to explain the structure of the lyric metres in Greek tragedy and comedy. His severer critics often tend to judge him by the textual emendations that he made or is supposed to have made 'out of the blue.' Since his edition of Horace is the book by which he is perhaps best known nowadays and the work most commonly subjected to adverse criticism, a brief discussion of it will serve the double purpose of showing that its merits greatly outweigh its defects and of illustrating the method that to a greater or less degree he followed in all his editorial work.[21]

In the first place the total number of Bentley's emendations for which he had no sort of manuscript authority is small, far smaller than is often assumed. On the other hand, there are innumerable places where he pointed out errors in the printed texts then available, basing his corrections on manuscripts, though some of these, as we now know after two more centuries of Horatian criticism, were inferior in quality. There has been a tendency to associate Bentley's name chiefly with certain famous alterations—*auspice Phoebo* for *auspice Teucro* (*Carm.* 1, 7, 27), *nitedula* for *vulpecula* (*Epist.* 1, 7, 29), *male ter natos* for *male tornatos* (*A.P.* 441)—which have not found favor with later editors. To judge Bentley fairly we must study the elaborate notes in which he built up his case and we must recollect the numerous places where he improved on the text as it was in his day by consulting more manuscripts than his predecessors and occasionally by giving fresh currency to forgotten readings or emendations in earlier commentators. The truth is that Bentley's own statements in his famous preface have been taken too literally. After remarking that a proper editor needs a certain power of divination in handling the text of his author, he continues: [22]

[21] An extreme example of hostile criticism is H. R. Jolliffe's *The critical methods and influence of Bentley's Horace* (Chicago dissertation; University of Chicago Press, 1939). The appendix of tables recording 'the extent to which Bentley's changes in the vulgate text of his day have been followed in some twelve important critical editions since' is a very useful compilation. The dissertation itself, however, falls into the same generic class of writing as certain modern biographies, whose aim is to 'debunk' their subject.

[22] Bentley's Latin is usually easily understood, but in this instance it is not without obscurity. For this reason I have preferred to quote the original Latin. I should interpret the passage thus: 'More of the changes offered in this edition of Horace are based on conjecture than on the help of manuscripts; and, unless I am utterly mistaken, the former are in general the more sure. For amid a variety of readings authority itself is sometimes illusory and beguiles the mistaken itch of the would-be-emendator away from the truth. But when we propose conjectures that are contrary to the testimony of all books (including MSS), hesitation and modesty whisper in our ear and reasoning alone and the

Plura igitur in Horatianis his curis ex coniectura exhibemus quam ex codicum subsidio; et nisi me omnia fallunt, plerumque certiora: nam in variis lectionibus ipsa saepe auctoritas illudit, et pravae emendaturientium prurigini abblanditur: in coniecturis vero contra omnium librorum fidem proponendis et timor pudorque aurem vellunt, et sola ratio ac sententiarum lux necessitasque ipsa dominantur.

We must also distinguish between the emendations admitted by Bentley into the text and the very numerous conjectures which he merely put forward in the notes. Of the former the greater part are supported by reference either to manuscripts existing in his day or to such as had been cited by previous editors. Again, how many readings there are which every modern editor prints without question, readings to which Bentley first gave currency! On other readings proposed by Bentley his successors are divided in their judgment. Among recent editors, before Klingner, Kiessling is probably the most sympathetic to Bentley, while the edition of Keller and Holder marks a reaction the other way. Vollmer's text is midway between the two. The latest edition, that by Klingner published in 1939, has in the text some Bentleian readings which both Vollmer and Keller-Holder had rejected.[23] In a majority of cases Bentley's readings have become obliterated, because the modern editor commonly prints only the variants from manuscripts. Only in a comparatively few instances, usually where the reading adopted is found in only one or a few manuscripts and is against the consensus of the majority, does Bentley's name appear in the *apparatus criticus*. It is not the least of Klingner's merits that he has inserted Bentley's name a good deal more frequently, and even when he disagrees with him, than some other recent editors of the poet have done. Any reader of Bentley's edition

---

clear light and very inevitability of our arguments hold sway.' It is possible that by *sententiarum* he means the author's not the critic's thought. In that case we should render the last clause, 'the clear light and very inevitability of the author's meaning hold sway.'

[23] E.g., manet (*Carm.* 1, 13, 6); Gyges (*ib.* 2, 17, 14 and 3, 4, 69); lyra—Berecyntia —tibia (*ib.* 4, 1, 22–23); flexus (*ib.* 4, 6, 21); silebo (*ib.* 4, 9, 31); sapiens (*Sat.* 1, 1, 38); versemur (*ib.* 1, 3, 60); amet (*ib.* 1, 4, 87); manibus (*ib.* 2, 3, 303); avet (*Epist.* 1, 14, 9); decentem (*A.P.* 92); tumentis (*ib.* 197).

can quickly satisfy himself that Bentley almost invariably gives reasons and quotes authority and parallel passages in support of his proposed changes. It is not then by the presence of its more drastic verbal changes, whether brilliant or capricious, that Bentley's *Horace* should be judged. The improvement that his text, taken as a whole, marks over previous editions and the immense erudition, ranging over the whole of classical Latin literature, displayed in the notes are what entitle his edition to rank for all time as one of the great productions of English classical scholarship. Editors will continue to dispute about this or that reading; they will be pro-Bentley or anti-Bentley, and the present writer has neither the qualifications nor the desire to enter those formidable lists. But he would suggest that the inevitable appearance of Bentley's name in the introduction and *apparatus criticus* of editions of Horace and of a great many other classical authors, Greek and Latin, is surely an incontrovertible testimony to his unassailable greatness as a scholar:

> Non fumum ex fulgore, sed ex fumo dare lucem
> Cogitat, ut speciosa dehinc miracula promat.[24]

[24] Horace, *A.P.* 143–144.

Michael Rostovtzeff's

The Social and Economic History

of the Hellenistic World *

The Social and Economic History of the Hellenistic World. By
MICHAEL ROSTOVTZEFF. 3 vols. (New York: Oxford Univ. Press.
1941. Pp. xxxii, 1779. $30.)

IT IS not long since the Hellenistic Age ceased to be the step-
child of ancient historians. Droysen's pioneer work, *Die Geschichte des Hellenismus,* was, it is true, published as far back
as 1836–43 and the last decades of the nineteenth century saw
more and more attention being given to Greek history after
the death of Alexander the Great. Yet your reviewer can remember that at his school the period was ignored; while in the university one read Theocritus, the *Argonautica,* and Herondas,
then a very recent discovery. One might even dip into one or
more of Mahaffy's books; but, in the main, Hellenistic history,
save those political aspects which were closely related to the
history of Rome, remained a closed book. Nowadays even the
briefest sketch of Greek history or civilization will include some
account of those long-neglected centuries. The reasons for this
changed outlook are well known. Many ancient sites have now

* *American Economic Review,* 32 (1942), 571–578. Reprinted by permission of
the American Economic Association.

been partly or wholly excavated on scientific lines and have yielded a rich harvest of archaeological material. Innumerable inscriptions of most varied content and importance have been recovered and published, while Egypt has rendered up thousands of papyri which have revolutionized our knowledge of that country under the rule of the Ptolemies.

But there is another side to the picture. Abundant as is the available material, it can never make up wholly for the loss of most of the formal histories written in the Hellenistic period. The archaeological remains and inscriptions are scattered over a wide area; material may be abundant for some regions and extremely scanty for others; it may also be abundant for one period of time and virtually nonexistent for another. In Egypt, too, the wealth of papyri has raised almost as many problems as it has solved, and their distribution in time is uneven, so that there is, for instance, much fuller information about the economic organization and life of that country in the third century B.C. than in the second. Finally, many of the excavated sites continued to be inhabited for centuries after Rome had gained control over the whole eastern Mediterranean, and usually the evidence for the Roman Imperial Age is far more ample and far better preserved than the Hellenistic material. We see this very clearly when we try to reconstruct the trade-routes and to estimate the volume of traffic between the countries bordering on the Mediterranean and the Middle and Far East. The story of Hellenistic trade has been to a great extent obliterated by the better attested story of Roman commerce; and to argue back from the later period to the earlier is always hazardous and sometimes positively wrong.

The publication of Professor Rostovtzeff's long-awaited work is an event of the first importance. These three finely printed and magnificently illustrated volumes are the fruit of many years of laborious study, involving all the ancient evidence and a vast modern literature as well, to which he himself has from time to time made notable contributions. Not without justice he criticizes earlier attempts to reconstruct the economic history of the Hellenistic Age for treating the whole period as a single whole; for, as he points out, what is true of Egypt or the Seleucid Empire in the third century is not necessarily so for the second or the first. He has therefore divided his subject into several broad periods and has sought to define and illustrate the peculiar character of each in the various countries concerned. The only drawback to this method is that it leads to a good deal of repetition; and even Mr. Rostovtzeff, though he warns against the danger of the practice, cannot always avoid using the evidence from one period to fill up gaps in our knowledge of another.

He begins by tracing briefly the political history of the Greek world from 323 to 30 B.C. and also gives his readers a useful *aperçu* of the ancient sources from 323 to 301, from 301 to 221, and from 221 onwards. Chapter II also is still of an introductory character and sketches the economic organization of the Persian empire and the Greek city-states in the fourth century. He stresses certain broad factors, such as the extensive trade relations between Persia and parts of Greece, and the dependence of European Greece on other regions both for food and for raw materials; he also shows the growth of economic independence which characterized the western Greeks at this time, as well as outlying areas like Thrace and South Russia. He concludes (p. 125) that the foreign commerce of Greece, "which defrayed the cost of its imported foodstuffs and raw materials, gradually declined and there was no hope of restoring the balance."

With chapter III, which covers the years from 323 to 281, the main subject of the book begins. The author discusses the policy of Alexander's successors within their own kingdoms and toward their Greek allies and subjects, the influence of the "wandering" armies on the economic and social life of the civil population, and the coinage. Chapter IV, which extends over nearly 400 pages and chronologically deals with the period from 281 to 221, is divided into three sections—Greece and the islands, the major monarchies (*i.e.*, Macedonia, Egypt, and the Seleucid empire), and the minor monarchies. This chapter in a sense forms the very heart and marrow of the book, covering as it does what was by all odds the most prosperous part of the Hellenistic Age. A clear indication of how unevenly the surviving evidence is distributed is the fact that, while 167 pages are devoted to Egypt and 120 to the realm of the Seleucids, 4 suffice for Macedonia! The material for the Greek cities also is tantalizing, being relatively full only for a few—Delos, Delphi, Athens, and certain islands, especially Rhodes. The author, unlike other recent writers, both here and later minimizes the effect of various institutions tending to make war more humane and its results less catastrophic than in the Classical Age. Conversely, he lays great, indeed exaggerated, emphasis on the extent of piracy and generally on the insecurity of life during these decades.

The section on Egypt under the first three Ptolemies is perhaps the most brilliant passage in the book. It describes the most complete, and for a time the most successful, planned economy of the ancient world, embracing alike agriculture, manufactures, and commerce. Even for Egypt it is still impossible to define with certainty every aspect of economic life. But, as the author points out, on the available evidence one can say that there was no branch of production which was not to some extent at least under royal control. The aim of the kings was to make Egypt and their overseas possessions, which at this date were considerable, as far as possible self-sufficient and also to secure a favorable balance in international trade and "thereby to secure a good influx of gold and silver from abroad." There are, on the other hand, many uncertainties. What was the population of Egypt, or indeed of any larger area in the Hellenistic world? What was the exact status of the foreign population in Egypt, which was so vastly important for carrying on the work of government, as well as in industry and commerce? How did Egypt pay for her considerable imports from the South? And what was the balance of trade between Egypt and Greece? Certainly, in spite of high tariffs, much was imported into Egypt from various areas, both essential raw materials, like metals, and non-essential goods for which the well-to-do were prepared to pay highly. Mr. Rostovtzeff, who offers at least a partial answer to most of these controversial questions, also very properly warns against the danger of drawing general conclusions from prices mentioned in papyri, since there was no standard measurement in use but the size of the *artaba* varied. Even so, one may mention in passing, weights and measures in modern India vary from district to district.

Information about Egypt is ample and detailed when compared with what is known about the Seleucid empire at the same date. Its rulers had a far less homogeneous territory to administer and, as the third century progressed, they steadily lost ground in the eastern parts of their dominions. They were also constantly at war with Egypt, and this circumstance Mr. Rostovtzeff would attribute in part to economic causes. He argues cogently for a rivalry between the two empires for the effective control through their respective territories of the trade from the Far East. It is certainly significant that the Ptolemaic currency, struck on the Phoenician standard, was seemingly excluded from the Seleucid empire, and that in Egypt and her dependencies no coins of Attic standard, which had been adopted by Alexander and continued by his successors in Asia, have been found. Still, after examining all the available data, the author is forced to admit that very little is known about the general fiscal policy of the Seleucids and he thus summarizes his conclusions (p. 517): "The principal achievements of Seleucid policy were these: the establishment of a uniform administration, the introduction of a systematic and, as far as possible, uniform taxation, the formation of a well organized royal army and navy, the construction and maintenance of a network of good roads between the various satrapies, the adoption of measures designed to provide a single abundant and trustworthy currency, a certain control of weights and measures, and, finally, the introduction of a uniform dating (the Seleucid era) and calendar, which were not only valid within the empire but were adopted by many of its neighbours and are still in use in some parts of the Near East." The last section of this chapter surveys conditions so far as known in Pergamum, Bithynia, Galatia, Pontus, the communities on the Black Sea, and the Bosporan kingdom.

The three chapters that follow (V–VII) deal in a similar regional way with the periods from 221 to 168, from 168 to c. 88, and from 88 to 30 B.C. The first of these was on the whole an age of depression and poverty in European Greece, even though the author's picture seems too lurid and overdrawn and the remarks of Polybius on the Greek passion for show, money, and a life of ease (*cf.* p. 624) smack too much of the philosophical schools to be valuable as evidence. The Greek cities of Asia Minor, however, were in spite of heavy taxation prosperous, while Rhodes during these fifty years reached the zenith of her political power and economic influence in the Near East. The power of the Seleucids suffered a marked decline which was only temporarily arrested by Antiochus III and there was a corresponding growth in the political and economic importance of Pergamum. One of Mr. Rostovtzeff's most interesting suggestions, based primarily on a study of extant coin-hoards, is the existence of a kind of economic *entente cordiale* between the Seleucids and the Attalids at this time (*cf.* pp. 656–657). His arguments for continued great prosperity in the Seleucid kingdom after Antiochus III's defeat by Rome and even under his two successors are far less convincing. I should myself hesitate to have much faith in Athenaeus's stories of royal magnificence; nor does great building activity on the part of kings prove general prosperity in their realms. At that rate the ages of Septimius Severus and of Diocletian could also be interpreted as times of rude plenty.

In Egypt this period marked the beginning of a steady economic decline which its rulers tried to arrest in various ways. Riots and even civil war caused a fall in revenues, and the difficulty of collecting taxes and arrears led to harsh compulsory measures and their attendant evils. Finally concessions were made, the main purpose of which was "the emancipation of private initiative from the heavy burden of state control"; in other words, a system which had worked efficiently during a large part of the third century, when Egypt controlled extensive areas outside Egypt, broke down badly when most of that extra-Egyptian territory was lost. A significant innovation, to which Mr. Rostovtzeff gives considerable attention, although its full purpose and effects are far from clear, is found in the matter of currency. The early Ptolemies, like other Hellenistic rulers, had operated on a bimetallic system. In the late third century, according to our author and others, this was changed to a trimetallic system, since the heavy copper coinage that was now increasingly used was not token money but represented its value in metal. Egypt also provides the only example of a serious currency inflation in the Hellenistic Age. This has quite recently been investigated afresh by A. Segrè,[1] who is sceptical about the real metallic value of the earlier copper coins but concludes that three types of drachma, one of silver and two of copper, were distinguished by the rulers of Egypt.

Brief mention must suffice for chapters VI and VII which tell the story of, first, the growing, and then the complete, domination of the eastern Mediterranean by Rome, a story which for that very reason is more familiar, at least in outline, to most readers. Again political changes brought drastic economic changes in their train—the partial decline of Rhodes and of Pergamum simultaneously with a general recovery in parts of Greece and especially in Athens, and the emergence of Delos as a leading emporium. Finally, there is the depressing tale of Rome's wars with Mithridates and her ruthless exploitation of the Near East in the first century.

The author ends his work with an eighth chapter of nearly two hundred pages, entitled Summary and Epilogue, which brings Volume II to a close. Readers who are not specialists in ancient history may do well to peruse this chapter before studying the rest of the book, which is not easy to read or to assimilate. Primarily this is due to the often intractable nature of the evidence, but at times one also feels that even the learned author is partially submerged by the mass of material which he is handling. There are, for example, avoidable repetitions. Was it necessary to devote two pages (74–75) to the pseudo-Aristotelian *Oeconomica*, which are fully discussed on pages 440–446? Such repetitions are not infrequent and sometimes extend even to individual sentences (*cf.* pp. 340 and 344). Again, the author, perhaps because his work was being composed over a long period, is not always consistent in his conclusions; nor are his data always fully coördinated, as the following instance will show. On page 242 he says of a medical tax (*iatrikon*) recorded in Cos that "it was probably a personal tax paid by the inhabitants of Cos for the maintenance of the public health service (hardly a tax

[1] *Am. Jour. Philol.,* Vol. 63 (1942), pp. 174–192.

paid by the doctors). On page 1092 he refers to the *iatrikon* in Egypt and remarks, "the tax has the same name as that levied in the Greek cities to finance the public medical service, and it could hardly have had another meaning in Egypt." But he has nowhere given any authority for the assertion that a public medical service was a regular feature in Greek cities, nor does he mention the most unequivocal evidence for the nature of the *iatrikon*. A Delphic inscription (*S.I.G.*[3] 437) of the early third century records that one Philistion, a metic, received exemption from a liturgy (the *choragia*) and the *iatrikon*. Even so the assumption that a medical service was a usual institution in the city-states is unwarranted. In the third place Mr. Rostovtzeff is sometimes very diffuse and pauses to discuss topics but remotely connected with the real subject of the book. A good example of this weakness will be found on pages 430 to 440.

The third volume is made up of nearly 350 pages of notes which provide ample references to the ancient sources and to the modern literature; they also contain a good deal of discussion of controversial matters. There follow four short excursuses on special topics by J. G. Milne, R. P. Blake, E. S. G. Robinson, and F. O. Waage, and two elaborate indexes. The notes are of the utmost value—indeed, they will be indispensable to any future investigator—but they also show certain unsatisfactory features. The author has a weakness for accumulating references which are superfluous, both in the occasional notes at the foot of the text and in the body of annotations in Volume III. Thus, the allusion to *O.G.I.* 10 is appropriate in connection with the text on page 463; it is pointless in note 42 on page 173. Again, on page 610 we learn that Rhodes and Eumenes II entered into close relations with Crete in order to check piracy, the authority for this being *S.I.G.*[3] 581 and 627. The former, a treaty between Rhodes and Hierapytna containing an antipiracy clause, is wholly to the point; but the other, an agreement between Eumenes and all the Cretan cities save one, is very fragmentary, and what survives is insufficient to support Mr. Rostovtzeff's inference. The same modern work is referred to again and again, and often eight or ten books are listed, half of which have no independent value because they merely repeat what is to be found in the others. Judicious selection would have made much of Volume III far more serviceable to the student. The author is not always critical in his selections. Suhr's monograph is neither accurate nor original (*cf.* pp. 28 and 34), while Stanley Casson's book on Cyprus is so bad in the earlier parts (*cf.* Gjerstadt's devastating review in *Jour. Hell. Stud.,* Vol. 59 [1939], pp. 142 *ff.*) that no wise reader will trust any portion of it. There was no need to refer to Jaeger's book on page 1321 or to Bilabel's article on page 1451, which is concerned only with the Roman period. Mr. Rostovtzeff's astonishing erudition will be patent to every reader of his book; it was unnecessary to parade his bibliographical knowledge at the cost of clarity and serviceableness.

A few doubts on general questions or criticisms of details may here find a place. On page 89 we read, "we know that in the fourth century Syria and Cyprus supplied Athens with grain." The author gives no references to the ancient authorities, for his note (p. 1326, n. 19) only indicates some archaeological evidence for general trade relations between Athens and Syria. There is in fact very little basis for the statement. The statement (p. 183; *cf.* p. 189) that Alexander's empire remained a political unit for about fifty years is to me utterly incomprehensible, since any such unity had disappeared at latest after the death of Antigonus I in 301. Even stranger, indeed positively wrong, is the assertion (pp. 530 and 533) that the Syrian Wars between the Seleucids and the Ptolemies were mainly fought in Asia Minor. The truth is that only in the second was Asia Minor the main scene of operations. On page 481 the author hazards the suggestion that the 10,000 *cleroi* owned by Syrian Antioch in the time of Julian the Apostate may "have been an inheritance of the remote past," that is, may have already been a part of that city in early Seleucid times. Even in the unchanging East such a survival through 600 years is more than unlikely; and Mr. Rostovtzeff himself knows better. On page 499, writing about Apamea, he points out that the cities of Seleucid Syria never ceased growing, and therefore it must be assumed that Apamea was smaller in the third century than in A.D. 6–7, when its population was 117,000. He makes full use of Josephus and pseudo-Aristeas for economic conditions in

Palestine, but strangely enough ignores the invaluable testimony of Sirach (Ecclesiasticus) 38, 24–34. This passage is interesting in two ways: it portrays vividly the daily work of the peasant, the signet engraver, the smith, and the potter, and it contrasts these manual workers with the superior caste of scribes.

"All these are deft with their hands, and each is wise in his handiwork. Without them a city cannot be inhabited, and wherever they dwell they linger not. But they shall not be inquired of for public counsel, and in the assembly they enjoy no precedence. On the seat of the judge they do not sit, and law and justice they understand not. They do not expound the instruction of wisdom, nor understand the proverbs of the wise; but they understand the work they have wrought, and their thought is on the practice of their craft." Then Sirach describes the ideal scribe, "who serveth among great men and appeareth before princes."

On page 777 we are told that the Rhodians in 163 were confirmed in their rights to private property situated in the former Rhodian dominions on the mainland, and Polybius 31, 4 is cited in proof of this statement. But Polybius relates that the Rhodians made two requests to the Roman senate: (1) that they should be allowed to recover Calynda; and (2) that Rhodians who had owned property in Lycia and Caria be permitted to enjoy that property as formerly (*i.e.*, before 168). A little later Polybius says briefly that the senate confirmed to Rhodes the possession of Calynda but there is not a word about the other request; the natural inference is that the senate rejected it. Mr. Rostovtzeff (pp. 927 *ff.*) accepts the conclusions of Otto and Bengtson regarding the date of Hippalus, discoverer of the monsoons in the Indian ocean. Ordinarily I distrust the *argumentum ex silentio* as much as the author, but in this case I find Strabo's silence inexplicable. Strabo had a keen interest in explorations and explorers, many of whom he mentions. Is it likely that he would ignore Hippalus, if the discovery had been made before Strabo's time? Besides, as Tarn has pointed out,[2] Otto and Bengtson's theory involves the outright rejection of

[2] *Jour. Hell. Stud.*, Vol. 59 (1939), p. 324.

the Elder Pliny's explicit statement that the discovery was made in or near his lifetime (*nunc*).

The author's observation that anti-Roman sentiments in the Greek world of the first century reach us "only very faintly" (p. 933) is an understatement, as has been shown by Harald Fuchs in his monograph, *Der geistige Widerstand gegen Rom in der antiken Welt* (Berlin, 1938), notes 42 and 43 on pages 43–44. Of Rome's "colonial" government in the first century Mr. Rostovtzeff remarks: "Such a government may be sometimes just and efficient, but it is always arrogant, arbitrary, selfish, and often ruthless and cruel." There is here a contradiction: If a government is just, it cannot according to any reasonable use of words be arbitrary. The truth is that the author's own political bias sometimes affects his historical judgment. We see this in his observations on the lower classes and wise aristocrats (pp. 611–612), but the most striking instance occurs in his analysis (pp. 1115–1134) of the bourgeoisie and the politically and socially less prominent "proletariat" in the Greek cities. The extreme contrast between them drawn by our author seems to me to go far beyond either the existing evidence or historical probability. Cicero's reference (see p. 1526, n. 92) to *sutores* and *zonarii* does not testify to the importance of the textile, but to that of the leather industry in Pergamum. Mr. Rostovtzeff confuses *sutor* (cobbler) with *sartor* (tailor), and the belts made by the *zonarii* were certainly of leather, not of wool or linen. Finally, I have noted a number of places in the annotations where Mr. Rostovtzeff's criticism of others not only lacks urbanity but is positively unfair. One example must suffice. On page 1534, note 126, he refers to two inscriptions and continues: "None of these documents nor the autonomy of Tyre are mentioned in the book by W. B. Fleming, *The History of Tyre*, 1915, pp. 65 *ff.*" But the two inscriptions were first published in 1918 and 1925 respectively!

Once or twice in a generation a book on some large topic appears and immediately becomes a standard work. It will be criticized and, as time passes and fresh evidence accumulates, it will be corrected on this point and on that, but its basic value will endure for many years. Such was Mommsen's *Römisches Staats-recht* or the late T. F. Tout's book on administration in medieval England. Such, if I am not mistaken, is Mr. Rostovtzeff's latest and greatest work.

⋘ 15 ⋙

Henri-Irenée Marrou's *Histoire*

de l'éducation dans l'antiquité *

HENRI-IRENÉE MARROU: Histoire de l'éducation dans l'antiquité. Paris: Éd. du Seuil 1948. 595 S. 660 Fr.

UNIVERSITY teachers who lecture on the history of Greek and Roman education have long been handicapped by their inability to recommend to the class a comprehensive, yet not too bulky, treatment of the subject. Not that it has been neglected by scholars, for the list of monographs and articles that have appeared since Grasberger's book is long. But, in general, these have dealt with only a part of the long period from Homer to the fall of the Roman Empire, or else they have been devoted to particular authors or to relatively restricted topics. M. Marrou's book fills a long-felt want admirably. He is thoroughly familiar with the ancient evidence, including inscriptions and papyri; his judgment on controversial issues is eminently sane; and his narrative, while fully documented, is still most readable.

After a short introduction, M. divides his subject into three chronological periods: 1. from Homer to the end of the fourth century B.C. (pp. 27–136); 2. the Hellenistic Age and the Ro-

* *Gnomon*, 21 (1949), 97–101. Reprinted by permission of the editor of *Gnomon*.

man Empire in the Greek-speaking world (pp. 139–309); 3. Rome and the Latin-speaking West to the fifth century a.C. (pp. 313–447). A brief epilogue, which traces the connection between antiquity and the Middle Ages in both East and West, is followed by a select bibliography and more than a hundred pages of notes (pp. 465–573), which serve a twofold purpose. They provide further references to the modern literature on various aspects of ancient education—references to ancient sources are given at the foot of each page in the main text— and they also enable M. to discuss controversial topics or to justify more fully the interpretations given in the narrative. Thus, for example, he shows convincingly (pp. 488–490) that the differences between Plato's views on education in the Republic and in the Laws are more apparent than real and that in reality the two works supplement one another. Or again, he discusses (pp. 497–499) the approximate number of young men enrolled in the ephebia from year to year, adding a chronological table based on inscriptions from 269/68 B.C. to A.D. 266/67. The relative space assigned to each of the three sections on the whole shows sound judgment; for the second and longest includes no less than seven centuries, and, besides, information especially about elementary education is vastly fuller for the Hellenistic and Graeco-Roman periods than for the preceding age. That the third section is relatively shorter is, with one reservation to which I shall return, also justified. Education in the western half of the Roman Empire from the first century a.C. onwards followed the Greek pattern so closely that a more detailed treatment would have resulted in needless repetition.

One general criticism suggests itself: While the size of the book is just right, one could wish that the description of physical education and athletics had been somewhat curtailed and that the space so saved had been used for a fuller discussion of the educational theorists. A goodly number of scattered references to Cicero's De oratore and Quintilian's Institutio are an insufficient substitute for a discussion of these works as a whole, and one misses any allusion to the newer style of rhetoric practised by the younger Seneca, to which Quintilian's theory with its emphasis on Ciceronianism marked a reaction. On this see the witty, if partial, paper by W. H. Alexander in the University of Toronto Quarterly 4 (1935), pp. 239–258. Tacitus' Dialogus is virtually ignored and so, strangely enough, are Arrian's Discourses of Epictetus which abound in educational doctrine. M. mentions neither Colardeau's Étude sur Epictète nor Halbauer's De diatribis Epicteti, though both books are still valuable. He gives some attention to the De liberis educandis of the pseudo-Plutarch and expresses a mild doubt whether the rejection of this treatise from Plutarch's genuine works is justified. But he has little to say about Plutarch's views on education scattered through the Moralia. This topic was well treated by Katherine M. Westaway, The educational theory of Plutarch (London, 1922), and the Munich dissertation (1926), Die Pädagogik Plutarchs und ihre Quellen, by Luise Müller, though immature, contains a useful collection of material. Dion of Prusa, to modern readers the most attractive among the writers of the Second Sophistic, receives little notice. Yet the reading-list (Orat. 18) that he sent to a middle-aged man desiring to take a more effective part in public life was worth a paragraph. It substantiates what we know from other sources about favourite school authors, but in addition to the Attic orators of the canon Dion also recommends for study more recent orators. Them we can hope to emulate. Demosthenes and the rest, because unapproachable, are in that sense discouraging. Again, in the dialogue between Alexander and Diogenes (Orat. 4) the Cynic philosopher's discussion of two types of education—divine and human—is not without interest. Finally, in spite of the author's disarming apology (p. 496, note 2), his neglect of Aristotle is hard to understand or to justify. We may agree that Aristotle's educational precepts in the Politics belong in the main to the Platonic phase of his thought; yet even in that book there are some things that are new, e.g., the emphasis on drawing and the three views about the ends of education which, according to Aristotle, were commonly entertained in his day. What of the impetus to scientific research given by Aristotle in his biological works and presumably in his teaching? And what of the Rhetoric and the logical works? The influence of both was great, so that, as late as the fourth century a.C., orthodox Christian teachers accused their Arian opponents of relying on the subtleties of Aristotelian dialectic to justify their pestilent heresies. Cf. on this the illuminating article by de Ghellink in Revue d'histoire ecclésiastique 26 (1930), pp. 5–42.

Some points of detail call for comment: M. gives a penetrating analysis (pp. 86 ff.) of the Sophists as teachers, but he seems to me to minimise their original contributions to political theory.

He accepts (pp. 125, 129) the total, "about one hundred," of Isocrates' pupils which is recorded in the ancient biographers, an estimate that seemingly goes back to Hermippus. On what did Hermippus base his figures? He is not likely to have had access to any official roll of students, so that probably he took into account only those who subsequently made some mark in the world as politicians or writers. Must there not have been others, some of whom indeed may have taken only a part of the four-year course of study?

M. remarks (p. 155) that strangers were not admitted into the Athenian ephebia on the same footing as citizens. This statement may need revision, for Reinmuth has recently argued (Transactions Amer. Philol. Assoc. 78, 433, where he also promises a fuller exposition of the evidence), mainly on the basis of IG II^2, 2033, that in time Attic citizenship "was granted to all who were admitted to the ephebia."

When discussing (pp. 143 and 494, note 5) the notion of world citizenship, the author contents himself with a reference to Mewaldt's semi-popular article, but ignores the more weighty contribution by W. W. Tarn, Alexander the Great and the Unity of Mankind. Published originally in the Proceedings of the Brit. Acad. vol. XIX, it can now be studied in revised and enlarged form in his Alexander the Great (Cambridge Univ. Press, 1948), vol. 2, 399–449.

The evidence for attendance by ephebes at philosophical lectures is surely better than M. suggests (pp. 258–261 with 527, note 5). It is true that in IG II^2, 1030 and 1031, the parts of the inscriptions that allude to philosophy have been restored; but this is not so in IG II^2, 1006 and 1028, to which M. himself refers on page 258. Indeed, in 1006 the two philosophical schools are specified by name—the Academy and the Lyceum. Similarly, a Samian decree in honour of Epicrates of Heraclea (SEG I, 368; c. 200 B.C.) describes him as a Peripatetic whose services to education consisted partly in public lectures, partly in private tuition of "young men desirous of learning."

The survival of Greek in the western half of the Roman Empire is admittedly a thorny problem, but M. seems to me too drastic in some of his conclusions. The absence of raillery in the younger Pliny's letters, when compared with Cicero's (p. 353), is surely due not to Pliny's less complete command of vernacular Greek but to his lack of humour, which is not conspicuous even when he sticks to Latin. When M. discusses (*ibid.*) the Christian communities, he unfortunately bases his argument on the evidence from North Africa. The truth is that that province was exceptional; for there, at a time when Greek was still widely understood in educated circles in the West, knowledge of Greek was very restricted. But the number of converts made in North Africa during the second century was great, and it is no accident that it was in Africa that the earliest Latin translations of the New Testament appeared. The first version of the *Vetus latina* may have been available by A.D. 150. The *libri et epistulae Pauli* named in the Acts of the Scillitan martyrs (c. 180) were surely in Latin, and a little later Tertullian, who composed some of his own works in Greek, used one or more versions of the *Vetus latina,* though at times he made his own translations of the sacred text. These pre-Hieronymic versions were composed in colloquial Latin, vernacular renderings which ordinary men with little education could understand. It was this feature which led educated pagans, who took the trouble to look at the Christian sacred books, to sneer at their lack of style and literary grace (cf. Lactantius, Inst. V 1). M. makes excellent use of the Hermeneumata (pp. 358 ff.), but says nothing of the oldest all-Latin glossaries. Yet their evidence, provided that they be rightly interpreted (cf. W. M. Lindsay in Bulletin du Cange 3, 1927, pp. 95–100), is of value, because they helped the early monastic students in the West to a better understanding of the more popular pagan authors. To the testimony for the decline of Greek in the West marshalled by M. should be added the ironical comment of Ambrosiaster (PL, 17, 255 B): *manifestum est ignorare animum nostrum, si lingua loquatur quam nescit, sicut adsolent Latini homines Graece cantare, oblectati sono verborum, nescientes tamen quid dicant.*

The reader unfamiliar with Quintilian will be seriously misled by M.'s comments (p. 382) on Quintilian's preference for Greek rhetorical terms. Four out of the five terms there listed are accompanied by their Latin equivalents, viz., *enumeratio* (Inst. orat. V 14, 11), *reticentia* (IX 2, 54 and 57), *dissimulatio* (IX 2, 44, but Q. prefers εἰρωνεία because it has a wider connotation), and *notatio* (I 6, 28). Q. gives no Latin equivalent for ἀναγκαῖον, but in both passages that it occurs (IX 2, 106.3, 99) he is quoting the younger Gorgias and Rutilius. The book by von Müller and Bauer (p. 466) has been superseded by Kromayer-Veith, Heerwesen und Kriegführung der Griechen und Römer (Munich, 1928). In place of the books recommended (pp. 524–525, notes 6 and 9) on Greek mathematics and astronomy, the reader should be referred to J. L. Heiberg, Geschichte der Mathematik und Naturwissenschaft im Altertum, and to Sir Thomas Heath's History of Greek Mathematics or his shorter Manual of Greek Mathematics, as well as to his monograph on Aristarchus of Samos.

The chapter entitled "Le christianisme et l'éducation classique" (pp. 416–434) is disappointing. It suffers from two faults: the treatment is too compressed and the author, who in the rest of the book maintains a nicely balanced judgment, here tends to lapse into dogmatic assertion and an arbitrary evaluation of the sources. Thus, in his description of catechetical instruction he lumps together all the surviving catechetical writings without distinguishing among them. Actually they illustrate three separate stages of teaching. Augustine's *De catechizandis rudibus* is a guide for Christian teachers preparing candidates for admission to the catechumenate. Of the many addresses by Cyril of Jerusalem eighteen give instruction to catechumens soon to be baptized and five to the same after baptism and admission as full members of the Christian congregation. Gregory of Nyssa's discourse, on the other hand, is intended for the guidance of Christian teachers themselves. M. ignores Niceta of Remesiana. But what remains of Niceta's addresses is peculiarly valuable because they exemplify the simple and unpretentious teaching which alone was suitable for baptismal candidates in a remote and only partly civilized region of the Empire. Incidentally it is clear from what he says (cf. A. E. Burn, Niceta of Remesiana, pp. 6 ff.) and also from Cyril 5, 12 (PG, 33, 520B–521A), that a proportion of candidates were illiterate. Hence it was part of the instructor's task to make them repeat the Creed and the Lord's Prayer after him until they had memorized both. More might have been said about Chrysostom's *De inani gloria,* since he explains to parents the simplest form of catechetical instruction suitable for young children. The story (p. 429), found only in Socrates and Sozomen, that at the time of Julian's edict the older and the younger Apollinaris composed epics, dramas, and dialogues in classical style but on Biblical subjects, is surely very suspect. Not a trace of such works has survived nor was the idea new; for in the West Juvencus had composed an epic on the Gospels fifty years earlier, while the Platonic dialogue, to say nothing of Gregory of Nyssa, had been adapted to Christian themes long before by Methodius. M., however, who does not question the accuracy of Socrates, proposes to reject outright Eusebius' testimony (H. E. V, 10) about the Christian school at Alexandria, except insofar as it refers to Origen. But Eusebius is writing of events close to his own times, besides being a far more trustworthy historian than Socrates or Sozomen. M. maintains that a school of Higher Christian Studies flourished in Alexandria only under Origen. Pantaenus is passed over in silence. Clement receives a bare mention, but his educational theories are ignored, though they have received considerable attention in modern times. The most recent book, Die christliche Lebenshaltung des Klemens von Alexandrien nach seinem Pädagogus, by Fr. Quatember (Vienna, 1946), no doubt appeared too late for M. to use. While it must be admitted that the evidence for the character of Christian studies in Alexandria after Clement and Origen is not free from obscurity, yet it does not justify the categorical statements of M., who denies the existence of any organized institution and assumes that instruction was confined to the informal contact between theologian and disciple. And what of Antioch? The method of scriptural interpretation taught by its theologians from Lucian to Theodore of Mopsuestia was distinctive. Is it justifiable to assume, what seems to me intrinsically unlikely, that this method also was handed on only through informal conversations between older and younger clerics and that there was no provision for more formal instruction and to more numerous pupils in the class-room? M. makes no mention of the school at Gaza. But there again there was a succession of teachers—Aeneas, Procopius, Choricius—and a remarkable combination of rhetorical and theological studies. Procopius, besides, was the father of those Catenae of Biblical passages which became so popular and which are a kind of Christian counterpart to the florilegia of pagan classical authors compiled in the Graeco-Roman world.

The suggestions and criticisms that have been offered above are made in no captious spirit. M. has carried through a difficult undertaking with conspicuous success. It is to be hoped that his book will be widely read and that there will soon be a demand for a second edition. If so, one appreciative reader who has learnt much from this book ventures to hope that the author may include in the new edition some treatment of topics which the need for compression has led him to omit or to handle too cursorily.

Bibliography of the

Publications of

M. L. W. Laistner, 1914-1956

Abbreviations

AJP   *American Journal of Philology*
AHR   *American Historical Review*
CP   *Classical Philology*
CQ   *Classical Quarterly*
CR   *Classical Review*
CW   *Classical Weekly*
HTR   *Harvard Theological Review*
Spec   *Speculum*

1914

"Geometric Pottery at Delphi," *Annual of the British School at Athens* 19, 61–69.

"The Excavation of the Kamares Cave in Crete," with R. M. Dawkins, *Annual of the British School,* 19, 1–34.

1921

"Dediticii: The Source of Isidore (Etym. 9.4.49–50)," *Journal of Roman Studies* 11, 267–268.

"Isocrates," *CQ* 15, 78–84.

"The Obelisks of Augustus at Rome," *Journal of Roman Studies* 11, 265–266.

1922

"Two Notes from the *Liber Glossarum*," *CQ* 16, 105.
"*Candelabrum Theodosianum*," *CQ* 16, 107.

1923

Greek Economics: Introduction and Translation (London, Dent), xlii, 204 pp.
"Notes on Greek from the Lectures of a Ninth Century Monastery Teacher," *Bulletin of the J. Rylands Library* 7, 421–456.
Survey of "Ancient History" in *Annual Bulletin of Historical Literature, No. XII, Publications of the Year 1922*, 1–9.
Reviews: P. N. Ure, *The Origin of Tyranny* (Cambridge, 1922), *History* 7, 288–289; J. T. Shotwell, *An Introduction to the History of History* (New York, 1923), *History* 8, 210–211.

1924

"Geographical Lore in the *Liber Glossarum*," *CQ* 18, 49–53.
"Abbo of St-Germain-des-Prés," *Bulletin Ducange* 1, 27–31.
"The Revival of Greek in Western Europe in the Carolingian Age," *History* 9, 177–187.
Survey of "Ancient History" in *Annual Bulletin of Historical Literature, No. XIII, Publications of the Year 1923*, 3–10.
Review: Joseph Wells, *Studies in Herodotus* (Oxford, 1923), *History* 9, 122–123.

1925

"Martianus Capella and His Ninth Century Commentators," *Bulletin of the J. Rylands Library* 9, 130–138.
"*Lista* and *Ruga*," *Bulletin Ducange* 2, 40–41.
"Flosculi Philoxenei," *CQ* 19, 192–195.
Survey of "Ancient History" in *Annual Bulletin of Historical Literature, No. XIV, Publications of the Year 1924*, 3–11.
Reviews: W. R. Halliday, *The Growth of the City State* (Liverpool, 1923), *History* 9, 328–329; T. R. Glover, *Herodotus* (Cambridge, 1924), *History* 10, 53–54; C. T. Seltman, *Athens: Its History and Coinage before the Persian Invasion* (Cambridge, 1924), *History* 10, 247–248.

1926

Glossaria latina: I. Glossarium Ansileubi sive Liber glossarum, ed. W. M. Lindsay, J. F. Mountford, J. Whatmough, F. Rees, R. Weir, M. L. W. Laistner (Paris, Les Belles Lettres), 605 pp. *II. Arma, Abavus, Philoxenus*, ed. W. M. Lindsay, R. G. Austin,

Bibliography

M. L. W. Laistner, J. F. Mountford (Paris, Les Belles Lettres), 291 pp. [*Philoxeni Glossarium,* pp. 123–291].

"The Decay of Geographical Knowledge and the Decline of Exploration, A.D. 300–500," *Travel and Travellers of the Middle Ages,* ed. A. P. Newton (London, Kegan Paul), 19–38.

"Celtis again,"*CQ* 20, 26.

Review: J. Vendryes, *Language: A Linguistic Introduction to History* (London, 1925), *History* 10, 364.

1927

Isocrates, De Pace and Philippus, edited with a historical introduction and commentary (New York, Longmans Green), 173 pp. [Cornell Studies in Classical Philology XXII].

"A Ninth-Century Commentator on the Gospel according to Matthew," *HTR* 20, 129–149.

Review: Henry Bett, *Johannes Scotus Erigena: A Study in Mediaeval Philosophy* (Cambridge, 1925), *History* 12, 152–153 and also *Philosophical Review* 36, 200–201.

1928

"Fulgentius in the Ninth Century," *Mélanges Hrouchevsky* (Kiev, Ukrainian Academy of Sciences), 445–456.

"The Date and the Recipient of Smaragdus' *Via regia,*" *Spec* 3, 392–397.

Reviews: Gustave Glotz, *Ancient Greece at Work* (New York, 1926), *CW* 21, 100–102; G. F. Abbott, *Thucydides: A Study in Historical Reality* (London, 1925), *CW* 21, 133–134; Publications of the Bibliothek Warburg, *History* 12, 366; Samuel Dill, *Roman Society in Gaul in the Merovingian Age* (London, 1926), and O. M. Dalton, *The History of the Franks by Gregory of Tours* (Oxford, 1927), *History* 13, 44–46; Ferdinand Lot, *La Fin du monde antique et le début du moyen age* (Paris, 1927), *AHR* 34, 102–104; Maud Joynt, *The Life of St. Gall* (London, 1927); J. M. Clark, *The Abbey of St. Gall as a Centre of Literature and Art* (Cambridge, 1926); and Dom Rombaut van Doren, *Étude sur l'influence musicale de l'Abbaye de Saint-Gall (VIII° aux XI° siècle)* (Louvain, 1925), *History* 13, 143–144; *Isocrates,* trans. George Norlin, I (London, 1928), *CR* 42, 223–224.

1929

A Survey of Ancient History to the Death of Constantine (Boston, D. C. Heath), xiii, 613 pp.

277

Reviews: J. B. Bury, *The Invasion of Europe by the Barbarians* (London, 1928), *History* 14, 64–65; Tenney Frank, *An Economic History of Rome* (Baltimore, 1927; 2d ed.), *Economic History Review* 2, 175–176.

1930

"Rivipullensis 74 and the Scholica of Martin of Laon," *Mélanges Mandonnet* 2 (Paris, Vrin), 31–37.

"The Influence of Isocrates' Political Doctrines on Some Fourth Century Men of Affairs," *CW* 23, 129–131.

"The Mediaeval Organ and a Cassiodorus Glossary among the Spurious Works of Bede," *Spec* 5, 217–221.

"Alcuin" and "Benedict, Saint," *Encyclopedia of the Social Sciences* (New York), I, 628–629; II, 510–511.

Reviews: B. D. Meritt, *The Athenian Calendar in the Fifth Century* (Cambridge, Mass., 1928), *Classical Journal* 25, 562–564; *Isocrate,* trans. Georges Mathieu et Emile Brémond, I (Paris, 1928), and *Isocrates,* trans. George Norlin, II (London, 1929), *CR* 44, 66–68; H. N. Couch, *The Treasuries of the Greeks and Romans* (Menasha, 1929), *American Economic Review* 20, 491–492; F. Heichelheim, *Wirtschaftliche Schwankungen der Zeit von Alexander bis Augustus* (Jena, 1930), *American Economic Review* 20, 716–717; Camille Jullian, *Au Seuil de notre histoire* (Paris, 1930), *AHR* 35, 903–904.

1931

Thought and Letters in Western Europe, A.D. *500 to 900* (London, Methuen), ix, 354 pp.

Reviews: John M. Warbeke, *The Searching Mind of Greece* (New York, 1930), *Philosophical Review* 40, 595–598; C. N. Cochrane, *Thucydides and the Science of History* (London, 1929), *History* 16, 54–55; H. H. Scullard, *Scipio Africanus in the Second Punic War* (Cambridge, 1930), *AHR* 36, 851–852; Camille Jullian, *Au Seuil de notre histoire,* II and III (Paris, 1931), *AHR* 37, 148; Franciscus Kleine-Piening, *Quo tempore Isocratis orationes quae peri eirenes et Areopagitikos inscribuntur compositae sint* (Paderborn, 1930), *CR* 45, 151–152.

1932

Greek History (Boston, D. C. Heath), xiii, 485 pp.

Reviews: Moses Hadas, *Sextus Pompey* (New York, 1930), *CW* 25, 110–111; Ferdinand Lot, *The End of the Ancient World and the*

Beginning of the Middle Ages (New York, 1931), *AHR* 37, 366–367.

1933

"Bede as a Classical and a Patristic Scholar," *Transactions of the Royal Historical Society*, 4th series, 16, 69–94.

"Source-Marks in Bede Manuscripts," *Journal of Theological Studies* 34, 350–354.

Reviews: A. J. Macdonald, *Authority and Reason in the Early Middle Ages* (Oxford, 1933), *Journal of Theological Studies* 34, 429–431; Piero Treves, *Isocrate: Il Panegirico* (Turin, 1932), *CR* 47, 137.

1934

"Seneca, Lucius Annaeus," *Encyclopedia of the Social Sciences* (New York), XIII, 662.

Review: S. J. Crawford, *Anglo-Saxon Influence on Western Christendom, 600–800* (Oxford, 1933), and A. J. Macdonald, *Authority and Reason in the Early Middle Ages* (Oxford, 1933), *History* 18, 362–363.

1935

"Xenophon," *Encyclopedia of the Social Sciences* (New York), XV, 508–509.

"The Christian Attitude to Pagan Literature," *History* 20, 49–54.

"The Library of the Venerable Bede," *Bede: His Life, Times, and Writings, Essays in Commemoration of the Twelfth Centenary of His Death,* ed. A. H. Thompson (Oxford, Clarendon), 237–266.

Reviews: C. E. Stevens, *Sidonius Apollinaris and His Age* (Oxford, 1933), *History* 19, 333–334; A. D. Nock, *Conversion* (New York, 1933), *Philosophical Review* 44, 81–82; W. W. Tarn, *Alexander the Great and the Unity of Mankind* (New York, 1933), *Philosophical Review* 44, 310.

1936

A History of the Greek World from 479 to 323 B.C. (London, Methuen), 492 pp.

"The Spanish Archetype of MS Harley 4980 (Bede's Exposition of Acts)," *Journal of Theological Studies* 37, 132–137.

Reviews: H. R. Patch, *The Tradition of Boethius* (New York, 1935), *Philosophical Review* 45, 426; Paul Henry, *Recherches sur la Préparation Évangélique d'Eusèbe et l'édition perdue des oeuvres de Plotin publiée par Eustochius* (Paris, 1935), *Philosophical Review* 45, 631–632; Oscar Leuze, *Die Satrapieneinteilung in Syrien und im Zweistromlande von 520–320* (Halle, 1935), *CR* 50, 40.

1937

"The Latin Versions of Acts Known to the Venerable Bede," *HTR* 30, 37–50.
Reviews: H. St. L. B. Moss, *The Birth of the Middle Ages, 395–814* (New York, 1935), *AJP* 58, 121–122; *Aristote, le second livre de l'économique,* ed. B. A. van Groningen (Leyden, 1933), *CW* 30, 8–9; *Prosopographia imperii Romani, Pars II,* ed. E. Groag and A. Stein (Berlin, 1936), *CW* 30, 142–143; J. D. A. Ogilvy, *Books Known to Anglo-Latin Writers from Aldhelm to Alcuin* (Cambridge, Mass., 1936), *Spec* 12, 127–129; C. H. Coster, *The Iudicium Quinquevirale* (Cambridge, Mass., 1935), *AHR* 42, 284–285; Walter Scott, *Hermetica IV: Testimonia* (New York, 1936), *Philosophical Review* 46, 560.

1938

"Was Bede the Author of a Penitential?" *HTR* 31, 263–274.
Reviews: *Cassiodori Senatoris Institutiones,* ed. R. A. B. Mynors (Oxford, 1937), *AJP* 59, 115–117; M. Boas, *Alcuin und Cato* (Leiden, 1937), *CR* 52, 179–180; *Sancti Caesarii episcopi Arelatensis opera, vol. I, sermones seu admonitiones,* ed. Dom G. Morin (Maredsous, 1937), *Spec* 13, 354–356; *An Economic Survey of Ancient Rome,* ed. Tenney Frank, III (Baltimore, 1937), *CW* 31, 63–64; A. R. Burn, *The World of Hesiod* (New York, 1937), *CW* 31, 55–56; *Inscriptiones Italiae, XI, Regio XI, Fasc.1, Augusta Praetoria,* ed. Piero Barocelli (Rome, 1932), *CW* 31, 187–188; E. M. Pickman, *The Mind of Latin Christendom* (New York, 1937), *Philosophical Review* 47, 544.

1939

Bedae Venerabilis Expositio Actuum Apostorum et Retractatio (Cambridge, Mass.), xlv, 176 pp. [Medieval Academy of America Publications, no. 35].
Reviews: Paul Henry, *Les États du texte de Plotin* (Brussels, 1937), *Philosophical Review* 48, 81–82; *An Economic Survey of Ancient Rome,* ed. Tenney Frank, IV (Baltimore, 1938), *AHR* 44, 861–863.

1940

"Some Reflections on Latin Historical Writing in the Fifth Century," *CP* 35, 241–258.

280

Bibliography

Reviews: J. T. Shotwell, *The History of History*, rev. ed. (New York, 1939), *CP* 35, 195–198; Gisela Schmitz-Kahlmann, *Das Beispiel der Geschichte im politischen Denken des Isocrates* (Leipzig, 1939), *CP* 35, 445–446; Werner Jaeger, *Demosthenes: der Staatsmann und sein Werden* (Berlin, 1938), *Philosophical Review* 49, 580–581; Joseph Vogt, *Kaiser Julian und das Judentum* (Leipzig, 1939), *AHR* 45, 947.

1941

"The Western Church and Astrology during the Early Middle Ages," *HTR* 34, 251–275.

Reviews: Bertram Colgrave, *Two Lives of St. Cuthbert* (Cambridge, 1940), and W. Douglas Simpson, *Saint Ninian and the Origins of the Christian Church in Scotland* (Edinburgh, 1940), *AHR* 46, 379–381; Harald Fuchs, *Der geistige Widerstand gegen Rom in der antiken Welt* (Berlin, 1938), *AJP* 62, 118–119; Gaetano de Sanctis, *Storia dei Greci dalle origini alla fine del secolo V* (Florence, 1939), *AJP* 62, 375–376; André Aymard, *Les Assemblées de la confédération achaienne* (Paris, 1938), and *Les premiers rapports de Rome et de la confédération achaienne, 198–189 avant J.-C.* (Paris, 1939), *AJP* 62, 507–509; Kurt von Fritz, *Pythagorean Politics in Southern Italy* (New York, 1940), *Philosophical Review* 50, 643–644.

1942

"Richard Bentley: 1742–1942," *Studies in Philology* 39, 510–523.

"An Addition to Bede in MS Balliol 177," *Journal of Theological Studies* 43, 184–187.

"The Palatine Migration of 1709," *New York History* 23, 460–464.

Reviews: Beryl Smalley, *The Study of the Bible in the Middle Ages* (Oxford, 1941), *Spec* 17, 146–148; C. N. Cochrane, *Christianity and Classical Culture* (New York, 1940), *AHR* 47, 314–315; Kenneth M. Setton, *The Christian Attitude towards the Emperor in the Fourth Century* (New York, 1941), *AHR* 47, 405; Michael Rostovtzeff, *The Social and Economic History of the Hellenistic World* (Oxford, 1941), *American Economic Review* 32, 571–578; J. W. Thompson, *Ancient Libraries* (Berkeley, 1940), *CP* 37, 229–230; L. F. Smith, *The Genuineness of the Ninth and Third Letters of Isocrates* (Lancaster, 1940), *CP* 37, 230–231.

1943

A Hand-List of Bede Manuscripts, with the collaboration of H. H. King (Ithaca, Cornell University Press), x, 168 pp.

Bibliography

Reviews: E. K. Rand, *The Building of Eternal Rome* (Cambridge, 1943), *CP* 38, 265–268; L. L. Howe, *The Pretorian Prefect from Commodus to Diocletian* (A.D. *180–305*) (Chicago, 1942), *CP* 38, 277–278; Edwin L. Minar, *Early Pythagorean Politics in Practice and Theory* (Baltimore, 1942), *Philosophical Review* 52, 324; John A. McGeachy, Jr., *Quintus Aurelius Symmachus and the Senatorial Aristocracy of the West* (Chicago, 1942), *AHR* 48, 847–848; E. J. Goodspeed, *A History of Early Christian Literature* (Chicago, 1942), *CP* 38, 61–62.

1944

"A Fragment from an Insular Manuscript of Isidore," *Medievalia et Humanistica* 2, 28–31.

Reviews: *The Vita Sancti Malchi of Reginald of Canterbury*, ed. L. R. Lind (Urbana, 1942), *CP* 39, 131–132; Joseph C. Plumpe, *Mater Ecclesia: An Inquiry into the Concept of the Church as Mother in Early Christianity* (Washington, 1943), *AHR* 49, 778.

1945

Reviews: *Traditio I*, *CP* 40, 57–58; T. G. Jalland, *The Church and the Papacy* (London, 1944), *Journal of Central European Affairs* 5, 64–65; *Medieval and Renaissance Studies I. 2*, *AJP* 66, 202–203.

1946

"The Influence during the Middle Ages of the Treatise 'de vita contemplativa' and its Surviving Manuscripts," *Miscellanea Giovanni Mercati* 2 (Città del Vaticano, Biblioteca Apostolica Vaticana), 344–358.

Reviews: Wilhelm Levison, *England and the Continent in the Eighth Century* (Oxford, 1946), *Spec* 21, 525–528; E. H. Clift, *Latin Pseudepigrapha* (Baltimore, 1945), *AHR* 51, 358–359.

1947

The Greater Roman Historians (Berkeley, University of California Press), viii, 196 pp. [Sather Classical Lectures XXI].

"Antiochene Exegesis in Western Europe during the Middle Ages," *HTR* 40, 19–31.

Reviews: Reto R. Bezzola, *Les Origines et la formation de la littérature courtoise en occident (500–1200) I: La tradition impériale de la fin de l'antiquité au XIᵉ siècle* (Paris, 1944), *English Historical Review* 62, 536–537; Pierre Courcelle, *Les Lettres grecques*

Bibliography

en occident de Macrobe à Cassiodore (Paris, 1943), and *An Introduction to Divine and Human Readings by Cassiodorus Senator,* trans. L. W. Jones (New York, 1946), *CP* 42, 254–257; Sister M. Thomas Aquinas Carroll, *The Venerable Bede: His Spiritual Teachings* (Washington, 1946), *AHR* 52, 358.

1948

"The Value and Influence of Cassiodorus' Ecclesiastical History," *HTR* 41, 51–67.

Reviews: C. A. Robinson, Jr., *Alexander the Great: The Meeting of East and West in World Government and Brotherhood* (New York, 1947), *AHR* 53, 311–312; E. A. Thompson, *The Historical Work of Ammianus Marcellinus* (Cambridge, 1947), *CP* 43, 205–207; André Lambert, *Die indirekte Rede als künstlerisches Stilmittel des Livius* (Zürich, 1946), *CP* 43, 278; D. Elizabeth Martin-Clarke, *Culture in Early Anglo-Saxon England* (Baltimore, 1947), *AHR* 53, 866.

1949

Reviews: Henri-Irenée Marrou, *Histoire de l'éducation dans l'antiquité* (Paris, 1948), *Gnomon* 21, 97–101; Ernst Robert Curtius, *Europäische Literatur und Lateinisches Mittelalter* (Bern, 1948), *Spec* 24, 259–263; Pierre Courcelle, *Histoire littéraire des grandes invasions germaniques* (Paris, 1948), *Spec* 24, 257–258; Wilhelm Levison, *Aus rheinischer und fränkischer Frühzeit* (Düsseldorf, 1948), *AHR* 54, 658; J. Oliver Thomson, *History of Ancient Geography* (New York, 1949), *AHR* 55, 103–104; Andrew Alföldi, *The Conversion of Constantine and Pagan Rome* (Oxford, 1948), and A. H. M. Jones, *Constantine and the Conversion of Europe* (London, 1948), *American Journal of Archeology* 53, 421–422.

1950

"Pagan Schools and Christian Teachers," *Liber Floridus: Mittellateinische Studien, P. Lehmann zum 65. Geburtstag gewidmet,* ed. Bernhard Bischoff and Suso Brechter (St. Ottilien, Eos Verlag der Erzabtei), 47–61.

Reviews: *Lactantius, Epitome of the Divine Institutes,* trans. E. H. Blakeney (London, 1950), *Spec* 25, 594–597; Joseph Vogt, *Constantin der Grosse und sein Jahrhundert* (Munich, 1949), *AHR* 55, 579–580.

1951

Christianity and Pagan Culture in the Later Roman Empire together with an English Translation of John Chrysostom's Address on Vainglory and the Right Way for Parents to Bring Up Their Children (Ithaca, Cornell University Press), vi, 145 pp. [James W. Richard Lectures].

"The Lesbos Manuscript of Chrysostom's de inani gloria," *Vigiliae Christianae* 5, 179–185.

Review: Fritz Schachermeyr, *Alexander der Grosse: Ingenium und Macht* (Graz, 1949), *AHR* 56, 335–337.

1952

"The Study of St. Jerome in the Early Middle Ages," *A Monument to St. Jerome: Essays on Some Aspects of His Life, Works and Influence,* ed. Francis X. Murphy (New York, Sheed and Ward), 235–256.

Reviews: *Martini Episcopi Bracarensis opera omnia,* ed. C. W. Barlow (New Haven, 1950), *CP* 47, 251–253; Ch. Wirszubski, *Libertas as a Political Idea at Rome during the Late Republic and Early Principate* (Cambridge, 1950), *Philosophical Review* 61, 112–114; Gérard Walter, *Caesar* (New York, 1952), *Yale Review* 42, 121–123; Beryl Smalley, *The Study of the Bible in the Middle Ages* (Oxford, 1952), *Spec* 27, 585.

1953

"Some Early Medieval Commentaries on the Old Testament," *HTR* 46, 27–46.

Reviews: Andrew Alföldi, *A Conflict of Ideas in the Late Roman Empire: The Clash between the Senate and Valentinian I* (Oxford, 1952), *AJP* 74, 444–446; Robert M. Grant, *Miracle and Natural Law in Graeco-Roman and Early Christian Thought* (Amsterdam, 1952), *Gnomon* 25, 549–550; *Cassiodori-Epiphanii Historia Ecclesiastica Tripartita,* ed. Walter Jacob and Rudolf Hanslik (Vienna, 1952), *Spec* 28, 558–561; *Satura: Früchte aus der antiken Welt Otto Weinreich zum 13. Marz 1951 dargebracht* (Baden-Baden, 1952), *CP* 48, 262.

1954

Reviews: *Aratoris subdiaconi de actibus apostolorum,* ed. A. P. McKinlay (Vienna, 1951), *AJP* 75, 210–212; Massimiliano Pavan, *La crisi della scuola nel IV secolo* (Bari, 1952), and Peter Wolf,

Bibliography

Vom Schulwesen der Spätantike: Studien zu Libanius (Baden-Baden, 1952), *Gnomon* 26, 205–206.

1956

Reviews: R. E. Smith, *The Failure of the Roman Republic* (Cambridge, 1955), *Yale Review* 45, 458–459; W. L. Westermann, *The Slave Systems of Greek and Roman Antiquity* (Philadelphia, 1955), *AHR* 61, 613–614; P. H. Blair, *An Introduction to Anglo-Saxon England* (New York, 1956), *AHR* 61, 939–940.